JOHN SULLIVAN DWIGHT

A BIOGRAPHY

Da Capo Press Music Reprint Series
GENERAL EDITOR
FREDERICK FREEDMAN
VASSAR COLLEGE

JOHN SULLIVAN DWIGHT
Brook-Farmer, Editor, and Critic of Music

A BIOGRAPHY

By
GEORGE WILLIS COOKE

𝄞 DA CAPO PRESS • NEW YORK • 1969

A Da Capo Press Reprint Edition

ML
423
·D9
·C7

This Da Capo Press edition of George
Willis Cooke's *John Sullivan Dwight: A
Biography* is an unabridged republication of
the first edition published in Boston in
1898 by Small, Maynard & Company.

Library of Congress Catalog Card Number 79-90210

Published by Da Capo Press
A Division of Plenum Publishing Corporation
227 West 17th Street
New York, N.Y. 10011

Printed in the United States of America

JOHN SULLIVAN DWIGHT
A BIOGRAPHY

very truly yours
John S. Dwight.

From a Painting by Caroline Cranch, 1884, in the possession of the Harvard Musical Association.

JOHN SULLIVAN DWIGHT
Brook-Farmer, Editor, and Critic of Music

A BIOGRAPHY
By
GEORGE WILLIS COOKE

SCIRE QVOD SCIENDVM

BOSTON
SMALL, MAYNARD & COMPANY
1898

PRESS OF GEORGE H. ELLIS, BOSTON, U. S. A.

TO THE HARVARD MUSICAL ASSOCIATION,

WITH WHICH THE SUBJECT OF THIS BIOGRAPHY WAS INTIMATELY
CONNECTED, FROM THE DAY OF ITS INCEPTION UNTIL HIS DEATH,
SERVING IT IN EVERY OFFICIAL CAPACITY, BEING ITS PRESIDENT
FOR TWENTY YEARS, THIS VOLUME IS RESPECTFULLY DEDICATED,
WITH THE HOPE THAT IT MAY HELP TO INDICATE HOW INTI-
MATELY THE MAN, THE ASSOCIATION, AND THE ART THEY AIMED
TO SERVE WERE UNITED TO EACH OTHER.

CONTENTS.

WHEN Nature was shaping him, clay was not granted
*   For making so full-sized a man as she wanted.*
So, to fill out her model, a little she spared
From some finer-grained stuff for a woman prepared ;
And she could not have hit a more excellent plan
For making him fully and perfectly man.
The success of her scheme gave her so much delight
That she tried it again, shortly after, in Dwight :
Only, while she was kneading and shaping the clay,
She sang to her work in her sweet, childish way,
And found, when she'd put the last touch to his soul,
That the music had somehow got mixed with the
*   whole.*

A FABLE FOR CRITICS.

PREFACE.

This biography of John S. Dwight was undertaken at the suggestion and request of Mrs. Ednah D. Cheney, and it has secured the benefit of her aid and revision. The aim kept in view in its preparation was to permit Dwight to speak for himself as far as it could be done, and to make the work autobiographic in so far as this was possible of accomplishment. As he was not a frequent letter-writer, resource has been had to the published words of his which throw light upon his career. Many of these are of an autobiographic nature, and they have been drawn upon frequently.

The letters written to Dwight by his friends have been freely used, especially where they interpret his own life or aid us in understanding his connection with men and women well known to the public. Among these will be found letters from Carlyle, Emerson, Dr. Channing, Lowell, Longfellow, Holmes, Theodore Parker, Hawthorne, Margaret Fuller, George Ripley, W. W. Story, Lydia M. Child, Elizabeth Peabody, Christopher P. Cranch, George W. Curtis, Charles T. Brooks, Henry James, William Henry Channing, E. P. Whipple, and Richard Grant White. The work contains at least twoscore interesting and valuable letters that have never before appeared in print.

An attempt has been made to understand the circumstances amidst which Dwight was placed, and to rightly interpret his social and intellectual environ-

ment.   To this end reminiscences from his personal friends and intimate associates have been secured, and among these are: Mrs. Julia Ward Howe, Mrs. John A. Andrew, Mrs. Ednah D. Cheney, Colonel T. W. Higginson, Mr. B. J. Lang, Mr. Arthur Foote, Mr. John Holmes, Mr. William F. Apthorp, Mr. Erving Winslow, Mr. S. Lothrop Thorndike, Mr. Ernst Perabo, Mrs. Laura A. Richards, and Dr. Cyrus A. Bartol.   If the book gives a true account of Dwight's life and character, it is due in large degree to these personal interviews and reminiscences.

Three phases of Dwight's life have been kept especially in view,— his connection with Brook Farm, his membership in the Saturday Club, and his work for music in Boston.   The chapter on Brook Farm gives, perhaps, a more distinctly inward view of its daily life than can be found elsewhere, due to the numerous letters it contains written from the farm by Dwight and his sisters.   It also deals more fully with the associationist movement in and about Boston than has been usual, and it shows that the influence of Brook Farm was felt for many years after it came to an end.

The Saturday Club has been frequently written of by Dr. Holmes and others, but various notes kept of its meetings by Dwight make the chapter here devoted to it final as to dates and members.   Its history is told more fully than it has been anywhere else, and with a view to showing how intimately Dwight was connected with the literary men of his time.

So important was Dwight's connection with the development of musical interest and taste in Boston that it was desirable some account of his work for music should be given to the public. His Journal of Music was a pioneer in its chosen field, and he made it an educational power in securing a just recognition of the claims of music as an art. He was intimately identified with almost every movement made in behalf of music for nearly a half-century in the city of his birth, and the history of that art in Boston cannot be written without the frequent use of his name. In his time every one looked to him for the right interpretation of music, and musicians trusted him as sincerely as did the general public. His work was therefore unique, and never likely to be repeated on the part of any interpreter of music. He was a fit man for the time, that time when music was securing its public, when musical culture was finding its opportunity, and when a man of literary skill was needed who could mediate between the art and the public.

The reference to Dwight in Lowell's "Fable for Critics," though brief, was just and appreciative. It shows how highly the poet thought of his friend, and it admirably expresses the interest with which Dwight's work for music was regarded by his associates. We do not think of him to-day as of intellectual kin with Hawthorne, but so he was thought of by our keenest literary critic.

Among the letters, etc., which came into my hands in the preparation of this volume was a series of

*letters from George William Curtis to Dwight.
These have been published in a separate volume,
which bears the title of "Early Letters of George
William Curtis to John S. Dwight: Brook Farm
and Concord." A few errors found their way into
that volume, which I take the liberty of correcting
here.*

*It was Curtis himself who invented the name
of Plato Skimpole for Alcott, and not Margaret
Fuller. Dickens's "Bleak House," in which Skimpole appears, was first published in 1852 in this
country; but Margaret Fuller went to Europe in
1846, and died in 1850.*

*Elizabeth Hoar was betrothed to Charles Emer-
son, and not to his brother Edward. In regard to
Charles Emerson the Hon. George Frisbie Hoar
writes me: "I suppose his was the most brilliant
intellect of any person ever born in New England,
if you may trust the testimony of so many authorities whose point of view is very different. His
brother Waldo, although eleven years older, said of
him that he looked to him as to a master, and that
he was the only person who made Shakspere seem
possible to him. Daniel Webster, in whose office he
studied, said, when he was consulted where he should
settle, that it made no difference where he settled. If
he opened an office in the midst of the backwoods in
Maine, the clients would throng after him. Dr.
Channing said of him, when he died, that all New
England mourned his loss; and Edward Everett
delivered a eulogy upon him at a Phi Beta Kappa*

dinner, which, I hope, will be brought to light if the long-delayed duty of writing a memoir of Everett shall ever be performed and his papers shall be published. When it is remembered that Charles Emerson died at about twenty-seven years, when he had scarcely begun the practice of his profession, you will perhaps be inclined to agree that my estimate of him is not a fond exaggeration."

The account which Curtis gave of the drowning of a young girl in Concord may be supplemented by the statement that her name was Martha Hunt, and not Mary. She belonged to the family of a well-to-do farmer in Concord, and was a beautiful girl, of sweet disposition. Had it not been for inherited insanity, she would have had no difficulty in finding a refined society suited to her capacity.

Elizabeth Randall was married at the house of Mrs. Cheney, and not at that of Samuel Hoar. It should also be said that Samuel Hoar was known in Concord as "Squire," and not as Judge. In his day he was one of the most famous lawyers in the country. Chief Justice Shaw said that he was the most powerful jury lawyer in Massachusetts. Starr King said of him that "he lived all the beatitudes daily." After his death tribute was paid to his memory by John A. Andrew, Emory Washburn, Charles Sumner, John G. Palfrey, Robert C. Winthrop, and James Walker. President Walker said of his relations to Harvard College that he was "venerable alike for his age and his virtues, a devoted friend to the college, whom he has been able to

serve in a thousand ways by the wisdom of his counsels and the weight of his character." He also said
of him, "Other men served the college: Samuel
Hoar saved it."

In his letter about Father Hecker, Curtis spoke
of a series of papers in the Dial, called "Ernest, the
Seeker," as written by William Henry Channing.
They were in reality written by William Ellery
Channing, the poet, one of Thoreau's most intimate
friends and his first biographer. One who knew
him well in his days of poetic activity has written of
him, "I shall be much mistaken if some of his poems
do not survive nearly everything that his generation
in this country produced."

One or two other errors may be corrected. Curtis
mentions the Nethake family in New York, not
the Vathek. The flower he found on his visit to
Wachusett was the potentilla. All these errors
have been corrected in the second edition. Some of
them were made by Curtis himself, and others came
from misinformation. I have to thank those persons who have kindly pointed them out to me.

The chapter on the Saturday Club was published
in the New England Magazine for June, 1898, and
is reprinted through the kindness of the publisher.
It has been revised, however, especially with reference to Horatio Woodman; and the facts in regard
to his life are now given, correcting false statements
that have been made about him.

G. W. C.

CHAPTER I.

ANCESTRY, YOUTH, AND COLLEGE LIFE.

THE Dwight family is a widely extended one in the United States, and has included a large number of statesmen, judges, authors, college presidents and professors, and other men of prominence and influence. Most of those who bear the name are descendants of Mr. John Dwight, one of the original settlers of Dedham, Mass. One branch of the family located in Shirley, Mass., about the middle of the eighteenth century. Captain John Dwight, a supposed son of John Dwight, of Medfield, who was descended from Michael Dwight, of Dedham, was born about the year 1705, became a sea captain, and was shipwrecked in 1744. He left a widow, and a son John, aged four, who was brought up in Boston. He moved to Shirley, where he spent his life as a farmer and a stone-cutter. He was in the Revolutionary army, and he was made partly deaf for many years from the effects of a wound received at the battle of White Plains. He died Oct. 6, 1816, as the result of accidental poisoning.

The children of John Dwight, of Shirley, were Susanna, John, Sally, Betsey, Francis, Priscilla, Pamilla, Sullivan. The eldest son, John, was born Dec. 22, 1776. He graduated at Harvard College in 1800, in a class which included Charles Lowell, D.D., Washington Allston, and Judge Lemuel Shaw. He studied for the ministry, but, before entering upon the work of his profession, found himself rejecting the severe Calvinism in which he had been educated. Then he studied medicine with the celebrated physician, Dr. John Jeffries, and settled in Boston. He was only moderately successful as a medical practitioner, his mind being largely occupied with mechanical invention. In religion he was a free-thinker, and of a very radical kind for his day. Sincere and truth-loving, he refused to accept what was unworthy of God and revolting to human affection. Speaking at his funeral, Theodore Parker remarked: " Our friend is said to have held opinions which are not popular. I know not of those opinions; but this I do know, — that, whatever they were, he was true to them. And greater praise could be given to no man."

Dr. John Dwight married Mary Corey, of West Roxbury, in 1812. She was a woman of "a very simple, modest, childlike nature, fresh in her feelings and instincts, and of a lovely disposition." She was a handsome woman, sweet, amiable, and sensible, of exquisite taste, and of a superior character. She was fond of reading, had good literary judgment, and a strong liking for poetry. Her nature was æsthetic and artistic in its preferences. She had a remarkable appreciation of beauty, and fine taste as to its character and quality.

To Dr. John Dwight and his wife Mary were born: John Sullivan, May 13, 1813; Marianne, April 4, 1816; Frances Ellen, Dec. 13, 1819; and Benjamin Franklin, Sept. 5, 1824. It was natural that the eldest son should take the name of his father, since it had for generations been a common Dwight name. The second name was that of his father's youngest brother, who was for many years a successful marble-cutter in Thomaston, Me., and a militia officer of some note.

John Sullivan Dwight was born in Court Street, Boston, in a house which is now standing. He first went to the infant school of "Marm English," who was patronized by many of the ministers and the best families. He next went to the grammar school in Derne Street, where he won a Franklin prize. He was a quiet, studious boy, fond of his books.

Young Dwight attended the Latin School, then taught by Benjamin Gould, where he took prizes whenever there were any, and secured a Franklin medal. One of his sisters remembers his holding a roll of paper in his hand, containing notes he had collected in preparation for the writing of a prize essay. His mother asked him if he would not have it tied with a ribbon, and he said he was willing to have it tied with a piece of twine if he could secure the prize. In the Latin School, Dwight made rapid progress, and took high standing in his class.

One of his sisters remembers that John first showed a taste for music when about fifteen, when he heard a brass band playing the "Hunter's Chorus"; and he followed it about. From that time music was an absorbing interest with him.

He was very fond of attending the "New England Museum," kept by Thomas Grainger, who was friendly with John's father, and gave the family free access to his place of entertainment. It was not the animals in which the youth took an interest, but the music. The boy was passionately fond of street music, and found delight in a street organ, even in later years.

John devoted much time to the piano and flute. From his mother he gained an exquisite love of the beautiful and a fine æsthetic sensibility. His father's mechanical skill he did not inherit in the least degree, but from his mother he acquired those intellectual qualities which determined all his after life.

In the summer of 1829 young Dwight entered Harvard College, "carrying thither," according to his own statement, "perhaps more Latin and Greek (technically, as to grammar, at least) than I [he] brought away." Having entered college better prepared than most of his classmates, he did not exert himself as he had done in the Latin School, but kept a respectable standing in his class. He was interested in music far more than in any prescribed college study, and it is because of that interest he is chiefly remembered by his companions. Music was then no part of the college course; but Dwight early joined the Pierian Sodality, a club of students for musical study and practice. It furnished the music for the exhibitions, which was thought to be very good. It was then the rule of the college that prescribed study hours should be kept by the students. From 12 M. to 2 P.M. was a time of intermission; and the moment the bell rang the noon hour Dwight caught up his flute, on which he played until the bell rang again for study, taking barely time to eat his dinner in the interval. One of his classmates has said that his heart seemed to be in music more than anything else.

Of this period Colonel T. W. Higginson furnishes these reminiscences: "I have always known John Dwight, ever since he and two other young men used to come to my mother's house in Cambridge, when I was about eleven, and play flute trios with my sister's piano accompaniment, she being a fine pianist. One was the late C. P. Cranch; and the third was William Negle Habersham, of Georgia. The latter had a silver flute; and I remember John Dwight's saying, ' It has a silver tone,' in the same dreamy and ecstatic way in which he always spoke of everything musical. He and Cranch were then divinity students, and Habersham an undergraduate. The latter graduated in 1836, so this must have been about 1835. I don't remember what music they played (my sister played Beethoven, who was then a novelty); but I remember that after being sent up to bed I was allowed to leave my door open, and went to sleep by music. Afterwards I read with pleasure of the boy in ' Charles Auchester ' who does the same."

In an account of the musical society called the Pierian Sodality, formed in 1808, and still flourishing, which Dwight wrote for the " Harvard Book," he gives some interesting reminiscences of his college days. " When the Sodality began to play at college exhibitions," he wrote, " or when the flutes came in, and, with those soft, persuasive instruments, of course the serenading, we are not informed. Both practices were fully in vogue when we first heard the Pierians, in 1827–28, and were kept up, with occasional interruptions, for many a year afterwards. Shall we forget the scene of the Exhibition Day, when the Latin School boy, on the eve of entering college, eager to catch a glimpse beforehand of the promised land, went out to University Hall, and for the first time heard and saw, up there in the side (north) gallery, the little group of Pierians, with their ribbons and their medals and their shining instruments, among them the protruding, long, and lengthening monster, the trombone, wielded with an air of gravity and dignity by one who now ranks among our most distinguished scholars, orators, and statesmen? Had any strains of band or orchestra ever sounded so sweet to the expectant Freshman's ears as those? And was not he, too, captivated and converted to the gospel of the college flute, as the transcendent and most eloquent of instruments? Nevertheless within a year or two he chose the reedy clarionet, wherewith to lead a little preparatory club,— the purgatory which half-fledged musicians of his own ilk had to pass through before they could be candidates for the Pierian paradise. This was called the Arionic Society; and, if its utmost skill was discord, the struggle of its members for promotion into the higher order was persistent. We think it was founded some years later than the Sodality, for which it was in some sense the noisy nursery. How long it lasted, we know not. The Sodality in our day, under the presidency of accomplished flutists (Isaac Appleton Jewett, Boott, and Graham), was comparatively rich in instruments. Besides the flutes (first, second, third, and several of each), we had the clarionet, a pair of French horns, violoncello, and part of the time a nondescript bass horn."

Dwight's love of poetry and the best literature was only less than his love of music. He read much in the best authors, and his literary exercises showed his strong literary taste. In his Junior year he read an original poem before the Hasty Pudding Club, in the middle of the Senior year he lectured on music before the Northborough Lyceum, and a few weeks before graduation he gave a paper on poetry before the Harvard Union. On graduation, July 17, 1832, Dwight furnished the class poem, which contained thirty nine-line stanzas. These facts hint at his excellent standing in a class which contained George Ticknor Curtis, Henry W. Bellows, Charles T. Brooks, Estes Howe, Samuel Osgood, and John Holmes, brother of the poet.

A part of his Senior year was spent by Dwight in teaching at Northborough. His letters do not indicate that he fully enjoyed the occupation or that the pupils he had under him were such as to enlist his intellectual sympathies. He introduced music into his school, and he found such comfort as he could in the social life of the place. In September, 1832, he entered the Divinity School of Harvard College. After taking up the studies of the next year, he left in October, and went to Meadville, Penn., to serve as a tutor in the family of Mr. H. J. Huidekoper. He greatly enjoyed his stay in that place, the family in which he was placed, the young people whose education he guided, and his own opportunities for reading and study. He was the leading spirit in organizing a lyceum in Meadville, before which he gave the first lecture, taking for his subject " Education." In August, 1834, he returned to the Divinity School; and he completed the course of study in August, 1836. On graduation he gave a dissertation on " The Proper Character of Poetry and Music for Public Worship," which was published in the *Christian Examiner* for November, 1836. This paper was a plea for the recognition of music on its own merits and as a means of genuine culture.

In the Divinity School, as in the college, Dwight's one great interest was music. Near his own were the rooms of his lifelong friends, Theodore Parker and Christopher P. Cranch. Parker had no love of music and no capacity for its production, but Cranch was only less devoted to it than Dwight. When the two music-lovers were one evening playing together, they heard a great din in the hall. On Dwight's opening the door, Parker was discovered sawing wood. When asked why he was so engaged in that place, he replied, " You disturb me with your music when I wish to study, and I will have my fun in return." He kept on with his sawing until the music was silenced.

On Exhibition Day in July, 1837, a number of graduates, who had been members of the Pierian Sodality, met with the students who were then members; and the conversation turned on the work of the little society. It was suggested that a society be formed of graduates for the purpose of meeting regularly at Commencement each year. A committee was at once appointed to prepare a plan for such society, of which Dwight was made a member. He wrote to Cranch: " The plan proposed has been very warmly met. Many gentlemen of high character have answered that they will come, and do all that they can to promote the objects contemplated. Some engage to contribute liberally towards a fund." On Commencement Day, August 30, a meeting was held in response to a circular sent out to all the former members of the Sodality, inviting them to attend. The report of the committee was prepared by Dwight, by whom it was read. He proposed two objects for the society contemplated, the first that of holding an annual meeting on Commencement Day of those interested in music, and the second that of securing the advancement of the cause of music, particularly in the university.

The society took the name of the General Association of the Members of the Pierian Sodality. Henry Ware, D.D., was elected the president, and Dwight the vice-president. In 1840 the name was changed to the Harvard Musical Association. In 1845 the society was incorporated, and in 1848 it began to hold its meetings in Boston. From the beginning the society took the position that "the science and art of music is worthy of a place in a system of liberal education, and deserving of cultivation by educated men." It took for its definite object to secure "the introduction of music as a regular branch of instruction, and the cultivation of musical taste and science in Harvard University."

CHAPTER II.

PREACHING AND TRANSLATING.

In July, 1836, John S. Dwight entered upon his work as a preacher; but three years and a half passed before he had a pulpit of his own. He was idle but few Sundays, but the parishes evidently were not wholly pleased with his preaching. He saw his own limitations with reference to his chosen profession. In a letter written in Boston, February, 1837, he said to Theodore Parker, "I am almost afraid that I cannot succeed as a preacher."

"You ask me to point out your faults," wrote Parker from Salem, March 14. "I can in no wise refuse, since you did me the same favor you ask. I fear to touch the subject, but will attempt it. Let me begin by stating some of your merits by way of offset to what is to follow. You have a deep love of the beautiful, strong likings and keen dislikings, a quick discernment, a deep love of freedom. I love the spontaneity of reason displayed in your mind and the beautiful active power of your imagination. But I must speak of 'faults' under each of these heads. You do not always see the beautiful clearly. The beautiful is not sharply defined, so you love vagueness, mistaking the indefinite for the Infinite, and, like Ixion of old, embracing a cloud instead of a goddess. You surround yourself with the perfumed clouds of music. You mingle the same perfume and melody in your sermons, but you carry all the vagueness of musical clouds where clearness and precision are virtues. Thus you will be feeble in expression where your feeling is strong. You place the beauty of action in unconsciousness. This is wrong,—profoundly wrong. Babes are unconscious. Instructed men act with will, therefore are they moral, god-like. You confound tranquillity and unconsciousness; but Tranquillity is the daughter of Volition and Love, their favorite though youngest child. You are deficient in will. This is the most important statement I have to make.

"Your strong likings sometimes lead you where you would not go. Your dislikes make you shrink from others who, you have a presentiment, are not congenial souls. Thus you are often misunderstood, often neglected by such as are really congenial, born of the same parent.

"Your quick discernment leads you away sometimes. What you catch at the first or second grasp, you hold; but you are not a patient thinker. This proceeds from want of will. You oftentimes go down very deep into the hidden things of nature and see visions; but you descry only half of a truth, which often leads to a whole error. If you would add reflection to your list of cardinal virtues of the mind, and apply it to the rich elements of thought which the spontaneous reason affords you, you will be a great man. This want of will-controlled thought has prevented your doing anything worthy of yourself. You have done fine things, but they are nothing to what you can and ought to do.

"Your love of freedom makes you despise law. Now a man is only free by keeping the law of his being, 'the law of the spirit of life,' as Paul calls it. You have not will enough to be free. Impulse assumes the place of will with you. Sometimes it carries you where reason would perhaps reluct to go. Now the will cannot be the impelling power, but it should be a directing. Without this man is like a straw in the waters. You have a beautiful sentiment; but you need a firm principle to give consistency, vigor, and *selbst-ständigkeit*. You have read the little note upon Schubert at the end of the Life of Schiller: it is full of instruction.

"I admire your imagination: it is really creative, not merely a sickly fancy; but it makes you dream when you should do. Duty, not dreaming, is for men. You must get a place in the real world before you can walk into the ideal like a gentleman. Nobody can scramble into heaven: even the giants piled Pelion upon Ossa before they attempted it. I have suspected that your ideals are incapable of realization. So are all, you will say. True, but only on account of the narrowness of Space and the lowness of Time; while I suspect yours of an intrinsic defect, that they sometimes involve a contradiction, and so would commit suicide before they were of age."

In writing to Dwight three months before the above letter was written, Parker had asked his friend to point out all the faults which he found most prominent in his character, both intellectual and moral. To this Dwight replied a few days later in these words: "I may hint to you something about your character, as I would to myself about my own, rather in the way of cautious suspicion than passing any actual judgment. I fear that I have not enough of the element of will in me. I cannot judge people. I can only regard what I see in them as the manifestations of a peculiar nature. I have strong likings, strong antipathies; but I do not feel it necessary to praise or blame. Still, I should be unworthy of the confidence you have reposed in me if I did not speak to you openly. I shall try to merit the confidence you have placed in my good will and candor, though I would not have you place too much in my judgment.

"I always thought you had faults; but, as I try to touch them, they slip away. Therefore, let me commence systematically; and, first, whatever may be your habitual principles, motives, tendencies, passions, you do not fail at all in the resolution to act them out. Whatever you wish, you will; and, what you will, you effect. This I have admired in you, perhaps because I am so passive. But yet even this virtue you carry to a degree which is disagreeable to me. I don't like to see a man have too much will: it mars the beauty of nature. You seem, as the phrenologist said, 'goaded on.' Your life seems a succession of convulsive efforts, and the only wonder is to me that they don't exhaust you. You continually recover and launch forth again. This circumstance makes me somewhat mistrust my own judgment about this trait. Still, it is painful for me to see a being whom I respect and love anything but calm. I like not impetuosity, except that of unconscious impulse. You distrust those who are unlike yourself. You fancy them restraints upon you, and then your faith in your own energies and ideas speaks out in a tone of almost bitter contempt for the world and those who do not think and feel as you do. You feel that such sentiments as you cherish ought to triumph, but you find the world courting men who pursue inferior aims. Coupled with your high ideal is an impatient wish to see it immediately realized,— two things which don't go well together; for the one prompts you to love, the other, soured by necessary disappointment, prompts to hate, at least contempt.

" I think your love of learning is a passion, that it injures your mind by converting insensibly what is originally a pure thirst for truth into a greedy, avaricious, jealous striving, not merely to know, but to get all there is known. Don't you often turn aside from your own reflection from a fear of losing what another has said or written on the subject? Have you not too much of a mania for all printed things,— as if books were the symbols of that truth to which the student aspires? You write, you read, you talk, you think, in a hurry, for fear of not getting all. Tell me if I conjecture wrongly, and pardon this weak but sincere attempt to answer your questions. Your friend and brother."

These letters indicate the sensitive, refined, and unworldly cast of Dwight's character, and the aloofness of his heart and mind from the commonplaces of the world. His letter to Parker reveals his own character more fully than does Parker's to him, and shows clearly his want of an incisive and dominating will-power. A letter from Rev. H. W. Bellows to Dwight, written in the autumn of 1836, hints of the fears Dwight's intimate friends had deep at heart as to his future. " A good many of your friends," his classmate writes, " who admire your genius, fear, I think, whether it is destined to have a full manifestation. Their fears and mine are founded upon a certain contempt you have for the details of life, for the common modes of usefulness, for the use of means. They fear for your stability. They fear for your nonconformity to circumstances. Have they any grounds? Do you feel any radical weakness of purpose, any consciousness that you are destined to dream bright dreams, and wake to weep over their vanity? You may have the character of being dreamy, irresolute, and impracticable, with a consciousness all the while of a lofty destiny of usefulness in the world. Forgive me for touching this matter, but I express a feeling that has sometimes cast a doubt upon my mind as to your prospects of happiness. I have feared that your fortunes might be those of genius too often without sympathy, too often disastrous."

Dwight did not always feel in the discouraged mood in which he wrote to Parker, and he had

more than one occasion for feeling that his work in
the pulpit was acceptable.   In 1837 Rev. S. D. Rob-
bins, of Lynn, wrote to him, " Your services were
not only acceptable, but more than profitable; and
I am grateful to you for their benefit." In 1839
Rev. E. Q. Sewall, of Scituate, wrote him : " I cannot refuse myself the satisfaction of letting you
know how exceedingly and universally pleased my
society were with your services.   It was delightful
to me to see the quantity of intellectual and moral
activity which seemed the product directly of your
word and theme."

In June, 1837, Dwight received a request from
Ralph Waldo Emerson that he supply the pulpit
of the church in East Lexington.   To this congregation, newly formed, Emerson had been preaching for about two years.   The people were of the
anti-slavery and radical type, to a considerable extent; and Emerson's preaching had been very satisfactory.   He had grown to strongly dislike the
pulpit as a place for himself, however; and he
quietly omitted on one Sunday the public prayer,
finding it not in consonance with his mood.   He
was anxious to find some one to take his place, and
to relieve him of the drive every Sunday from Concord.   Dwight spent a few Sundays with this little
congregation; and in February, 1838, he received
this letter from Emerson : —

" I was at East Lexington yesterday, and explained my wish to relinquish the charge of the
pulpit to Mr. Morrill; and he talked with the com-

mittee. They are very glad to know that you are disposed to come,— the committee for themselves, — and they think it agreeable to all. But they are so systematically prudent that they think it will for the present be better if I engaged to supply the desk, and then send you, than if they agree with you at first hand.

"So I am to come once or twice in person between now and the first of May, when my engagement expires; and then, if agreeable to you, I am to renew the engagement, but with the understanding that you are to take the entire charge, only calling me in if any particular contingency should make it desirable. I am agreeably astonished at arriving at the dignity of patronage, and you may be sure I shall be sufficiently ostentatious of it. Meantime I shall depend on you to go there next Sunday, and thereafter. When I see you, I will fix some day when I should go before May."

For something more than a year Dwight continued to supply the East Lexington pulpit, being absent, however, more than half of the time. His preaching did not wholly satisfy the congregation, and he was not invited to settle. He is still remembered in the parish with much regard for his enthusiastic love of nature and his passionate devotion to music. "He was all music," say those who knew him,— full of interesting talk about the art, and constantly improvising on the piano, when one was within reach. He was shy, bashful, diffident in the extreme, sensitive to surroundings and especially as to persons, and caring little for those not of his own taste and quality. He was also greatly interested in German; was then giving much time to its study, and to translation of the German poets. In his visits to the parish, German books and music, and whatever books he happened to be interested in at the time, went with him, and were freely talked of to those who would listen to him. His sermons were often written on Saturday night and Sunday morning, a considerable part of the night being devoted to them. This practice he kept up so long as he occupied a pulpit.

Dwight was dependent upon those who heard him for whatever success he attained in the pulpit. If people did not hear him gladly, he felt at once the depression of the situation; but, where he was cordially welcomed, his mood rose to the highest level. In May, 1839, he spent three Sundays in Bangor, Me., in the pulpit of Rev. F. H. Hedge. On the second Sunday he wrote to one of his sisters: " I enjoy myself exceedingly, and I feel fifty per cent. better every way than when I left Boston. I receive the most cordial and constant attentions from the people; in fact, never was made nearly so much of anywhere. So many call upon me, or invite me to ride, to tea, and what not, that I get little time to work or to brood over my thought; and that is just what I want. There is much more refined society than I anticipated in Bangor. Mr. Hedge's society includes the most of this better part. What makes me feel doubly at home here is the fact that Mr. Emerson was here some years ago, and interested the people very much. I have never got so cordial a hearing for my free utterances as here. They are an active, public-spirited people, and are not afraid."

During these years of waiting Dwight was not idle with his pen. In 1838 he wrote reviews of Tennyson's "Poems" and Gardner's "Music of Nature" for the *Christian Examiner*. During 1839 he wrote on Schiller's "William Tell" and Dickens's "Oliver Twist," and in 1840 he furnished to the same review an article on "Spenser's Poems." It was good work he put into these criticisms, somewhat youthful and enthusiastic, but sound and wholesome. His review of Tennyson was the earliest published in this country, and was marked by his independent and appreciative spirit.

His chief work at this time, however, was the translation of the minor poems of Goethe and Schiller for the series of volumes edited by his friend George Ripley, under the general title of "Specimens of Foreign Standard Literature." The second volume in this series appeared in the latter part of 1838, with the title "Select Minor Poems, translated from the German of Goethe and Schiller, with Notes." Dwight translated most of the poems from Goethe, and somewhat less than half of those from Schiller; and he edited the volume, furnishing the eighty pages of notes. The plan of the volume is given in a letter which Dwight sent to Rev. James Freeman Clarke, then at Louisville, Ky., asking for his aid in its preparation : —

"Knowing you to be a friend of Goethe and Schiller, I may venture to ask your assistance in the volume which I am preparing, and which is to consist of the principal 'minor poems' of those two authors. My plan is to present a faithful translation of all the most characteristic and important lyrics of these two men, so selected and arranged as to exhibit as much as possible of their spirit, and in some measure to tell their internal history, to mark the different phases through which their minds passed, to show them as they were acted upon by the circumstances of their terrestrial education. Thus of Schiller I should wish to give some specimens of his earliest and most impassioned poetry, and then some which is more tinged with his philosophical speculations, and all of those riper and calmer productions of thought and views of life. Of Goethe I would not omit his pantheistic pieces, which come under the general title of 'God and the World,' although these will be very difficult to accomplish.

"I am to have the assistance of Professors Longfellow and Felton, of Rev. Dr. Frothingham, of Miss M. Fuller, C. T. Brooks, etc., all of whom have entered upon the work with spirit. But we must fill out three hundred and fifty pages, and execute all with great care, so that we need a good deal of assistance. I hope you will take mercy upon me in my desperate expedition, and send me something.

"As to the method of translation, I wish in all

cases to preserve the form as well as the spirit; for in lyric poetry the form is part of the substance. To retain the very idea of the author, with the exact rhythm and rhyme, and the fervor and grace of expression, is the ideal to which we ought certainly to aim; and then it will not be our fault if we fall short."

Besides those persons mentioned in this letter, Dwight had the assistance of George Bancroft, William H. Channing, Frederic H. Hedge, and Christopher P. Cranch. He did not have the aid, however, of Felton and Longfellow.

Into the notes much labor was put, and of a helpful kind. The first one was of considerable length, and presented Dwight's theory of translation. The other notes gave the circumstances of the writing of the poems, and such explanations as made them readable by those not familiar with the literary history of the two poets.

An interesting incident in connection with this book was its dedication, in these words: " To Thomas Carlyle, as a slight token of admiration and gratitude, this volume is respectfully inscribed by the Translator." In October, 1838, Dwight wrote in this wise for permission to insert this dedication: —

" My friend, Mr. R. W. Emerson, whom I had desired to write to you and make a rather presumptuous request in my behalf, has exhorted me to do the thing myself. As a young student of German letters, following out gratefully, but unworthily, the impulse which he owes in great part to your writings, and now about to present some of the first-fruits of his studies to the public, in the shape of translations, will you allow me the gratification of dedicating them to you? The whole task has been pleasant to me, though I fear for the result. It has been, on my part, active conversation with greater minds, and an attempt to get nearer to them by striving to reproduce some of their works. What I have to show for it will show most unworthily, no doubt; but it has been honest, hearty labor, and has met with such sincere encouragement from a circle of friends whose judgment I respect, and whose sympathies are with the highest, that I have determined to let it go forth, and to let Goethe and Schiller appear in such imperfect copies as I have been able to make of some of their divine lyrics in the moments when they have most filled my fancy and spoken to my experience. That I have done them in this way is. my only hope for them.   It makes them sweet memorials to myself, though they may look poorly to others.   In filling up a volume, however, some things have had to be done mechanically, more for completeness' sake, and for others, than from any special impulse of my own; and this the more as I have adopted and carried out the principle, in translating these poems, of preserving the *form* always with the spirit, as being, in fact, inseparable from it in a lyric.   Generally, I have caught the music of the piece, and walked about with it ringing through me, while I pondered and digested the substance, and in this way has the literal imitation become natural and free.

"The book is to be one of the series of 'Specimens of Foreign Standard Literature,' edited by Rev. George Ripley, and will be entitled 'Select Minor Poems from Goethe and Schiller.' It will contain a pretty full collection of the songs, ballads, etc., of those men, and many of the philosophical and art poems and dithyrambics of Goethe. I have selected chiefly such pieces as have struck my fancy, such as steal upon my memory at times as fit representations of inward experiences, wherein all must recognize something of their own. Several translations have been contributed by my friends, among whose names, possibly, you will recognize one or two acquaintances. This account of the plan of the work, of the feelings and methods with which it has been growing together most naturally and pleasantly, I have felt bound to give you before asking leave to connect your name with it in any way. Most pleasant of all will it be, when it is all done, to inscribe one page to the most successful interpreter of the beauties and deep wealth and wisdom of German mind to the English people, with whom, in spirit at least, we younger and ruder Americans, New Englanders, claim to be numbered. Most pleasant will it be to acknowledge many a deep inward obligation, which the young man in his self-culture feels to the friendly spirit that goes before him, leaving such a pure

light behind him, to surprise and invite the humblest onward."

"Your very courteous letter has just been
handed to me," Carlyle wrote in reply. "I answer
without delay, what you have reason to expect, that
I am flattered and honored by your proposal; that,
if such a dedication can seem in any way desirable
to you, it cannot be other than gratifying to me.

"My best wishes go with you in your enterprise.
Among the Germans are to be found true singers:
the only true ones we have had for a great while,
with any such compass of melody; the last we are
likely to have, I think, for a great while. You do
well to unseal their voices for them in that great
western land. They are countrymen, kinsmen of
ours, these Deutschen; and truly, in the speaking
or singing department, the chief of the family at
present. In the doing and divining department,
again we Saxons, Englanders New and Old, may
set up for the first. Honor to each after his kind!

"Your mood of mind is the right one for a translator. The *tune* of a Poem, especially if it be a
Goethe's Poem, is the soul of the whole, round
which all, the very thoughts no less than the words,
shapes and modulates itself. The tune is to be got
hold of before anything else is got. And yet each
language has its genius, its capabilities. Your task
is a difficult one. For the rest there is no alchemy
like good will.

"It is several years now since I quitted that
province of things, but I feel still and shall ever

feel its great importance to the whole modern
world; and it is a real pleasure to me, on looking
round, to observe so many generous fellow-laborers,
on this side of the ocean and on that, who have
taken up the cause in such a fashion as to insure
fair play to it in the long run.   Go on, and prosper.

"May I ask you to present my kind remem-
brances to Mr. Ripley?   I have many friends in
your country whom I know not how to thank.   If
you see Emerson, say I wrote to him lately out of
Scotland, and mean to write again in some two
weeks by a speedier conveyance."

On the appearance of the book a copy was at
once sent to Carlyle, with a note of thanks and ex-
planation.   In due time there came in reply the
following characteristic letter : —

Cheyne Row, London, 14 *March,* 1839.

My dear Sir,— Your letter by the " Royal William " reached me yesterday.   The Book it referred
to had not then arrived.   But, strangely enough,
Kennett, the dilatory Kennett, inspired by I know
not what good genius, had in those same hours be-
thought himself and set his messengers in motion;
and so, returning from a friend's late last night, I
found your Packet lying safe in waiting for me.
Mrs. Austin and Miss Martineau are both in town.
They shall have their copies, if they have not already got them.   Mrs. Jameson is gone to Germany and Dresden some days ago, so that hers,
I suppose, must lie till her return, which was not

expected to be very distant.   Such a volume would have been a welcome thing to carry round with her to Weimar.   However, it will doubtless find its way thither by and by, and be welcome, arrive when it may.

For myself I thank you very cordially for this Gift, for the copy specially assigned me, and for the kind Inscription prefixed to all the copies.   It is good news that any one esteems us, better and better when our favorer is one whom we ourselves can esteem.   Of course, I have not yet been able to give your volume such an examination as I well design for it; but I have looked here and there, read largely here and there, read your notes nearly altogether, and know tolerably whereabouts you are.   It seems to be a volume creditable to New England, to yourself and all your coadjutors, well worthy of the creditable publication it forms part of.   With great pleasure I recognize in you the merit, the rarest of all in Goethe's translators, yet the first condition, without which every other merit is impossible, that of understanding your original. You seem to me to have actually deciphered for yourself, and got to behold and see the lineaments of this great mind, so that you know what it means and what its words mean.   I have heard from no English writer whatever as much truth as you write in these notes about Goethe.   I might say nowhere else at all among English writers anything but partiality, misapprehension, non-vision, gleams of insight bewildered in a mass of hallucinations, leaving no image for us but at bottom that of a vague large blamable *Impossibility*. Interpretation of detached pieces in such circumstances is hopeless. In the contrary circumstances there may be hope in it. I like many of the versions very well. Your songs seem to me to be the best, far better than one has seen hitherto, than one could have expected to see. The Epigrammatic Aphoristic matter, too, is sometimes wonderfully successful. At other times the quaint felicity of the expression is lost (I know nothing in writing more difficult to preserve), but the sense even in these cases is there. Schiller was much easier to do. On the whole, I must congratulate you on getting through so handsomely. It was an enterprise wherein failure to a very high degree need not have been dishonorable. Among your helpers I notice my old acquaintance Channing, and greatly approve of his " Kennst Du das Land ? "

How the public will receive your book is perhaps very doubtful, perhaps not very momentous. One great acquisition you have infallibly made, far beyond what any Public could do for you,— the acquisition of a Teacher and Prophet for yourself. Alone of men, very far beyond all other men, Goethe seemed to me to have understood his century, to have conquered his century, and made that, too, for himself a portion of universal Time, a portion of Eternity. Glory to the strong man ! say I. Joy over all the race of men ! Such a man is as a Prometheus, who in a time of midnight and spectres miraculously brings fire and light out of Heaven itself; and his sacred urn is burning here among us still for long generations, whereat the rest of us can, according to our need, *kindle* lights. What all this means, I believe you know. It is now long that I have ceased to speak much about such things; but they are not forgotten for all that. There is a time to speak of them, there comes also a time to be silent of them, and, if possible, do better than speak.

Your scheme of activity pleases me well. Taken up in singleness of heart, with modesty, with cheerful courage to do and to endure, it cannot but lead you towards a good goal. Neither must poverty depress you overmuch. Poverty is no bad companion for a young man. No degree of poverty whatever can permanently hold down a man in wrong courses. Nay, the best and highest course for a man, where his duty and blessedness do lie, is often enough one of great and greatest poverty. Heed not poverty. Speak to your fellow-men what things you have made out by the grace of God. A far fataller enemy than poverty is one to which not many of us, but all of us, are liable in this career: the thrice cursed sin of Self-conceit, bred oftener by riches than by Poverty! God deliver us all from that, send us whatever of "ill fortune" is needful to deliver us from that!

I write in great haste, but with little prospect of speedy leisure, and therefore to-day rather than to-morrow. Pray thank Mr. Ripley for *his* valued book, which lay nearly a year hidden somewhere, but did appear in fine.

With best wishes and thanks,

Yours very sincerely,

T. CARLYLE.

In writing to Emerson, under date of April 17, 1839, Carlyle said: " I received Dwight's book, liked it, and have answered him: a good youth of the kind you describe. No Englishman, to my knowledge, has uttered as much sense about Goethe and German things." In March Emerson had written to Carlyle: " I hope you liked John Dwight's translations of Goethe and notes. He is a good, susceptible, yearning soul, not so apt to create as to receive with the freest allowance; but I like his book very much."

In the letters of these years there are hints of various activities and interests, hymns written for the ordination of Theodore Parker and on other occasions, a visit full of satisfaction to Dr. Channing at Newport, attendance upon the meetings of the little company of Transcendentalists, intimate friendship with Ripley, a cordial correspondence with Brooks, Parker, Samuel Osgood, Bellows, Hedge, Elizabeth Peabody, Mrs. George Ripley, and others.

CHAPTER III.

AT NORTHAMPTON.

IN 1839 there came the promise of a pulpit of his own to Dwight. During that year he preached with acceptance at South Boston, Dover, N.H., and Northampton, Mass. In each of these places it seemed probable that he might be invited to settle. He went to Northampton for a few Sundays in July. He became at once interested in the society, and he threw himself most actively into the work of visiting and building up the congregation. Early in the next year he was asked to preach again at Northampton. He was invited to become the minister of the little Unitarian parish, and he was ordained in May.

From the first the people were not wholly satisfied with Dwight's preaching and methods of work. It was only a little more than fifteen years before that the church had separated from the original parish of the town, which still strongly retained the impress of the work of Jonathan Edwards. Calvinism was strongly intrenched in the Connecticut Valley in 1820, and the worst features of the revival methods were still in vogue. Those who withdrew from the Edwards parish in 1823 were Unitarians of the most conservative type, and they were not prepared for other innovations than those they had already made. Into this town of Puritan traditions came a young man full of modern ideas and methods, a Transcendentalist when Transcendental-

ism was condemned everywhere, and one not con-
tented until he had tried his own experiments and
put his own devices into operation.   There was
much debate, long hesitation, and a final invitation,
but with a considerable number lukewarm or opposed.

It must not be understood, however, that Dwight
was an extremist at this time.   His long statement
of belief furnished to the parish would now be regarded as conservative, and would doubtless suffice
to admit him into not a few evangelical churches
of the present day.   It was in what he omitted of
conventional words and forms and in the new
methods he introduced that the cause of hesitation
on the part of the congregation was to be found.
At last, however, all objections seemed removed;
and Dwight accepted the call offered in February.
He was to receive a salary of six hundred dollars.
He was ordained on May 20, the sermon being
preached by his friend George Ripley, and the
charge given by Dr. Channing.

On the Sunday following his ordination Dwight
wrote to his sister: "In the full blaze of morning
I woke in terror.   More than half the sermons still
remained before me.   Then came an intense day.
Somehow mysteriously I got through it, as I had
no right to hope.   I scratched away in the morning, and got one done, and went and preached it.
It was on 'The Church,' an attempt to set forth the
true and simple idea of a Christian community,
which should be unsectarian, exclusive in nothing,

and based on the common interests and sympathies of all humanity. The text for the whole day
was from 1 Corinthians: 'Though I be free from
all men, yet have I made myself servant unto all,
that I might gain the more.' This opened three
topics: (1) the end of the ministry to increase the
church,—'that I might gain the more'; (2) the minister as a minister or servant of the church,—' I
made myself servant unto all'; (3) the minister as
a man, the independence of the minister,—'though
I be free from all men.' I preached the first head
in the morning, and it gave great delight. I mention it because it was the most liberal view ever
presented of the church. I hurried home, and
sketched something rapidly for the P.M. on the
other two heads, which I filled out extempore. It
was an exceeding trial, both for the intense mental
exercise in planning and executing and on account
of the mortification it cost me on account of my
delinquency. The church was unusually full,— if
anything, fuller than on Wednesday. I spoke earnestly, but blundered and stammered not a little,
repeated myself, and left out most things, and came
down from the pulpit in confusion. But, to my
great surprise, every one was satisfied, and many
enthusiastic. And so I learned the lesson: a true
purpose is power, though it have no hands.

" After church I walked down with Judge Lyman
and Dr. Channing to visit old Judge Hinkley, who
is near his end. I could not help thinking again
how Providence, in all things, favors me; that, on

the first time of my being called to the trying and
new situation of administering peace at a death-
bed, Dr. Channing, of all men, should be with me.
His talk and his prayer were most touching. I
visit the old judge daily since, with confidence.
Then I ran half-way up Round Hill, and sat on the
grass an hour, drinking the beauty and the melody.
How this beauty revives one! I was tolerably
rested by it, and proceeded up to Edward Clarke's,
and took tea with the Channings, the Lymans, and
Mr. and Mrs. Rogers, the most beautiful company
which could be assembled on a beautiful evening
on a glorious hill. At sunset we all went down to
Mrs. Hunt's, where we had a conversation meeting,
at Dr. Channing's suggestion. The house was
crowded. We talked over the morning's sermon
and the 'church.' Dr. Channing talked a great
deal, and closed with a prayer which was inspiration. The effect of his visit has been most happy
on all the people. He has been the true friend and
godfather here to me. He knows half my people,
is interested in our church, and thinks he sees the
first signs of true life and progress. I spent most
of Monday morning with him, and then took leave
of him in sadness." A few days later Dr. Channing
sent him the following letter about his sermon: —

My dear Sir,— I return " Bettine " by Miss Lyman.
There was one part of your sermon about which I
did not speak to you. You said the minister was to
have *his friends.* True, but he must here practise

some self-denial.   He must avoid all exclusiveness, and beware of giving real ground for jealousy. He must wait, too, long enough to understand those around him, that he may not rashly give a confidence which he must afterwards withdraw.   In this way the young minister brings on himself silent but real dislikes.   I hope I am legible, for the state of my hand hardly allows me to write.

Yours truly, etc.,

Stockbridge, May 29.

W. E. C.

A letter written to Dwight on the day of his ordination, by Miss Elizabeth P. Peabody, gives indication of one of his limitations as a preacher. It is such a frank and generous letter as only a friend can write. " What I am going to say," she writes, " respects some part of your services.   A certain want of fluency in prayer has been the real cause of your want of outward success more than any other thing; and, even in the place where you are, it is felt, although overlooked in the estimation of your many high and beautiful gifts.   Now it has always seemed to me as if a few hints from another would remedy this deficiency, but I felt there was a difficulty in giving them while you were yet a candidate, because there would be something painfully embarrassing to a mind noble and delicate as yours in the consciousness of praying with reference to the criticisms of an audience.   I suppose the evil has originated in your idea of being spontaneous. You have thought there was falsehood, perhaps, in making an exercise of this kind a subject of meditation and composition. You have heard so much formal praying that you have shrunk from it as the only evil. But in your case it was hardly to be feared: you might premeditate and even write, and still there be no danger of your losing sight of God or losing feeling. Moreover, I think that, even on your own plan, if you would be very short, and as soon as you feel yourself hesitate should close, you would outgrow it, especially as now you will find yourself much more at ease. I remember Mr. E[merson] said that once you had a theory about preaching of the same kind, and did not put enough intellectual labor into the composition of a sermon. But you have got over that, and hence I infer that you may change your mind about prayer. It is right for me to say that, when I heard you preach last, I felt nothing but pleasure in the prayer, which seemed to me full, free, and rich, and should have supposed that the difficulty was completely outgrown, but that I have heard what is said about it at Northampton and elsewhere. I certainly know no one else in such a state of palpable growth as yourself, save and excepting Mr. E. I was charmed and interested by your first sermons, but felt your improvement in practical talent to be very great. The last years of your life, in which you have borne an apparent failure with such courage, dignity, and beauty, have done for you, palpably, what no outward success could have done. It has turned you visibly from a child into a man in bearing; and, in hoping for you now a continued prosperity, I can hope for nothing more than that you should adorn it as you have adorned adversity."

With the aid of George Ripley the ordination services were printed in full in a neat pamphlet, in Boston, during the autumn. In the summer and later on there was correspondence with Charles T. Brooks about a volume of German poems, which Brooks was translating, and in the preparation of which he desired, and received, Dwight's help. From letters to his family and friends, his doings and thinkings may be briefly chronicled.

"Had a fine day Sunday with old sermons," he wrote September 4. "The people looked so glad and expectant. After services I rode out with the Lorings to Mrs. Child, and spent one of the most delightful evenings of my life." This was Ellis Gray Loring and Lydia Maria Child. "I have lived in high clover this week," he wrote October 12. "Two whole Sundays from Cranch! He has completely won the hearts of our people. I have never listened to four sermons all so noble and so inspiring. I feel eclipsed in his success. He ought to be renowned and sought for in the churches, but his day is coming. Nothing has gratified me more since I have been here than to witness the warm response of our people to his bold and stirring declarations of truth. I feel as if the victory was won in regard to liberty of opinion here, and he feels that it is the freest and most genial atmosphere in which he has spoken."

A week later he wrote: " I enjoyed Cranch's visit prodigiously. Saturday I taught singing-school, had conversation meeting in the evening, at which I taxed my mind more than usual, and made the fullest statement, which I have ever yet succeeded in getting out, of my idea of Christ and Christianity."

" When I got back," he says November 8, " I found a beautiful present from New York,— Beethoven's opera ' Fidelio.' The same night I found a letter from Dr. Stedman, written in behalf of Ditson, the music publisher, asking me to make a translation from the German of Matthison's ' Adeläide,' and adapt it to Beethoven's music for publication. The letter contained a copy of Beethoven's letter of dedication to Matthison. These two things came in upon me together, just as one of my old Beethoven fits was growing upon me. I have played through ever so many sonatas this week."

Writing to one of his sisters under date of Jan. 12, 1841, Dwight gives an account of his work in detail: "Shall I give you the order of performances for one week? Sunday evening, a conversation or a teachers' meeting; Monday, Shakspere; Tuesday, Glee Club; Wednesday, choir meeting; Thursday, the Ladies' Whist Club, alias ' The Sociable '; Saturday, singing-school for children,— not to mention parties and such like. Then there are things to be written, things to be read. I incline to books, and would pass the day with them if it were possible. They give me more satisfaction than men just now. The *Dial* I have nearly devoured since Sunday. It even clipped the borders of my sermon some, it was so irresistible a dainty. It is a splendid number; and I cannot but thank the good souls who wrote in it, they have given me so much of inward comfort and beautiful thoughts. You shall have it erelong."

The conversation meetings which Dwight mentions several times were not an invention of his own. He probably took the idea of them from Dr. Charles Follen, who was for several years the minister of the little church in East Lexington. It was Dr. Follen's idea that the religious services of the churches were too stiff and formal, not sufficiently spontaneous, and did not give the people opportunity enough to ask questions and to express their own opinions. He planned a church at East Lexington, with the pulpit near the centre, wherein pastor and people could freely interchange ideas. His hope was that a new life would be awakened by this free spirit in the church, and that there would result a deepening of the religious life. His death on the ill-fated steamer "Lexington," as he was returning from New York to the dedication of the church, prevented his realizing his idea of a free church, in which the service should be the joint expression of the worshipful spirit of both the minister and congregation. His abilities as a scholar, his free spirit as a thinker and social reformer, and his deeply religious instinct, would have led him to use wisely the fresh and earnest methods he proposed. Dwight took from him the idea of meetings for conversation on religious subjects, wherein all should speak freely, and in which it was sought to cultivate the spirit of devotion in simple earnestness.

Dwight read the *Dial* with much interest, and procured several subscribers for it in Northampton and Greenfield. He was a contributor to the first volume, the opening number publishing one of his sermons under the title of " Religion of Beauty," and an article by him on " Concerts of the Past Winter," being those of Boston. In the third and fourth numbers appeared a sermon under the title of " Ideals of Every-day Life." Some of his interest in this publication may be understood from a portion of a letter to him from Mrs. George Ripley: "We are heartily rejoiced that you like the *Dial* well. George, Margaret, and Theodore [Ripley, Parker, and Miss Fuller] all run it down unmercifully. It has not fire and flame enough for them, but the reflected approbation of the public makes them seem more truly to appreciate it now. It is thought by many — myself among the number — a very charming book. Miss Peabody says: ' It is domestic, giving the every-day state of feeling and thought of the writers. There is no effort about it, and much strength behind.' The next number will be great. We cannot answer your inquiries with regard to the poetry in the *Dial*, especially that 'sweet, sad melody' you speak of. Margaret supplies the poetical department from the confidential deposits of private friendship in her portfolio; and we agree not to know the names of the pieces we most admire, that we may always have an answer for those who ask us."

"You have seen the *Dial*, of course," wrote Ripley in July. "I hope you like it better than I do. It is quite unworthy, I think, of its pretensions; and unless the everlasting hills, to which we have looked for help, give us something more than this, they had better cease to be parturient. Pray send us the remainder of that homily on 'The Church at Work,' etc., or whatever you may have stronger and better. I like your 'Rest' still more in print than I did in MS. It is an exquisite expression of a noble and true thought. Your article on 'Concerts' is an atoning offering for the many sins of the *Dial*. I do not fancy the 'Religion of Beauty' so much as I expected to do. It is unfinished. Almost every sentence promises something better than we get, and the sum total is a feeling of disappointment. Do give us some truly artistic product, be it ever so small. Your beautiful improvisations are a sin against your own soul; and, unless you repent and mend your ways, you will be damned when the day of judgment comes."

"How glad I am that you like the *Dial* so well!" wrote Ripley a month later, "and that the saints in Northampton and Deerfield also have an eye for its merits. The best judges, though, I think, generally are disappointed. It was not *prononcé* enough.

They expected hoofs and horns, while it proved as gentle as any sucking dove. The next number, I trust, will make amends. Still, this has produced a decided sensation. I feared it would fall dead; but there is no dread of that now. People seem to look on with wonder; while the Philistines, who dare show out, are wrathy as fighting-cocks. Pray send on your articles without delay; and, if you have any more such dainty verses as the last, let them come, too."

At the end of Dwight's first contribution to the *Dial* appeared a poem bearing the title " Rest," to which Ripley refers with words of praise. Although immediately following the article on the " Religion of Beauty," it does not form an integral part of it. This poem has been frequently reprinted, and for many years it was popularly supposed to be a translation from the German of Goethe. It was written by Dwight himself, and it is the one poem of his that has become popular and secured the honor of familiar quotation. It will be given here in full as the *Dial* first printed it: —

REST.

Sweet is the pleasure
    Itself cannot spoil !
Is not true leisure
    One with true toil ?

Thou that wouldst taste it,
    Still do thy best ;
Use it, not waste it,
    Else 'tis no rest.

Wouldst behold beauty
    Near thee, all round?
Only hath duty,
    Such a sight found.

Rest is not quitting
    The busy career :
Rest is the fitting
    Of self to its sphere.

'Tis the brook's motion,
    Clear without strife,
Fleeing to ocean
    After its life.

Deeper devotion
    Nowhere hath knelt;
Fuller emotion
    Heart never felt.

'Tis loving and serving
    The Highest and Best!
'Tis onwards! unswerving,
    And that is true rest.

Dwight had other literary tasks in hand than that of contributing to the *Dial*. He writes to Brooks of a "great parcel of songs for Lowell Mason, most of which were more imitations than translations." "I am under engagement to Ripley," he wrote Aug. 14, 1840, "to make a volume of Herder about that terrible Spinoza, etc., this autumn. I have postponed it all summer, and have but just got a chance to begin." In April the next year he wrote, "I have promised Ripley to make a volume or two from Goethe's prose, which ought to be

half-done by this time, but is scarcely begun."
Neither of these tasks was completed, and it is
doubtful if they were ever really undertaken.

When the anniversary of his ordination came
round, Dwight took occasion to review his year's
work, to point out in what ways it had not satisfied
him, and to indicate how it might be improved.
He spoke freely of some criticisms made upon his
preaching which had come to him; and he said
that the objections arose from the fact that the
people were worldly, and therefore not desirous of
having the truth freely spoken. These sermons
revived the discontent, and gave occasion for its
breaking out in a serious manner. He attempted
to heal the breach, sought to explain his words, to
reconcile the malcontents, and to restore harmony.
Ten days after the outburst he wrote: " I have
never felt in better spirits than since the painful
effort of yesterday. In the first place, I feel that
I have done my duty. In the next place, it has
shown me who are my friends, and what warm and
true friends they are."

" From all that I have discovered," he wrote
June 22, " of the character of the individuals of
whom my society is composed, I feel more and
more convinced that the relation between us never
could have been lasting, that I never entirely understood the heterogeneous compound, that, had I
done twice as much as I have, had I neglected no
means or precaution which occurred to me, it could
not have altered the case. The truth is, the true

state of things was from the first concealed from me. The enthusiasm of that ordination time deceived us. There were many who came reluctantly into the measure of my settlement. But all went on so quietly that I had reason to suppose that everybody was interested as much as could be expected. As it is, I know that a great many have been and still are deeply interested in my services, and are grieved exceedingly that a separation should take place. Very nearly all the women, and a majority of the men, I count upon confidently. But the favor with which I am looked upon by the female portion seems to be one chief offence. It is strange that my friends and my opposers know so little of each other." A few days later he wrote: " I am free! I heard nothing of the doings of the parish meeting till three days after. It was very thinly attended, and most of my friends were absent."

Dwight spent the summer and autumn in Northampton, enjoying the beauties of nature and devoting himself to literary labors. He preached a few times in neighboring towns, and he spent much time in wandering over the hills. His letters show an exquisite appreciation of all the quieter phases of nature around him. He was planning and preparing for the future. August 20 he gave a lecture before the American Institute of Instruction on " Simplicity of Character as affected by the Common Systems of Education." Before the Harvard Musical Association, August 25, he gave an address on music, which was published in _Hach's Musical Magazine_ for September.

"The days are quite filled up," he writes September 24; "yet I have done little but study and read and muse with reference to the coming lectures. I have just got through two long jobs,— the writing off and correcting my two addresses for the press, which I have sent to Boston. The musical address will appear soon in _Hach's Magazine_, and a few copies will be done up separately in pamphlet form. I have nearly doubled the length of it in writing it over, and I feel now that it is the happiest statement of my feelings about music which I have yet written. As I delivered it, it seemed loose and badly hung together, though it had a unity in my mind. I have now put a backbone into it, which holds all the parts firmly and systematically together."

The lectures referred to were on music, and they were prepared before his return to Boston in November. Early in the summer he wrote his friends in behalf of a course of popular lectures on music, and he soon had a number of engagements for their delivery. The winter was devoted in part to this work and to other literary employments.

After leaving Northampton, Dwight preached half a dozen times, and then quietly dropped out of a profession which he felt was no longer congenial. In reply to an invitation from Dr. Flint, of Salem, to fill his pulpit for a few Sundays, Dwight wrote from Brook Farm, under date of June 18, 1842:

" The truth is, my mind has been for some time past verging more and more away from the clerical profession.   Already I had resolved never again to be settled (even if I could be, which is doubtful); and now, just as I received your request, I was seriously deliberating the question whether to preach again at all.   I have doubts about the Church.   I agree with Parker mainly as to the essence of Christianity.   I disincline more and more to the forms, especially public prayer.   I have less sympathy than I had with the prevailing spirit of the churches, and less hope of ever being able to mould the Church and the profession to my idea, so that I could be true to my conviction while continuing in them ; and, in this state of mind, while I cannot go heartily and with my whole soul into a pulpit, I feel that it would be false to do it at all, either from old habit or for the sake of the livelihood, or respectable connection which I might derive from it. For the present, therefore, I decline all invitations to preach, not pledging myself with regard to the future, but yet seeing little prospect of my being reconciled to the profession or the profession to me.

" What pangs this costs me, what breaking of old hopes fondly cherished, and what plunging upon a .new sea of uncertainties, I have not time or spirit to detail to you.   But I know you will approve my course of action, such being my state of mind, and will give me credit for all willingness and desire to help you, were it only consistent with my sense of duty."

CHAPTER IV.

BROOK FARM.

IT was a time of intense intellectual ferment when Dwight began the work of his life. The Transcendental movement was just getting under way, and he entered into the spirit of it with great enthusiasm. The stir of social discontent he fully shared with many of his friends. The eager wish for a pure and rational religion was his in a large degree. In these and other directions he was a child of his time in the truest sense, sharing its hopes, joining in its aspirations, and ready to labor for the realization of its ideals.

When the Transcendental Club was started in Boston, he was a member from the first. He was intimately connected with all the men who belonged to it, and had known them as friends for some years. They felt him to be one of themselves, a sharer in their convictions and one worthy of their confidence. They saw in him fine traits of character, capacity for noble achievements, and somewhat of the high gift of genius. If they saw any limitation in his character, it was that he was not sufficiently self-seeking to push his way to the highest successes, and that he lacked the assertive will which is the promise of great achievements. He won their affection, however, and secured their loyal friendship. He fully shared in their intellectual hopes, and he was not behind any of them in that loyalty to conviction which counts not the cost for the sake of truth.

These qualities of his character were well brought out by his connection with Brook Farm. His intimacy with George Ripley and his wife, which had been of several years' duration, undoubtedly had something to do with his interest in that experiment. It was not this alone, however, which led him to join his friends in this effort at practical reform. Far more than Ripley himself, he was by nature destined to cast in his lot with such an effort to regenerate society. A born idealist, by temperament an enthusiast, and by conviction a come-outer from the conventionalities of society and religion, he was one who could see the promise of such a movement, and forsake all things cheerfully for its sake. It was not a young man's day-dream which led Dwight to Brook Farm. He never outgrew the convictions of that early time. To the day of his death he held firmly to the motives and aspirations which made him a member of the Brook Farm community.

Dwight was not one to drop into the common ways of the world and be content therewith. Wherever born or reared, he would have looked at the world with his own eyes, and been unwilling to accept the traditional methods of explaining it. Refined and gentle in all the habits of his mind, an intense lover of the beautiful, and æsthetic in his tastes and preferences, he seemed not to have in him any of the stuff of a reformer. He certainly was not an iconoclast or one in any way inclined to the destruction of what is old and venerable. It was his love of beauty, his instinctive yearning for what is pure and noble, and his keen desire for moral justice which led him to join with those who desired a better form of society. It was his wish to show how a finer and purer life could be lived when men turned away from greed and gave themselves to what is right and just.

One of the most characteristic enthusiasms of the time found its best expression at Brook Farm. It was not mere enthusiasm, however, which led to that experiment, but a careful and serious study of the needs of humanity. George Ripley was a man of sound intellect, tempered moral purpose, and wise insight into human needs. He calmly reasoned out a method for saving society, and his theories were shared by some of the most judicious men and women of his day. He went to Brook Farm in March or April, 1841, with deliberate purpose and high hopes. His wife and a few friends went with him to try the experiment of an industrial and social life which should be guided by rational aims, and in which all should jointly share in securing the good of all. The Articles of Association of this community were drawn up on September 29, and officers were elected. On the first of November the Brook Farm Institute of Agriculture and Education was organized, and to it were transferred the farm and other property which Mr. Ripley had purchased.

The objects had in view in the establishment of Brook Farm may be best stated in the words of

George Ripley, its founder and leader. "Our objects," he wrote, "are to insure a more natural union between intellectual and manual labor than now exists; to combine the thinker and the worker, as far as possible, in the same individual; to guarantee the highest mental freedom by providing all with labor adapted to their tastes and talents, and securing to them the fruits of their industry; to do away with the necessity of menial services by opening the benefits of education and the profits of labor to all; and thus to prepare a society of liberal, intelligent, and cultivated persons, whose relations with each other would permit a more simple and wholesome life than can be led amid the pressure of our competitive institutions." The articles of agreement, drawn up in Boston during the winter of 1840–41, somewhat more explicitly set forth the purposes had in view: "To substitute a system of brotherly co-operation for one of selfish competition; to secure to our children, and to those who may be intrusted to our care, the benefits of the highest physical, intellectual, and moral education which, in the present state of human knowledge, the resources at our command will permit; to institute an attractive, efficient, and productive system of industry; to prevent the exercise of worldly anxiety by the competent supply of our necessary wants; to diminish the desire of excessive accumulation by making the acquisition of individual property subservient to upright and disinterested uses; to guarantee to each other the means of physical support and of spiritual progress; and thus to impart a greater freedom, simplicity, truthfulness, refinement, and moral dignity to our mode of life."

When Ripley went to the farm in West Roxbury, he was accompanied by his wife, Sophia Willard Ripley, a woman of ability and learning, self-denying, and a capable leader, fit to adorn any society, and yet accepting the most menial tasks in behalf of her faith in the ideal; and his sister, Marianne Ripley, a teacher of experience and skill, devoted to her brother's interests, but somewhat Puritanic and inflexible in character. Soon after they were joined by George P. Bradford, a graduate of Harvard College, a gentle and refined soul, a lover of good literature, an able teacher, to which profession his life was devoted; Warren Burton, a graduate of Harvard and a Unitarian preacher, a writer of two or three delightful books on educational subjects, especially one on the district school as it was; and Minot Pratt, a printer and student, a lover of flowers, and a writer on agricultural themes, a gentle and lovable man, with his wife and children. On the 12th of April Nathaniel Hawthorne joined the little community, and a few weeks later he set down in his journal an enthusiastic account of the life at the farm. William B. Allen became the farmer of the association. In the autumn Charles A. Dana, who had been a student at Harvard, joined his interests with the others; and in November John S. Dwight became a member. When the association was organized, in the autumn of 1841, Ripley was assigned the position of chairman and leader, Dana was made the secretary, and Mrs. Ripley took charge of the educational interests.

The word " association " was used by the residents at Brook Farm to describe their life, private property was permitted and encouraged, all paid for board and lodging, and all received wages for the work they performed. It was a definite attempt to bring out and develop individual talent and character, and every effort was made to prevent sameness of thought and expression. At first there was an inclination to an excess of individual action, and to what Margaret Fuller called "grotesque freaks of liberty." This tendency grew less insistent in time; but the right to individual belief was acknowledged to the fullest extent, and it was duly respected. Without doubt this freedom of action was one source of weakness in the association; for it hindered united effort, and the needed discipline was not secured.

For the first three or four years the association devoted itself mainly to agriculture and education. The farm was not a good one, but a considerable effort was made to add to its productiveness. An experienced farmer was secured to direct the farm operations, and all the men were expected to devote a part of each day to the farm-work. A return to nature was much preached at that time, and it was thought by many that the cultivation of the soil was the only natural form of labor. It was maintained that no one could be sound in body and mind who did not cultivate the earth. " So, in order to reform society, in order to regenerate the world, and to realize democracy in the social relations," as Mr. Dana stated the objects had in view by the founders of Brook Farm, " they determined that their society should first pursue agriculture, which would give every man plenty of outdoor labor in the free air, and, at the same time, the opportunity of study, of instruction, of becoming familiar with everything in literature and in learning."

From the first the educational object was made more prominent at Brook Farm than agriculture itself. In describing the association, George Ripley wrote, " We are a company of teachers." And again he said, " The branch of industry which we pursue, as our primary object and chief means of support, is teaching." The educational forces of the association were carefully organized. There was an admirable primary school, which was followed by one preparatory for college, and another which devoted three years to a practical training in agriculture and horticulture. George Ripley taught philosophy and mathematics; George P. Bradford, literature; John S. Dwight, music and Latin; Charles A. Dana, Greek and German; John S. Brown, agriculture; Sophia W. Ripley, history and modern languages. In the primary school the teachers were Marianne Ripley, Abby Morton (afterward Mrs. Diaz), Georgiana Bruce (afterward Mrs. Kirby), and Hannah B. Ripley. In this department many others took part as time went on, and among them Dwight's sisters. Among the students were a considerable number who became known to the world for their intellectual ability or their interest in practical reforms. Much attention was also given to the intellectual interests of the adult members of the association. Clubs were organized, lectures were given, and books were freely loaned from his library by Mr. Ripley. In fact, an intellectual atmosphere surrounded the whole community. All were at school who belonged to it, for many gatherings were held that provided instruction and intellectual stimulus to all the members. In the mingling of old and young in the process of education the association was unique in its methods, few restraints being put upon the young, while the old were constantly invited to keep fully alive their intellectual interests.

The life at Brook Farm was very simple, and it was marked by a spirit of co-operation and sympathy. There was a common table, and all the members joined together in providing social entertainment. The life was a very happy one. The work of the field or kitchen was relieved by conversation, song, or jest; and the men did not fail to assist in the severer labors of the women. Every kindly office of helpfulness the members freely bestowed upon each other, if it was seen to be needed; and the young found endless amusement in games of every kind.

On the farm, when it was bought, was a large
house; and this was named " The Hive." It was
added to, and provided kitchen, dining-room, parlor,
and office, as well as many sleeping-rooms. Across
the road was a much smaller farm-house that was
rented for some months for school purposes, and
was christened " The Nest." In time there was
built on the highest point of land a large house
that therefore took the name of " The Eyrie," which
was occupied by the Ripleys, and used for school
purposes, as well as the keeping of Mr. Ripley's
library. Here, also, were the pianos, with the aid
of which Dwight carried on musical instruction. A
cottage was also built, that has been frequently
named after Margaret Fuller, but was not built or
occupied by her. The Pilgrim, or Morton, house
was built by two brothers from Plymouth for their
families, but soon came into the control of the
association. Then was undertaken the great
Phalanstery that was burned before completion.
Barns, a large workshop, and greenhouses were
also added to the buildings on the farm.

On leaving Northampton in the autumn of 1841,
Dwight became a member of the community at
Brook Farm. In a few remarks made by him, at
the close of an address on Brook Farm by Rev.
O. B. Frothingham, he gave an account of his life
there. They explain his purpose in joining the
association, and his mature judgment as to the
outcome of the experiment.

" It was my privilege," he said, " to know Mr.

Ripley very intimately for a number of years before he conceived that experiment. When I came out of the Divinity School at Cambridge, he was my first warm, helpful, encouraging friend. I was at his house almost daily during that famous controversy with Andrews Norton. I knew the whole of it as it went on. I talked with Mr. Ripley, and heard him read his manuscript.

"After I lived in Northampton, I was very much attracted to his idea which resulted in Brook Farm. His aspiration was to bring about a truer state of society, one in which human beings should stand in frank relations of true equality and fraternity, mutually helpful, respecting each other's occupation, and making one the helper of the other. The prime idea was an organization of industry in such a way that the most refined and educated should show themselves practically on a level with those whose whole education had been hard labor. Therefore, the scholars and the cultivated would take their part also in the manual labor, working on the farm or cultivating nurseries of young trees, or they would even engage in the housework.

"I remember the night of my first arrival at Brook Farm. It had been going on all the summer. I arrived in November. At that time it was a sort of pastoral life, rather romantic, although so much hard labor was involved in it. They were all at tea in the old building, which was called the Hive. In a long room at a long table they were taking tea, and I sat down with them. When tea was over, they were all very merry, full of life; and all turned to and washed the dishes, cups, and saucers. All joined in,— the Curtis brothers, Dana, and all. It was very enchanting; quite a lark, as we say. Much of the industry went on in that way, because it combined the freest sociability with the useful arts.

" The idea of most of us was that, beginning with what we felt to be a true system, with true relations to one another, it would probably grow into something larger, and that by bringing in others we should finally succeed in reforming and elevating society and put it on a basis of universal co-operation. Communism it was not, because property was respected. Some were allowed to hold and earn more than others. Only justice was sought for in the matter of labor and in the distribution of any surplus, if there were any, which seldom occurred. Capital, labor, and skill each had their fair proportion in the division; and the same person might share under each of these heads. It gave labor the largest share, five-twelfths; capital, four-twelfths; and skill, three-twelfths. By skill is meant the organizing head to industry. That was the whole of our equality.

" The great point aimed at was to realize practical equality and mutual culture, and a common-sense education for the children in a larger sense than prevails in ordinary society. The educational phase consisted partly in our education of one another and partly in the school, which was also one of the means of support of the community. Pupils were taken from outside, who lived there, and were taught by Mr. and Mrs. Ripley and others. There were some young people who came and lived there simply as boarders, from a certain romantic interest in the ideas, but not committing themselves to them by membership.

" The social education was extremely pleasant. For instance, in the matter of music, we had extremely limited means or talent; and very little could be done except in a very rudimentary, tentative, and experimental way. We had a singing class, and we had some who could sing a song gracefully and accompany themselves at the piano. We had some piano music; and, so far as it was possible, care was taken that it should be good,— sonatas of Beethoven and Mozart, and music of that order. We sang masses of Haydn and others, and no doubt music of a better quality than prevailed in most society at that date; but that would be counted nothing now. Occasionally we had artists come to visit us. We had delightful readings; and once in a while, when William Henry Channing was in the neighborhood, he would preach us a sermon.

" Hawthorne was there then, but he left at about that time. He knew very little about it as an organized industrial experiment. But he was pleased to live on a farm, and he liked to drive oxen; and he would drive until he got himself tired through the day, and shut himself up in his room in the even-

ing.   So it was wholly a mistake that the 'Blithe-
dale Romance' describes Brook Farm.   There is
nothing of Brook Farm in it except the scenery.
None of the characters represent people at Brook
Farm.   It has been supposed that the heroine was
Margaret Fuller, but she was never a member.
She was only an occasional visitor, a friend of Mr.
and Mrs. Ripley.   She made us delightful visits.

"We were never more than a hundred, often not
that; and we had very little means and a poor
farm, nearly two hundred acres, mostly grass and
woods, and found it hard to get people enough of
the right kind to do what work was required.
Everybody went into the work heartily, and everybody tried to help every other.   There was a great
sweetness and charm in the sincerity of the life.

"I do not think Brook Farm was wholly a
dream.   This aspect has been too strongly presented.   I think it was very practical, for we had
very practical and common-sense men and women
among us.   It was a great good to me.   Every one
who was there will say it was to him, though it is
extremely hard to tell of it.   The truth is, every
resident there had his own view of it.   Every one
saw the life through his own eyes and in his own
way.   Naturally, they formed groups; and one
group was not like another.   Certain ones were
just as individual as in any common society.   I felt
and still think that it was a wholesome life, that it
was a good practical education.   I have no doubt I
should not have been living at this day if it had not

been for the life there, for what I did on the farm and among the trees, in handling the hay and even in swinging the scythe. Those who have survived, and been active in their experiences, have certainly shown themselves persons of power and faculty, with as much common sense, on the average, as ordinary men."

As Dwight has said in these reminiscences, the school was opened almost from the first. Persons who were in sympathy with the purposes of the community sent their children, as did others who were intent only on finding the best possible instruction for their children. The prices were moderate, the surroundings delightful, the moral atmosphere wholesome; and it was in a fair degree successful.

Dwight directed the musical life of the community. His enthusiasm for the musical art found scope for expression at this time. The materials he had at command were not of the best, but he made the most of them. He cultivated a taste for the better kinds of music, talked so enthusiastically about the divine mission of music, and gave so much time to bringing out the best musical qualities of the members of the community that he succeeded in impressing his own tastes and convictions upon all around him. His work for music has been described by a member of the community, Miss Amelia Russell, writing in the *Atlantic Monthly* for November, 1878, where she says that he was "of a most delicately sensitive organization;

and discords of every kind were as antagonistic to him as were false chords in music. His whole life," she says, "seemed one dream of music; and I do not think that he was ever fully awake to all the harsh gratings of this outer world. We were indebted to him for much of the pleasure of our evening social life. He was too really musical to endure the weariness of teaching beginners the first rudiments of his own art, although for some time he was our only teacher. I must say he was wonderfully patient, considering his temperament, in the task he had assumed; for his nerves must have been most fearfully taxed in some of his labors, but his outward demeanor did not bear testimony to what must often have been his earnest desire,— to tear his hair out by the roots."

In giving a boy's recollections of life at Brook Farm, in the *New England Magazine* for May, 1894, Arthur Sumner says that Dwight "used to come in from his toil in the hot sun at noon to give me a lesson on the piano; and, after doing that job, he would lie down on the lounge and go to sleep, while I played to him. What a piece of nonsense it was to have a man like that hoeing corn and stiffening his eloquent fingers! But the idea was, I think, that all kinds of labor must be made equally honorable, and that the poet, painter, and philosopher must take their turn at the plough or in the ditch. Mr. Dwight had a quite feminine sweetness and delicacy of nature."

Another member of the community has written

of the time when Dwight joined it, and of his earliest efforts to develop a musical interest and taste among the members. " This winter," we are told, " brought to us a cordial sympathizer and earnest laborer, John S. Dwight, and with him all sorts of talk about the meaning and use of music, and much delicate improvisation. Soon there was a class of little ones crowding around the gentle, genial master, singing from the first ' Boston School Singing Book '— has there been so sweet a collection since? — and later a larger class who attacked the gems in ' Kingsley's Choir,' and presented Mozart's Seventh and Twelfth Masses. How modestly he speaks of the Mass Clubs which sprang up about that time, not only at Brook Farm, but in Boston, and of the writing and lecturing on the great masters, as if he himself had not been the sole instigator and unwearied worker, assisted, no doubt, by the articles of Miss Fuller! First, it was necessary to create a larger want for something better than the Swiss Bell Ringers and mangled psalmody. Then he set himself to work to cause to be assembled the talent that would supply, while it increased the demand. It will never be known by what studied and persistent manipulation a sufficiently large public was brought to believe that Beethoven's symphonies and Mozart's masses were divine creations, and as such their performance should be called for by all lovers of fine music."

The reference in the above to Dwight's mention of Mass Clubs is to his paper on " Music as a

Means of Culture," published in the *Atlantic Monthly* for September, 1870. In that essay he gave some reminiscences of the Brook Farm period, and especially of the awakening of musical interest at that time. In that awakening he was the chief factor, and it was his own enthusiasm which kindled to a glow the musical interest of others. The Mass Clubs were the result of his work for music at Brook Farm and in Boston, and of his effort to make people acquainted with the great composers and their productions. His own ardor and persistence were so great as to arouse in others a like passionate love of music as an art and a means of true culture. The lecturing on music he mentions was done by himself, for the most part; but it fell in with the general intellectual movement of the time. What Emerson was doing for the intellectual life of the time, Parker for its religion, Ripley for its economic life, Dwight was doing for its music, spiritualizing it, giving it force and character in intellectual convictions, and bringing it into close relations with all the higher human interests.

"It is a fact of some significance," Dwight says, " that the interest here felt in Beethoven began at the same moment with the interest in Emerson, and notably in the same minds who found such quickening in his free and bracing utterance. It was to a great extent the great souls drawn to ' Transcendentalism' (as it was nicknamed), to escape spiritual starvation, who were most drawn also to the great, deep music which we began to hear at that time. For, be it remembered, the first great awakening of the musical instinct here was when the C Minor Symphony of Beethoven was played, thirty years ago or more, in that old theatre long since vanished from the heart of the dry-goods part of Boston, which has been converted into an 'Odeon,' where an 'Academy of Music' gave us some first glimpses of the glories of great orchestral music. Some may yet remember how young men and women of the most cultured circles, whom the new intellectual dayspring had made thoughtful, and at the same time open and impressible to all appeals of art and beauty, used to sit there through the concert in that far-off upper gallery or sky-parlor, secluded in the shade, and give themselves up completely to the influence of the sublime harmonies that sank to their souls, enlarging and coloring thenceforth the whole horizon of their life. Then came the Brook Farm experiment. And it is equally a curious fact that music, and of the best kind, — the Beethoven sonatas, the masses of Mozart and Haydn, — got at, indeed, in a very humble, home-made, and imperfect way, was one of the chief interests and refreshments of those halcyon days. Nay, it was among the singing portion of those plain farmers, teachers, and (but for such cheer) domestic drudges that the first example sprang up of the so-called 'Mass Clubs,' once so in vogue among small knots of amateurs. They met to practise music which to them seemed heavenly, after the

old hackneyed glees and psalm-tunes, though little
many of them thought or cared about the creed
embodied in the Latin words that formed the convenient vehicle for tones so thrilling. The music
was quite innocent of creed, except that of the
heart and of the common deepest wants and aspirations of all souls, darkly locked up in formulas, till
set free by the subtile solvent of the delicious harmonies. And our genial friend, who sits in Harper's 'Easy Chair,' has told the world what parties
from 'the Farm'— and he was 'one of them'—would
come to town to drink in the symphonies, and then
walk back the whole way, seven miles at night, and
unconscious of fatigue, carrying home with them a
new good genius, beautiful and strong, to help
them through the next day's labors. Then, too,
and among the same class of minds — the same
'Transcendental set'— began the writing and the
lecturing on music and its great masters, treating
it from a high spiritual point of view, and seeking
(too imaginatively, no doubt) the key and meaning
to the symphony, but anyhow establishing a vital,
true affinity between the great tone-poems and all
great ideals of the human mind. In the *Harbinger*,
for years printed at Brook Farm, in the *Dial*, which
told the time of days so far ahead, in the writings
of Margaret Fuller and others, these became favorite and glowing topics of discourse; and such discussion did at least contribute much to make music
more respected,— to lift it in the esteem of thoughtful persons to a level with the rest of the 'humani-

ties' of culture, and especially to turn attention to the nobler compositions, and away from that which is but idle, sensual, and vulgar.

"The kind reader will grant plenary indulgence to these gossiping memories, and must not for a moment think it is intended by them to claim for any one class the exclusive credit of the impulse given in those days to music. Cecilia had her ardent friends and votaries among conservatives as well. But is it not significant, as well as curious, that the free-thinking and idealistic class referred to — call them 'Transcendental dreamers' if you will: they can afford to bear the title now — were so largely engaged in the movement that among the 'select few' constant to all opportunities of hearing the great music in its days of small things here so many of this class were found? The ideas of those enthusiasts, if we look around us now, have leavened the whole thought and culture of this people, have melted icy creeds, and opened genial communion between sects, have set the whole breast of the nation heaving, till it has cast off the vampire of at least one of its great established crimes and curses, have set all men thinking of the elevation of mankind. These are the conquering ideas; and with them came in the respect for music, which now in its way, too, is leavening, refining, humanizing, our too crude and swaggering democratic civilization. A short pedigree, but great ideas, by their transforming power, work centuries of change in a few years.

" The great music came in, then, because it was in full affinity with the best thoughts stirring in fresh, earnest souls. The same unsatisfied, deep want that shrank from the old Puritan creed and practice, that sought a positive soul's joy instead of abnegation, that yearned for the '*beauty* of holiness,' and for communion with the Father in some sincere way of one's own without profession, that, kindled with ideals of a heaven on earth and of a reign of love in harmony with nature's beauty and the prophecies of art, found just then and here unwonted comfort, courage, and expression in the strains of the divine composers, of which we were then getting the first visitations. It was as if our social globe, charged with the electricity of new divine ideas and longings,— germs of a new era,— were beginning to be haunted by auroral gleams and flashes of strange melody and harmony. Young souls, resolved to keep their youth, and be true to themselves, felt a mysterious attraction to all this, though without culture musically. Persons not technically musical at all would feel the music as they felt the rhythm of the ocean rolling in upon the beach. They understood as little of the laws of the one as of the other fascinating and prophetic mystery. Beethoven, above all, struck the key-note of the age. In his deep music, so profoundly human, one heard, as in a sea-shell, the murmur of the grander future. Beethoven, Händel, Mozart, found no more eager audience than among these 'disciples of the newness' (as some sneeringly called them), these believing ones, who would not have belief imposed upon them, who cared more for life than doctrine, and to whom it was a prime necessity of heart and soul to make life genial. This was to them 'music of the future,' in a more deep and real sense than any Wagner of these later times has been inspired to write."

For a time, at least, Dwight gave himself up with enthusiasm to the new life around him, and to its absorbing interests. His pleasure in the idyllic side of the life he was living is well expressed in a note to Lowell, written about seven months after he had taken up his residence at Brook Farm. " May I not hope to see you at Brook Farm in this fine season ? " he asks. " I should delight to have you long enough to conduct you about our wood and river walks, or take you out in our boat, when we might discuss matters human and divine, or, better yet, deliver ourselves up to the water-sprites and to our own wayward fancies, whether of noisy talk or silent reverie, like Nature's happy children. I have forgotten how to write or think or picture out a scene or thought in words. I only feel. Perhaps you will bring a sprig or two from the poetic plants which have been springing up under your still fostering hand this summer. When are we to have the book ? "

He had not wholly dropped his pen, however ; and an article on " Griswold and American poetry " went to the *Christian Examiner* at this time. In the autumn Henry T. Tuckerman asked him to contribute translations from his favorite German poets to the *Boston Miscellany*. At the same time Lowell was writing to him in behalf of his own venture, the *Pioneer*. Lowell's letter indicates fairly well the position which Dwight had gained as a literary worker and as a musical critic : —

"*My dear Friend,*— On the 1st of next January a magazine will be started in Boston, of which I am to be the editor. It is to be a *free* magazine, and is to take as high an aim in art as may be. I wish to notice every branch of art, and do it in an artistic way. To this end I wish to get those who know something to write for me in its several departments. I shall give them *carte blanche* as to what they say, not wishing to cut the opinions of those who know more than I do of the subjects on which they write down to my own level.

"If you are willing, I should like to have the musical criticism under your charge. At first I shall not be able to pay as much as I wish. But I will give at the least $10 for every article of three pages or more, and $2 a page for less. The possibility of raising our people's taste in this divine matter must be a part of your reward at first. If the magazine succeeds, I shall be able and glad to pay you as you deserve.

"If you come into Boston, will you come and see me, that we may talk it over? If you cannot, will you write to that effect? Yours in love and hope,

J. R. LOWELL."

A fortnight later Dwight wrote: "Not finding you in, I take the liberty of sitting down in your office to reply to yours of a fortnight since. I was hoping to see you in Boston before this, or I should have written. Your project pleases me exceedingly. I have only time to say that it will give me pleasure to be connected with it in any way in which I may further its success. It would be a great pleasure to me to have a corner in which I may freely whisper from time to time what I have to say on Musical Art; and in these hard times I shall be glad of any additional resources, however small, to eke out what is exceedingly small.

"I shall try to call this afternoon, if peradventure I may find you in your office, and hear you expose the noble project further. Meanwhile I rejoice to find you grown so Pan-theistic, since in that I can subscribe myself your sympathizer and well-wisher."

"I intended fully to have seen you on Sunday," Lowell wrote a week later, "but found myself so happy at Frank Shaw's that I had not the heart to go away. It is truly a gladness to me that you are willing to write my musical criticisms for me, for I do not know any one who can do it so well.

"Can you write something about the symphony which the Academy are to 'bring out' this winter? Say three or four or five pages of the size of the *Boston Miscellany*. Three of your MS. pages will probably fill a printed page of that size. When I specify the length, I do not wish you to curb your-

self: if it should be longer, never mind. I should
also like to have a notice of Bohrer, if you have
heard him, to go in fine print among the notices
of the month. Any essay on music that you are
prompted to write, I shall be glad to print and pay
for. I should like to see you when you are in Boston, but am generally out of town Saturday after-
noons. Always your friend."

Dwight did write on the Academy of Music
and other subjects, but the *Pioneer* was short-lived.
In 1843 he contributed to the *Democratic Review*
articles on Haydn, Händel, and Mozart; and he
wrote on other subjects for the same periodical.
When Mrs. Eliza Lee was translating from Richter and publishing his biography, Dwight lent her
valuable assistance. " I regret exceedingly," she
wrote him, " that I could not have had the benefit
of your revision of my book at an earlier period;
for I feel that your correction of the translation has
been a benefit which nothing can repay."

The interest in Dwight's lectures on music led
to a desire for their publication on the part of his
friends. What that interest was is hinted at in a
note sent him by Margaret Fuller, who wrote: —

"*My dear Mr. Dwight,*— I enclose the sum I
vainly attempted to rob from the musical public
under cloak of your reputation. I shall not be able
to hear your lecture, as it is the last evening my
sister Fanny passes with us before a separation like
to be a long one, but trust you will give your audi-

ence as much pleasure as you did last time. The expressions of obligation that I heard were numerous. If there is a concert or rehearsal at the Odeon on Saturday evening, will it be convenient for you to escort Caroline and myself? With regard.

S. M. FULLER."

The desire to see his lectures put into a volume was voiced by Ellis Gray Loring, who wrote Dwight in August, 1842: "I have had true satisfaction in reading the lectures on Händel and Mozart, and doubt not they will realize for me what must be your chief purpose; that is, that your readers shall always hereafter enjoy and appreciate better the compositions of those masters. I wish your various writings on music might be collected and published. I think they would make, in every sense, a successful work." The same wish was expressed in a letter from George W. Curtis, written in January, 1844, who said: "When Charles Dana came running to me with what he thought Emerson's poem, how could I help saying, It is mine? In that case, at least, it was sympathy for Emerson's reputation that prompted the speech. There is something that pleases me much in the united works of young authors. Imagine the united literary works of Dwight and Curtis rotting in an odd drawer of Ticknor's or James Munroe's; could we ever look each other in the face again? What a perpetual suspicion there would be that the one swamped the other! Do you not mean some day to gather your musical essays together, and suffer them to expand into a book? though not with the cream-colored calyx that Ticknor affects, I beg. Nay, might you not make some arrangement with Greeley to publish them here in a cheap way, if you would make money? for those who valued them would, of course, obtain more desirable copies. If not, and you would think dignity compromised, some of the regular publishers might be diplomatized with. They would make a unique work. You know we have nothing similar in American literature, no book of artistic criticism, have we? Why will you not think of it, if you have not done so? and, 'what so poor a man as Hamlet is may do, you shall command.'"

In 1845 there was correspondence with a New York publisher about a "History of Music," and encouragement was given; but the book was not completed. At the same time Dwight proposed the plan of putting his *Dial* essays into a book; and the publisher wrote: "I have read a part of the 'Ideals of Every-day Life' with more care since writing you, and am highly pleased with it, so much so that, if you will let me have it after you shall have enlarged it enough to make fifty or seventy-five printed pages of a 12mo, I will add a few choice things, and publish it. I should not expect to make anything on it, but would just make it pay for itself by paying you a reasonable compensation. The chief object would be to dissemi-

nate the pure principles which those sermons incul-
cate, and to make known your name as a writer
through the large list of the press which is now on
our exchange list from every State in the Union.
I should give away three hundred copies, at least.
Will you not let me have it at a small compensation?" This scheme also fell through, probably
because of more urgent interests demanding attention at Brook Farm.

His enthusiastic interest in music Dwight expressed in a letter written on Christmas Day, 1843.
It also gives hint of his feeling of deprivation in
being shut out from opportunities to cultivate
music as he desired. The cordial, friendly, and
even enthusiastic letters of Mrs. Child were full of
spirit and courage; and especially was her delight
in Ole Bull of a most exuberant nature.

"*My dear Friend Mrs. Child*,— All things con-
spire to make me write to you. It is Christmas night.
Mr. Benzon is here to remind me of you (though I
need no reminding), and to take my letter; and,
above all, you have spoken to me irresistibly in
that splendid letter to the *Courier* about 'Ole
Bulbul.' This last, I believe, I must thank for
effectually breaking the spell of my strange, un-
pardonable,— to myself even,— inexplicable silence.
I will no longer respond only in silent feeling, but
in visible tokens, in words; for therein you speak
like my other self, therein you speak to *me*, — not
for the first time, surely. Have I not for two whole

years been receiving the kindest and sweetest
recognitions from you, and, like a selfish dog,
hoarded them up in silence, answering not a word?
Verily, you have heaped coals of fire upon my head.
First, that noble, soul-stirring appeal in behalf of
Mrs. Colt, which I did not answer because the result went against my heart; then message after
message of kindest sympathy and remembrance,
which have been to me among my great encourage-
ments in a life of perplexity and loneliness; then
your beautiful, your most cheering and inspiring
book,— a book which I prize and reperuse with
double fondness, for the golden sunshine in it and
for associations with the author and the giver;
and now, finally, this outpouring of your true soul
about music, which no one should respond to more
promptly or fervently than myself.

" How shall I ever repay you for all my debt?
If thoughts and feelings answering to yours, and
having a most conscious reference to you,— thoughts
by you suggested and suggesting you,— were letters,
I should have written to you every day in the year.
Alas! I hope my friends know expression with me
is no measure of regard. You certainly will bear
me out in saying it is never too late to repent.
And this is the holy, happy Christmas,— a good
time to shuffle off the coil of old indolent habit, and
to present myself before you in the clean robes of
new and good intentions. You will not give me
up for hopeless. I hereby rebuke, renounce, and
cast out from myself the dumb spirit. If he has

occupied so long as to have somewhat weakened my original faculty of speech, and made me slow and awkward at concocting a letter (for my dumbness has been to all my friends, not to you alone), this, too, you will pardon, and accept a first lame effort encouragingly.

" I shall not rest until I hear your Bulbul. They tell me that in him is the living presence of commanding genius in music; and that is what I have hardly, perhaps never, met. I have divined, recognized (through a glass darkly), genius in the works of great composers through the imperfect medium of uninspired performers, or through my own poor efforts to study myself into their meaning by slow and painful transfer of the printed notes to the keys of my piano. I have been charmed, transported, robbed of my sleep, and haunted for days by the wonderful performances of violinists and pianists.

" But I do not feel quite sure that music has yet spoken to me through one of her appointed organs, through one of her chosen sons, in the person of a performer. And yet I have heard something so near to inspiration that I require the presence of Ole Bull to show me whether it was not that.

" During the last week my sleep was broken, and all my habitual scenes and functions made stale and wearisome and obsolete, as it seemed to me, by hearing, not indeed a Persian nightingale, but a something between a canary bird and a thrush. I mean Vieuxtemps. He is the perfection of art, if nothing more; and he must be more, to be that.

Of his tones, what you say of Bulbul's would not be an exaggerated description. Sometimes there was nothing earthly in them. They were like spirit disembodied: they did not contradict or limit my soul, as all things material or finite do, as all things must do which have not perfect beauty. My soul was free with them. Like the stars and the tints of the sky at all hours, I enjoyed them with an entire surrender of myself and with a sweet response. Then they were wild, nervous, and electrifying. Indeed, the bold certainty, bold yet calm, the sudden flashing energy with which he always attacked a theme, was a perpetual surprise and a perpetual conquest. The melody was certainly new-born under his hands: there was no possibility of its becoming old or wearisome. The nature of the instrument, too, its appetizing harshness, its racy, sharp violinity, came honestly out, more eloquent and musical than if it were all sweet. His compositions, not very profound or impassioned, were beautiful, were original. This made it seem cold and only artistical to many. But there was a uniform subdued sensibility and a quiet earnestness in his whole air that would not let me believe him without a soul. He moved my soul. Could he have done it unless he had played from at least an equal depth? Could he have caused me to feel if he did not feel himself? He was born for the violin, I know. A youth of twenty-three, he has exhausted its known powers. The most experienced critics cannot discover a want in his performance. Perhaps you think, if the critics cannot, the simple hearts can. Well, he delighted me with the peculiar delight of finding something perfect in the outward. Modest and unconscious, not thrusting himself between his music and you, he seemed to be the artist in a high and holy sense, to be filled with the true idea and sentiment of art, to lose himself in exercising an infallible mastery over his instrument. But not an infallible mastery over this most wonderful, most common instrument, this human heart? He certainly has not conquered the multitude like Ole Bull. Perhaps, though a true artist, he yet lacks genius. If he has it, it is not of the popular recognizable sort. One thing was most wonderful to think of afterwards,— that his art, so admirable, so inspiring, seemed at the moment nothing strange or difficult, nothing but the simplest,— no more marvellous than daylight, but yet as marvellous, as hard to explain or analyze. I say he is between a canary and a thrush, because he is such a polished singer on the one hand, and yet, so far from being a tame one, he has plenty of 'gism.' He laughs and mocks like the thrush. He is wild and wood-like and mysterious and inimitable like him.

" *Wednesday*, 27*th.*— I am just from the Fourier convention, where I spend day and night. It is intensely interesting, probably the only great audience in this world where most exciting controversy could be carried on in a perfectly sweet spirit on both sides. How much of this is owing to the 'spirit that moves over the face of the troubled waters' when William Channing's voice is raised! But I cannot tell you of it in this. Here I feel with new force the divine significance of music. You have said the truest thing ever said about it when you called music the 'soprano, or feminine, principle of the universe,' the principle of all things, etc. That music is so becoming recognized as the art of arts, the soul of them all, at the very same time when the law of social harmonies is being announced, is a fact not without significance. Were it not worth while to give a life to develop the analogy?"

In October of the next year Mrs. Child wrote, urging Dwight to prepare an article on Ole Bull for the *Democratic Review*, and offering to secure him free admission to the great violinist's concerts if he would do so. Dwight promptly replied; but the first part of the letter, which touched upon personal experiences and sorrows, was cut away and destroyed by Mrs. Child. In a fragment of it which remains, he says: "The truth is, my friend, I am oppressed with sadness. I have had heavy sorrows to bear in these later times which have quite checked the elasticity that seeks expression." The part of the letter touching upon music and Ole Bull explains why Dwight did not give more time to literary pursuits, and is as follows: —

"Now as to Ole Bull. I heard him twice last winter. Excepting only a symphony of Beethoven or a mass of Mozart, nothing ever filled me with such deep, solemn joy. I had spoken warmly of Vieuxtemps, and still he is very beautiful in my memory. The popular award of 'artistical perfection' to Vieuxtemps and 'genius' to Ole Bull is not quite just to the former. I felt in him more than he gave me to hear. I do not believe that he has exhausted himself yet. But Ole Bull is undoubtedly the stronger and greater man. I should doubt if he were the more simple of the two. He is certainly the most original, the most never-failing and commanding. He does inspire as the other cannot. The most glorious sensation I ever had was to sit in one of his audiences, and to feel that all were elevated to the same pitch with myself, that the spirit in every breast had risen to the same level. My impulse was to speak to any one and to every one as to an intimate friend. The most indifferent person was a man — a living soul — to me. The most remote and proud I did not fear nor despise. In that moment they were accessible,— nay, more, worth reaching. This certainly was the highest testimony to his great art, to his great soul.

"Frederic Rackemann, the pianist, who has himself the fire of genius, was intimate with him. He would speak, by turns, of Bull and of Vieuxtemps as the greatest, and that, apparently, with the most entire unconsciousness of any inconsistency. Yet I judge that his sympathy was more with Bull. Once he said that 'Vieuxtemps was altogether the greater artist'; but, on being pressed, he said that

Ole Bull could do all that he could, with a little study, and a great deal more. It was plain where his enthusiasm shone forth.

" I should really delight to do the thing you propose, were I only sure of one thing,— my ability. I have, to be sure, very, very little time, my musical and literary life being almost indefinitely postponed. But I would contrive to steal time. Let me say that I will expose myself to the temptation of doing it, but I will not promise. Hear him more, I certainly should; and your kind suggestion about the pecuniary facilities would be highly acceptable,— nay, indispensable; for now that I am so lost to intellectual society in Boston, so identified with a despised sect, and so absorbed here as to lose the run of musical acquaintances, free tickets are not at my command, as they once were. One thing more: I want to know Ole Bull; yet in my obscurity I cannot seek him out, surrounded as he is always by a brilliant crowd. Is it not possible that the frankness and originality of our community life might interest him enough to warrant his riding out to Brook Farm? Mr. Chickering or Schmidt would gladly show him the way. Were I in the city, I certainly should know him. I cannot answer your question about counterpoint. With warmest acknowledgments to Mr. Hopper, I am sincerely and gratefully your friend,

" J. S. DWIGHT."

Brook Farm has been subjected to much of criticism, and to not a little of amusing comment. That it should have been the subject of banter and sarcasm is not in the least strange, especially as it was viewed by those who were not in sympathy with its purposes. It has also suffered from the reminiscences of its own members, who have treated it as one would a youthful escapade, while they commented freely on the serious purposes of its older and more responsible leaders. Though it has been written of often as if it were a holiday picnic, yet it did not wear such an aspect to those who were responsible for its policy and its success.

Dwight, not less than Ripley, believed in Brook Farm, and devoted to it the whole of his capacities while it continued in existence. He belonged to the inner circle of its leaders, helped to shape its policy, and felt the responsibility of its success or failure resting upon him personally. While he was one of the leaders in the social life of the community, he was also a wise counsellor in the administrative management. Not a fluent speaker, and restrained by his diffidence from public utterance, his voice was often heard in the meetings of the community when visitors were to be welcomed or the general interests discussed. During the period when the teachings of Fourier were under consideration and the policy of the community was being reshaped, he was one of the most practical in suggestion and fertile in plans and wise in counsel of any of the leaders. No one else, not even Ripley, was superior to him in the work of distinctly shaping the future plans of the community.

It may be frankly said, however, that Dwight had no financial skill, and that his administrative gifts were limited; but he had in him a deep, strong, practical common sense, a capacity for touching life on the side of its every-day interests, and he greatly admired men of common sense and executive power.   While of a most refined and sensitive organization himself, delicately alive to every æsthetic interest, and of exquisite tastes, he was no dilettante, and in no sense over-refined or finical. He mingled freely with the people of the Farm, keenly sympathized with the toils and deprivations of workingmen, and was eager to do what he could to improve the condition of those hard beset in the struggles of life.   He had no inclination to despise those who were not cultured, but freely appreciated the genuine gifts of all persons.   He loved genuineness and thoroughness wherever they were found, and he exercised a large and wholesome influence in putting these virtues into the working policy of Brook Farm.

Far too much emphasis has been laid on the social side of Brook Farm by those who have written about it; but, in fact, at all the meetings of the community — even little tea parties — the talk was likely to run on high and serious themes. During the first two or three years it is true that the social interest was a prominent feature, and much time was given to amusements and entertain-

ments of all kinds. As those who have written of
the life at the Farm were nearly all quite young at
this time, it is very natural they should have given
most attention to describing what to them was
then the interest which left the deepest impression. The life was never sombre or lugubrious,
but always bright and sympathetic, a wise freedom
being allowed to all. Yet it is true that a thoughtful and earnest spirit pervaded the whole life of the
people. Serious subjects were discussed more than
is usual elsewhere, and a tone of culture and refinement made itself felt on every hand.

A hint of what the social life was at Brook Farm
may be gained from a letter written Jan. 27, 1845,
describing a little coffee party planned by Amelia
Russell, and attended by Mr. and Mrs. Ripley,
Charles and Maria Dana, Albert Brisbane, John
Orvis, John, Marianne, and Frances Dwight, Os-
borne, Eunice, and Fanny Macdaniel, Sarah White-
house, and Frederic Cabot: "Coffee was handed
round, a few puns perpetrated. Meanwhile a holy
aspiration from high heaven was stealing quietly
and unseen over the souls of all present. Mr. Ripley proposed for a toast Albert Brisbane, the first
apostle of Fourierism, and made some interesting
and rather humorous remarks about the great assistance he had afforded us in the convention and in
the framing of the new constitution. Mr. Brisbane
disclaimed it all, grew eloquent in reply, spoke of
Brook Farm society and the friendship he had enjoyed here, the pleasure of receiving many kind

offices at the hand of friendship, etc. I cannot attempt to repeat the toasts that were given, they
were so numerous and all good, nor the excellent
remarks that were made by Ripley, Dana, Brisbane, and Dwight. Suffice it to say that I never
heard either of them speak better. It was all
beauty and inspiration. There was true humor, eloquence, elegance, deep earnestness, and sacred solemnity. After those present were toasted, beautiful tributes were paid to the absent. Fourier;
William H. Channing, the priest and poet of association; Greeley; and other New York friends,—
were remembered, and each toast prefaced by interesting remarks. Charles Dana proposed his friend,
Parke Godwin, spoke of him with deep feeling and
all the earnestness of affection, and, just as he was
concluding, Fred added, 'God wins always in the
end.' So appropriate and good a pun was universally applauded. We set it down for Fred's best,
but afterwards found that he also was encircled
with a heavenly halo, and everything he did that
evening was his best.

"As the speeches became higher and holier and
more beautiful, and the broadest principles were
uttered from golden lips, and our emotions grew
more elevated and solemn, Charles Dana spoke of a
meeting in New York where they all joined hands,
and pledged themselves to the cause of association;
and he called upon us warmly and fervently to do
the same. With one impulse we all arose, and
formed a circle around the little table; and, hand

in hand, we vowed 'truth to the cause of God and humanity.' It was a solemn moment, never, never to be forgotten. Then our circle of friendship was toasted. What beautiful allusions Dwight made to our circle, and to circles within circles, that it was not exclusive, but that endless circles might be drawn around it, all having the same centre! Mr. Ripley wished, very humorously, that our Phalanx might grow till we could join hands around Palmer's woods, around Cora Island, across the river. Mr. Brisbane would have the circle surround the globe. Then Mr. Brisbane, after Mr. Ripley had been speaking of circles, said he had omitted the ellipse,— the emblem of love centred in two foci,— and made beautiful remarks upon that. Dwight made a good pun, saying Mr. Brisbane had supplied the ellipse — or omission — in Mr. Ripley's speech. Dwight toasted the coffee-pot in this wise: 'Our patient friend, the coffee-pot,— though drained of its contents, it has not lost its patience: if it is not spiritual, it certainly is not material (is immaterial).' Mr. Ripley jumped a foot and turned directly round at so good a pun. Fred gave a toast with no little wit and humor: 'John Allen,— may his wisdom grow to his love.' Immense applause. Dwight gave a beautiful toast to the memory of the dead,— the dead moon, and all the events in the dead past which have led us on to possess any real life. I wish I could remember every word, it was so poetical and beautiful. Allusion had been made to Mr. Orvis as Orpheus,

Dwight ending with saying, 'God bless the sun, and also Orpheus: God bless the moon, and also Morpheus.' Mr. Ripley made quite a long and humorous speech upon a glass of punch —quintescent punch — which he drank at a New York meeting, and which roused a dull company into great activity, since it was so exquisitely compounded that, if it had made a man quite drunk, it would not have injured his intellect. This called out two puns. Dwight asked if the party was a Punch and Judy spree (*jeu d'esprit*); and Fred said that it seemed only necessary to punch Mr. Ripley to get a good speech from him. In the early part of the evening Mr. Brisbane alluded beautifully to Dwight, calling him the fringe in the great associative movement, not a common fake, civilized fringe, but one that was centred deep in inward principles, and manifested itself outwardly in various forms of beauty, like the odor and color of flowers. Very beautiful were his words, but my memory fails. So it ended at twelve o'clock; and we separated to pass a sleepless night in the company of solemn, pleasing, and exciting thoughts. You must imagine a great deal I have described so poorly! Our entertainment was one of a regular series, ascending gradually from a few jokes to the highest spiritual emotions, and then gradually descending again."

All this was sentimental and somewhat extravagant, but it shows the enthusiasm of youth. An enthusiasm like this, however aroused, has a real meaning, and shows soundness of life in that which produces it. There was something here to bind these men and women together in closest ties of fidelity to an idea.

In religion the greatest freedom existed. Very little of formal piety showed itself, and the attitude of the leaders was one that was radical almost to an extreme. In an unconventional and informal way, religion was a powerful influence throughout the life of the community; and a strong religious feeling and conviction existed. Though Ripley and Dwight had left the church, and many of the others did not attend church services regularly, yet there was a truly religious spirit in the community and a deep devotional feeling. It took the form of a strong desire for social justice, and was a pervasive influence in this direction among the more thoughtful and intelligent. When William Henry Channing spent a Sunday at Brook Farm, he preached to the people, and with great effect. He was the oracle and religious guide of the community, its confessor and saint. He had a wonderful gift for planting in the minds of the impressionable the seeds of devotion and consecration to high ideas and ideals. In this way he exerted a powerful influence over the minds of all the younger members of the community.

Dwight lived in the Eyrie, the first house built by the community, and so named because it was located on a rock,— the highest point on the Farm. Here he had the Ripleys for house neighbors, here the library was located, and here, also,

the classes met their teachers.   In this house the
more intelligent members of the community met
for recreation and discussion in the evenings, and
within it the musical culture of the community was
developed in personal study or in club training.

After he had been at the Farm for some time,
Dwight was joined by his parents and sisters, who
remained members until the end came.   On Christmas Eve, 1846, his sister Marianne was married to
John Orvis.   Marianne Dwight had been an assistant and then a preceptress in Mr. Bailey's " High
School for Young Ladies " in Boston.   She was
the teacher of drawing at Brook Farm, and an
assistant in Latin.   Frances Dwight was as much
a lover of music as her brother, shared in his study
of it at this time, and assisted him in teaching it to
the children.

At the end of 1844 a change began at Brook
Farm in the agitation about the teachings of
Fourier.   His chief apostle in this country was
Albert Brisbane, and a visit of his to Brook Farm
is described in a letter written by one of Dwight's
sisters, Dec. 22, 1844 : —

" Brisbane arrived last evening.   This morning
we assembled at half-past ten to hear what he had
to say.   He promised us for the forenoon merely
the history of his travels in Europe; but it was
mingled with so much philosophy, his views were
so broad and deep, his language so eloquent and
forcible, that we could not but feel gratified and
instructed.   What he said of nationalities was very

fine,— that in each nation we see a predominating sentiment, which characterizes it throughout. In England familism is predominant. This marks the English landscape, dotting it with cottages and manor houses. This pervades the industry of the nation, in which the useful always predominates. In France cabalism is the ruling sentiment. Social feeling, love of variety, amusements, etc., mark the people. In all their manufactures they have the elegant in view. The destiny of France has been to break down the feudal spirit of the Middle Ages, to destroy Catholicism and aristocracy. He gave a fine picture of the history of France up to her present speculative time, and asserted that only in that country, amidst such a people, could such a genius as Fourier have been born.

" This afternoon Mr. Brisbane spoke on the prospects of association in France, which he considers rather miserable and hopeless. Here is the field, and here at Brook Farm must the efforts of all be concentrated. Probably Mr. Brisbane will come and live with us. But I have no time to tell you anything that was planned and devised for this next year's operations. It is hopeful, is it not, that we have this first year a dividend of profits amounting to $1,445?

" Our sister associate, M. A. Williams, was this morning released from her severe sufferings by death,— the first death that has occurred here. A beautiful grove of cypress-trees back of our house has been selected for her grave. She has been taken care of in the best and kindest manner, and received universal sympathy. Nowhere else could this poor woman, who has no near relatives and no property, have fared so well. Here is one of the pleasantest blessings of association."

The same person gave an account of a visit of Robert Owen to Brook Farm, and her letter opens up an interesting view of the inside life of the community: —

" To-day I have wished for you to enjoy with us a most delightful visit from Robert Owen. Never was I so agreeably disappointed in any one. The old man has a beautiful spirit of infinite benevolence. I really love and reverence him. He is seventy-four, full of energy and activity, very courteous, attends carefully to every little etiquette, pats the children on the head, and has a smile and a pleasant word for all. Last evening he gave us a lecture on socialism, and another to-day. I am astonished at his views,— to find that we differ much in speculations and in details,— yet we have one and the same object, and can meet on a common ground. After his lecture he gave us an account of his experiment at New Lanark, which he carried on with two thousand persons for thirty years, and then left in the care of others. These persons were of the very dregs of society, when he took them. Now they are mentioned in statistics as being the most moral population of Great Britain. The whole story was very interesting. So was his account of the Rapp community. I have always associated his name with New Harmony, but he says this was conducted by people who understood not his principles.

"After he had finished, Mr. Ripley rose, and paid him a very handsome tribute, inviting him to be with us whenever he could, and expressing our sense of the honor we felt he had conferred upon us, proposed Robert Owen as a sentiment, wishing he might always enjoy in his own mind that sublime happiness that will one day be the portion of the human race. Owen expressed himself as much pleased with our experiment, and wondered at our success. He is going to England, to return here in September. He has taken the common sense path to association. I wish I could see you, to tell you more of this interesting forenoon."

In December, 1843, a large convention was held in Boston of the friends of association. The communities at Hopedale, Northampton, Skaneateles, and others were represented. Rev. Adin Ballou spoke for Christian communism, Charles A. Dana advocated the Brook Farm type of social co-operation, and Brisbane strongly urged the claims of Fourierism. Among the speakers were Ripley, Greeley, William H. Channing, and several others. So great was the interest of the meeting that it continued into the first week of 1844, and all the sessions were crowded with eager listeners. The object of the meeting was a free interchange of views on the part of associationists, communists, socialists, and other advocates of a social reforma-

tion.   The desire was to find some common basis
of action in furtherance of social reform.   Ripley
and Channing were, at first, very reluctant to accept the teachings of Fourier, which were advocated
with great eloquence and persistency by Brisbane.
Gradually, however, they were won over to a more
favorable consideration of the methods for organizing industry which had been developed by Fourier
in his writings.

During the year 1844 the Fourierite theory of
organized industrial life was put into practice at
Brook Farm, so far as it was possible to do so with
its limited numbers and resources.   From this time
on Dwight became much more active in his interest
in the community, and more thoroughly identified
himself with the spirit of social reform which it
exemplified.   The change in Brook Farm began, in
fact, early in 1844, partly as the result of the discus-
sions then going on and partly as the result of newspaper attacks.   The New York *Herald* made such
an onslaught on Brook Farm at this time that pupils
and boarders withdrew on account of it, and the
question of income had to be seriously considered.
An effort was now made to increase the productiveness of the farm and to enlarge the number of paying industries.   Two letters of this time will give
glimpses into the efforts which were making to
adjust the life of the community to the new conditions : —

"I belong to a group," wrote one of Dwight's
sisters, "for making fancy articles for sale in

Boston.   We have been very busy at it of late, and
Amelia Russell and I are very much amused at the
idea of our having turned milliners and makers of
cap-tabs.   Our manufacture is quite workmanlike,
I assure you.   We realize considerable money (!)
from this, and hope, women though we are, to have
by and by the credit of doing some productive
labor.   We are now having frequent teachers' meetings to improve our educational practice, and ap-
proximate it to our plan.   In all this I feel a deep
interest."

"A chosen body of our people are exceedingly
busy making a new constitution.   I guess we shall
have a good one, and such a one as will make civilizées open their eyes wide with astonishment.   I
wish you could have seen the pictures Mr. Brisbane
has of a phalanstery and its domain in full harmony.   They are magnificent in design, and give
one a pretty clear glance, at least, into the kingdom
of heaven that is to come on earth.   Mr. Brisbane
and Mr. Macdaniel are still here.   I like them very
much.   We have had some very pleasant social re-
unions, some walks and glorious coasts."

The great building, or Phalanstery, begun in the
summer of 1844, in which the Fourierite idea of
communal life was to find full expression, was burned
on the evening of March 3, 1846.   The next day
Marianne Dwight wrote to one of her friends an
account of the fire, which is of much interest as
showing the attitude of the people toward this
calamity.   The account shows the spiritual earnest-

ness and the moral devotion which Brook Farm
developed in its members to a large extent.

"I must, with what poor words I can, attempt to
put you in possession of the particulars about the
burning of our Phalanstery. The council had just
appointed a committee to superintend the finishing
of the Phalanstery, and had dispersed, when Mr.
Salisbury, passing the building, saw a light in the
upper part, and put his head into a window to learn
the cause thereof. Men had been at work there all
day, and a fire kept in a stove. He found the room
full of smoke, and ran instantly to the Eyrie and
told Mr. Ripley, who was the first on the spot.

"Then came the sudden, earnest cry, 'Fire! the
Phalanstery!' that startled us all, and for a moment
made every face pale with consternation. I was
in my room, and ran to the front of the house.
Flames were issuing from one of the remote windows, and spreading rapidly. It was at once evident that nothing could be done. It seemed but
five minutes when the flames had spread from end
to end. Men ran in every direction, making almost
fruitless attempts to save windows and timber. The
greatest exertions were made to save the Eyrie,
which at one time was too hot to bear the hand,
and even smoked. Our neighbor Mr. Orange went
first on the roof, and worked like a hero, and not
in vain.

"Would I could convey to you an idea of the
scene! It was glorious beyond description. How
grand when the immense heavy column of smoke

first rose up to heaven! There was no wind, and it ascended almost perpendicularly. I looked upon it from our house until the whole front was on fire: *that* was beautiful, indeed. The whole colonnade was wreathed spirally with fire, and every window glowing. I was calm, felt that it was the work of heaven, and was good; and not for one instant did I feel otherwise. Then I threw on my cloak, and rushed out to mingle with the people. All were still, calm, resolute, undaunted. The expression on every face seemed to me sublime. There was a solemn, serious, reverential feeling, such as must come when we are forced to feel that human aid is of no avail, and that a higher hand than man's is at work. I heard solemn words of trust, cheerful words of encouragement, resignation, gratitude, and thankfulness, but not one of terror or despair. All were absorbed in the glory and sublimity of the scene.

"In less than an hour and a half the whole was levelled to the ground. The Phalanstery was finished. Not the building alone, but the scenery around was grand. As it was to be, I would not have missed it for the world. I assure you the moral sublimity with which the people took it was not the least part of it. The good Archon [Ripley] was like an angel. Mrs. Ripley alone was for half an hour too much overcome to look upon it.

"People rushed here from Roxbury, Dedham, Boston, and Cambridgeport. Engines could not help us much. There was such a rush of the

world's people to the Hive. We gave them what
we could,— made hot coffee, brought out bread and
cheese, and feasted about two hundred of the
fatigued, hungry multitude. Mr. Orange brought
us provisions from his house, and ran through the
street for milk. About midnight I wrote letters to
Orvis and Allen, for I thought they would be in
agony for us if they did not get their first intelligence directly from home. I had one short sound
sleep, and was up early, writing to Frank. I looked
at the bare hill this morning, I must say, with a
feeling of relief. There was an encumbrance gone.

" Heaven had interfered to prevent us from finishing that building so foolishly undertaken, so
poorly planned and built, and which again and
again some of us have thought and said we should
rejoice to see blown away or burned down. It has
gone suddenly, gloriously, magnificently; and we
shall have no further trouble with it. Just what
the effect will be to us, it is impossible now to tell.
The contract was lately given into our own hands;
and, I suppose, ours must be the loss. About
$7,000 had been spent on it. We must take deep
to heart a good lesson. We have been through
about every other trial: now we have been through
the fire. We needed this experience, and I pray
we may come from it like pure gold. It leaves us
no worse off than before we began it, and, in some
respects, better. May Heaven bless to us the
event !

" I feared it would look ugly, dismal, and smutty

this morning; but the ruins are really picturesque. A part of the stone foundation stands like a row of gravestones, the tomb of the Phalanstery. Thank God, not the tomb of our hopes! Charles Dana returned from New York an hour since, and, I am happy to say, takes it as cheerfully as the rest of us. We breakfasted an hour later than usual to-day, and our hired carpenters have gone back to Dedham. I see no other change. The day is calm and beautiful. All goes on as usual. We look toward the hill, and all seems like a strange dream. You cannot think how it struck me last night towards the close of the fireworks, when, after watching the constantly rolling flames for two hours, I looked up to the sky, and saw Orion looking down so steadily, so calmly, reminding me of the unchanging and eternal."

Two letters written by the same hand, one in March and one in April, only a few weeks after the fire, give farther proofs of the courage and moral earnestness and loyalty of the people who then made up the Brook Farm community.

"Last evening," she wrote, "we had a new flowering of the tree of life that seems to have taken such deep root in this spot, in spite of the soil. Our friend and associate, W. H. Cheswell, wishing to celebrate the anniversary of his arrival at this Eden, invited everybody to attend his regular dancing school. I felt very unlike it, had been almost ill with the headache all day; but, as friend Cheswell has always looked with a jealous eye upon the aristocratic element, John thought it would be best to go, and persuaded me into it. And right glad we are that we went. The dancing went off in fine style: it could not have been better. About ten o'clock, two by two, we were all marched out of the dining-hall into the parlors, to await the setting of the table. When notice was given, each gentleman took his lady, and we marched back again, and seated ourselves at the table, which extended through the centre of the room from end to end, and offered us the tempting luxuries of hot coffee, cake, crackers, and cheese. After partaking of these dainties, Charles Dana rose, and announced that he would read the toasts which had been prepared for the occasion. They were very excellent, and some of them not a little amusing. The different groups were toasted, from the printing group to the plain sewers, and individuals called upon for speeches. These were ready and admirable. We had fun and wit, poetry and sober good sense, earnestness and solemnity. There was a new consecrating of each and all to our work here at Brook Farm,— a pledging of the groups to faithful, devoted, needful action, and the very heartiest expression of hope, faith, and union.

" The one discordant note that has sounded in our ears lately came round into harmony; and thunders of applause burst forth as Charles Dana, with recovered strength and energy, expressed his deep faith that the cause of association and its work must and would be carried on to some extent here at Brook Farm. The Archon, unluckily, was not present, and says he wants to have it over again. It was such a meeting as never happens but once. Charles Dana and John Orvis were the only persons present of our usual speakers. Indeed, it was all the better for that; for there was no restraint. Anybody could get up, and, in his way, say the good word; and I do say it was one of the very best parties I ever attended. Do tell Mr. Channing, if you see him, that I would have given the world to have had him present, or perhaps behind the scenes. It would have done his heart so much good to have seen this new development of the good spirit that is working in us and binding us together in strength. In truth, we are a Phalanx."

"We are now starting in what appears a common-sense way," she wrote a month later. "We have reduced our plans somewhat, but I trust a higher ideal is before us than ever. One thing is certainly very encouraging, and to me it is really providential. How is it that the people who are not calculated to help us, who, though good in their way, yet lack that refinement which is indispensable to give a good tone to the place, do actually withdraw in the pleasantest manner, wholly unasked, and without any chance of feeling that their withdrawal is desirable to us? I cannot call it chance. God wills it. God means something by it. We have lately felt it really necessary that certain people should leave. We have not known how to

bring it about. Well, all at once comes a call
to them, a better prospect opens to them outside.
In these changes there is something trying to our
feelings, but they are well. We are thankful that
they have come about so pleasantly. Those of us
left are capable of improving by living together,
and feel very closely drawn together. We feel our
brotherhood with those who have gone, but it
always seemed to me a great mistake to admit
coarse people upon the place. Now we need not
fear subjecting our pupils to evil influences from
such quarters. Indeed, I see not why we cannot
now offer as good or better moral influences than
could be found at any other boarding-school.

" My interest now must centre in the school. I
do know what a good school is. I know well why
we have not had a good one here, and I see clearly
that we can easily have the very best. I am sol-
emnly determined to use my utmost efforts to bring
it about. I have offered myself to the work, have
just been elected chief of the teachers' group, which
gives me, together with Mrs. Ripley (chief of the
educational series), and, indeed, more than she, the
superintendence of the school. Her health requires
that I should give her this relief ; and I enter upon
the duties with alacrity and cheerfulness, with diffidence, to be sure, and yet with confidence. Think
what aid I can command,— the Ripleys, Charles
Dana, John S. Dwight, Fanny, Miss Russell, etc.

" The change we make in our organization will
secure to each group greater independence than

before. Each will transact its own business, make its own sales and purchases. We need money to invest in some departments, and for this purpose a subscription is now going on. We feel that we have a right to call upon citizens to help us with their money to accomplish what we can toward building up a true system of life."

One effect of the change made in the internal organization was the establishment of a printing-office at Brook Farm, and the publication of a weekly sixteen-page, three-columned paper called the *Harbinger*. It was devoted to the interests which Brook Farm represented; but it had wide sympathies, and was not in any sense partisan. A tone of intellectual earnestness pervaded the whole paper, its literary character was of the best, and a spirit of cultured manliness infused itself into every page. Into the *Harbinger* went a good part of the best life of John S. Dwight for the next three years. He wrote much for it, and he was actively connected with its literary management. A few letters will indicate something of the nature of his editorial labors. When the paper was being planned, he wrote to Emerson for aid; and the reply is characteristic.

"Your letter was very kind and friendly," Emerson wrote, "and one is always glad that anything is adventured in the midst of so much excusing and impediment; and yet, though I should heartily rejoice to aid in an uncommitted journal,— not limited by the name of any man,— I will not promise a line to any which has chosen a patron. We shall never do anything if we begin with being somebody else. Then, though I admire the genius of Fourier, since I have looked a little into his books, yet it is only for his marvellous tactics. He is another French soldier or rather mathematician, such as France is always turning out; and they apply their wonderful ciphering indifferently to astronomy, chemistry, war, or politics. But they are a sub-type, as modern science now says, deficient in the first faculty, and therefore should never be allowed the lead in grand enterprises, but may very well serve as subordinate coadjutors, where their power as economists will stand in good stead. It seems sadly true that the scholars and philosophers, and I might say also the honest and well-disposed part of society, have no literary organ or voice which is not desperately sectarian; and we are always impelled towards organization by the fear that our little power will become less. But, if things come to a still worse pass, indignation will perhaps summon a deeper-voiced and wiser muse than our cool New England has ever listened to. I am sure she will be native, and no immigrant, least of all will she speak French. But she will, I doubt not, have many wreaths of honor to bestow on you and your friends at Brook Farm; for courage and hope and real performance, God and man and muses love.

"You see how little and how much faith I have. As far as your journal is sectarian, I shall respect it at a distance. If it should become catholic, I shall be found suing for a place in it. Respectfully and affectionately yours."

He had better success with Lowell, who not only sent a poem, but wrote of efforts to serve his friend in other ways : —

"Leigh Hunt, in one of his pleasant essays, says that he often pleased himself while he wrote with thinking that this or that thought or expression would please some one in particular of his friends. In writing the poem which I send for the *Harbinger*, I said to myself, J. S. D. will like this, and so I send it. The images are perhaps a little too bold for our close-clipped American public, who, nevertheless, would be willing to sit quietly once a week under the reading of the book of Job, thinking all the while that for inspiration it compares unfavorably with Pope. But I have a notion that it will be very much to your mind. Maria, who is my public, likes it; but do not print it unless you do. Please see to the proof-sheets, — for I have been martyred several times that way, — and do not let your compositor make lumberer into slumberer, as, from my knowledge of the compositor turn of mind, I am sure he will be desirous to do. Do you think finned isles too outrageous an expression for innocent whales? You remember how they thrust their hilly backs above the water and lie asleep, and Sinbad's adventure also.

"I carried your sister's drawings to Dr. Gray, but found that he keeps an artist. He did not at all appreciate them, looking at them (though I told him over and over that they were not drawn for scientific purposes) with the eye of an anatomist, counting the pistils and stamens, and wholly incapable of perceiving their wonderful dramatic propriety (I know no other term for it), which quite shamed his scientific artist's productions. However, he was Gray-cious enough to say that, with a little botanical study, your sister would do exceedingly well, and that, if he lost his 'artist,' of which he had some fears, he should be glad to employ her pencil. It was a furnace-hot day when I carried them down, and I was drenched with sweat enough to have earned my bread for life (if the terms of the Adamic curse could be strictly complied with); and Dr. Gray looked so cool and clean, and so insensible to my pictures (for I had made them mine by the interest I felt in them), that I went away provoked to even greater heat. Nevertheless, Dr. Gray is one of the best men I know,— the ideal of a professor,— simple-hearted, and an enthusiast for his science. It is not his fault that Providence did not give him a poetic eye.

"Duyckinck writes me doubtfully about the essays. He says he likes very much those he has seen, but doubts their salableness, especially as some of them have been printed once. As he himself knows nothing whatever of music, I think his liking is an equally strong argument for their sale. Perhaps it would be well to send him such as you can. He is only an acquaintance of mine, but I spoke of them as warmly as I could without injur-

ing them in his man-of-the-world opinion by too
great anxiety.

"If you print my poem and have two numbers
to spare, send them to me. Do not forget your
engagement to visit us at Commencement. I began
a review of Lord's poems for you, which I will fin-
ish and send to you. The heat cut me short in it."

The poem was printed in the *Harbinger* for
Aug. 2, 1845, under the title of "To a Pine-tree,"
and may be found in Lowell's poetical works with
a few emendations.

Dwight was a constant contributor to the pages
of the *Harbinger* during the whole period of its
publication at Brook Farm. He wrote for it edi-
torials on association, music, and literary topics, he
reviewed many books, and he sometimes contributed poems. He also translated several works from
the French of Fourier, Victor Considerant, and
other associationist writers. During the progress
of the third volume he became intimately connected with the editorial management of the paper.
He assumed with Ripley the responsibility of conducting it, and devoted much of his time to its
management. In this volume, appeals were made
in behalf of the paper; and a guarantee fund was
raised among the friends of association. Before the
end of the fourth volume the paper became distinctly the organ of the American Union of Associationists, which organization assumed its control
and the financial responsibility of its publication.
At this time Ripley and Dwight were elected the

editors, and the sum of five dollars each per week was voted them by the Union.

In the first number of the *Harbinger*, Dwight reviewed the musical defects of this country in the past, maintained that the new social spirit gave the highest promise for musical development in the future; and he set forth his purpose to devote a portion of the *Harbinger* to the furtherance of musical taste and knowledge. "We wish," he wrote, "to consider music as one of the expressions and as one of the inspiring causes of the restless but prophetic spirit of these times. Of course, then, we shall not say much of mere musical trifles. It shall be our business constantly to notice and uphold for study and for imitation music which is deep and earnest; which does not merely seek to amuse, but which is the most enlightened outpouring of the composer's life. ... Three things we shall have in view: (1) the criticism of music as an art; (2) the interpretation of it as an expression of the life of the age; and (3) the development of its correspondence as a science with other sciences, and especially with the science of the coming social order and the transition through which we are passing towards it."

This programme was carried out with earnestness and success, and the *Harbinger* became one of the best musical journals the country has ever possessed. The criticisms were strong and effective; and the interpretative articles were in good literary form, incisive with keen artistic insight, and adapted to give the art real meaning as a source of culture.

In October, 1847, the *Harbinger* came to an end at Brook Farm, and was transferred to New York, where it appeared in a new form, but with much the same spirit. Dwight continued his connection with it as one of the Boston editorial contributors, the other being W. H. Channing. To the seventh volume he made thirty-seven contributions, including a translation from the columns of the *Démocratie Pacifique*, the Fourierite daily journal of Paris, of a work of Victor Considerant on "Harmony." He wrote on music in Boston, three articles on "What made you an Associationist?" two on a plan for an associative dwelling, one on the associative theory of property, and several literary reviews. As an indication of the literary judgment, appreciation, and skill with which Dwight dealt with the books which he reviewed, a letter from Longfellow, bearing the date of Dec. 10, 1847, may here be presented: —

"I should have written sooner," said the poet, "to thank you for your most friendly and cordial notice of 'Evangeline' in the *Harbinger*; but by some adverse fate I could not get a copy of the paper till some ten or fifteen days after its publication. It would hardly be modest in me to tell you how much satisfaction it gave me; but, setting modesty aside, I thank you for it very heartily, and this rather for the sympathy than the praise. There are so many persons who rush forward in front of one, and, seizing one's Pegasus by the rein, give him such a jerk as to make his mouth bleed, that I always feel grateful to any one who is willing to go a few paces side by side with me. I think you will agree with me that what a writer asks of a reader is not so much to like as to listen. You I have to thank for both; and, I assure you, I have seldom, if ever, read a notice of any work of mine which gave me so much pleasure as yours of ' Evangeline.' "

In its new form and place of publication, at first the *Harbinger* gave promise of success; and it was proposed that Dwight should go to New York and devote his time wholly to its pages. To this effect is a letter to him from Parke Godwin, which also shows Dwight's continued interest in association. "Ripley informs me,' wrote Godwin, "that you hesitate about coming on to the meeting of the American Union of Associationists; but I hope you will be enabled to do so. We want to see you much. There is a great deal to talk about, especially in reference to the *Harbinger*. It is an important time in other respects. Come by all means! Besides, we want a word from you touching your *Opera* here. You will see the artistic department here is wofully neglected. We have no one to do the work, yet it is indispensable that something should be done. Would that you could be with us permanently, or at least a part of the time! With your co-operation *here*, we should be able to make the best paper in the United States.

As it is, I know of none better, *me judice;* but, with a few modifications and improvements, everybody else would be made to know the same thing, which is of more consequence to our success. By the way, what has become of the Boston editor? or does he mean to write only once in six weeks? Please stir him up. The *Harbinger* has done very well in its pecuniary receipts the last month. Tweedy, who has an eye for business, is quite encouraged. I see no reason why we cannot make the paper pay for itself; *i.e.*, with a little industry and enterprise. I think it can still be greatly improved in the arrangement and character of its matter, all of which we shall try for, hard."

We must now return to the period immediately following the burning of the Phalanstery at Brook Farm. Dwight went to New York a few days later, to give a course of four lectures on music. During his stay in that city he was domiciled with his old friend and classmate, Rev. Henry W. Bellows. The fire gave another purpose to his visit than that of musical propagandism, and he made the interests of Brook Farm and association an almost constant topic of discussion among his friends. He wrote to George Ripley of his efforts in behalf of Brook Farm, especially.

"My days are crowded full; and I get little time for writing, even on my lectures. At the first lecture there were about one hundred and twenty persons present, some of the subscribers failing on account of short notice and other accidental reasons.

The impression was far better than I had hoped. I believe it gave universal satisfaction to those who heard, although I extemporized association at the end of it. Dr. Dewey was highly delighted, and has paid me much attention. On Saturday the weather was so unpromising I was advised to postpone. By this I gained time to see our association friends. I had quite a talk with Greeley. He wrote upon the paper which I took with me, ' I give up all my stock unconditionally, and will subscribe, besides, the first $100 I get which does not belong to somebody else.' Marcus Spring gives up his, and expresses a wish to subscribe something. He says that he has got something which he is holding in reserve to aid this cause; but he fears that Brook Farm, in its present locality, cannot do much. I convinced him, I think, that it is indispensable for us to go on, and to go on where we are for some years more, at least. He says he will aid, but he does not wish to encourage any large expenditure on our present operations. He believes that we Brook Farmers are the real and only nucleus of the association to be first realized in this country.

" I met him again at Miss Lynch's party in the evening, and had more talk. The result was to invite me over to Brooklyn last night (Sunday) to meet the Christian Union people. So, after holding private matins with Fred Rackemann, who opened to me the gospels according to Beethoven, Mendelssohn, and other minor prophets, and after dining with George Curtis, and attending 'Vespers' at the Catholic church, and walking six or seven miles, I (with Cranch) arrived at Marcus Spring's, and took tea and had music. Then we adjourned to Mr. Manning's, where some thirty people were assembled. I held forth for the whole evening on the history and condition and prospects of Brook Farm, answering everybody's questions, and going very fully into the matter. I told the strict truth, and found that to most people it was not near so bad. as they had expected. Every one seemed deeply interested, and anxious that Brook Farm should go on.

"Mr. Hicks relinquishes his stock. Mr. Manning gives his to Channing, to dispose of as he pleases. Mr. Hunt is willing to do anything; and Mr. Benson, of his own accord, said that some effort must be made in New York to help out the subscription in Boston. Tweedy seems deeply interested, and is more and more a Fourierist, having attained to it by much the same internal process that I did. He is a man much after my own heart. You may consider the whole of the stock held in New York as cancelled. As soon as a clear plan shapes itself on our part, there will be something done here.

"I talk association everywhere. Everybody questions me, and I have removed prejudices from a good many minds. With Mr. and Mrs. Bellows I have talked hours and hours,— in fact, all the time, — and think they entertain the idea rather more willingly. Of gastrosophic adventures I have too much to tell: that shall be for Brook Farm evening chats. Parties, music, dinings out and in, and hosts of visitors, besides the tremendously long walks, and hitherto unfortunate attempts to write on my last lectures, crowd my days to the fullest. Every day I am belated, run away with, lost, and wearied. But I can stand it some time longer; and it is wholly profitable, I think. I have had real pleasure in Dr. Dixon and lady, and mellifluous Rev. Mr. Hart; so, too, in Kempel, who is extravagantly delighted with my lecture. Had a beautiful evening also at Godwin's, where were Miss Sinclair, Margaret Fuller, Mrs. Kirkland, Dewey and daughter, etc."

To one of his sisters he wrote: "My lectures in one sense were very successful; that is, they produced a deep impression, and were even received with enthusiasm. But, pecuniarily, the result will not be what I expected. I shall hardly realize over one hundred dollars instead of two. This is owing to the great expense of hall and advertising. The audience doubled on the second night, and shrank a little after that. It was owing partly to the inertia of my enthusiastic friends about noticing in the newspapers. But it will be a fine opening, I think, for another time. More of this when I get home.

"I have had a wonderfully fine time, socially. William Story and a party of friends from Boston have been here some days. We all, with Cranch and his wife, were at Mrs. Child's on Sunday evening. Mrs. Child's enthusiasm about my lectures is unbounded. She presented me a beautiful bouquet at the close of the last, and says they have given her the only fresh feeling of interest since Ole Bull. On the subject of that gentleman we frankly differ, but she tolerates my heresy."

"And so my estimate of your lectures was not one of my exaggerations, after all!" wrote Mrs. George Ripley to Dwight. "Tributes to the merits of the first one are coming in upon us; and yet I cannot think the audience, unaccustomed to your mode of expression, to your somewhat associative dialect, can have gone into the depths of the thought. I feel as if a repetition of them would be demanded, and am trying to get used to the thought of a slightly prolonged absence on your part. I wish you could have seen the group in the reading-room last evening after supper, the tall ones stooping over and the short ones standing tiptoe to read the notice of you in the *Tribune*. Can I tell you the pleasure with which your letter was received? Your description of the luxuries of civilization seemed very like a story I once read of Aladdin's wonderful lamp, and your deep sense of the more abundant wealth to be found in the circle of pure Phalansterians was most cordially responded to. What a rich and varied life you are at once drawn into! and, in the midst of it you find your home circle of every-day Brook Farm friends. You have an unusually grand standpoint from which to speak to the public.

"Thank you for Mr. King's letter. That little sentence in which he speaks of our loss as bringing us again into harmony with universal laws is worth all he has written for months. How true, too, that we can see a Providential guidance in our all being led back to our primitive occupations, and having somewhat collected our scattered forces and brought them to bear on definite objects of real value, before we were thrown into dismay by our calamity! We had in some sort, and almost unconsciously, planned our new mode of life before we were burned out of the old one.

"We earnestly wish for you back at every moment and every turn; and yet, surely, this is a better time for your absence than later. Everything now is preliminary. The general council meets every night. They have been reviewing all departments, looking over accounts, etc., I think all minds tending towards the decision that it will be best to give up our property and begin anew (this, of course, entirely private), let school, paper, painting and domestic industry necessarily connected with them, constitute the associative centre, and our band of farmers (stanch and noble-minded yeomen as they are) take the farm under some new arrangement, including more responsibility on their part. Mr. Shaw says the school and paper must not be given up for a single week. His interest is reviving under the light of a new hope, and he comes with cheerful spirits almost every day. Mr. Russell is much engaged about the school, and says he can do something for it. . . .

"Mr. Orvis came home Tuesday, rather worn down and disappointed, but with undying hope, faith, and devotion. He went to town yesterday to make some more active arrangements about the subscription. Much can be done if we are in a situation to avail ourselves of it, which we are not just at present. One thing you will be glad to know,— that all minds in the least degree capable of it are thinking and deciding for themselves. There is no crushing influence bearing upon them. I never knew them more free. Last night a grand letter came from John Allen, full of glowing love, expressed in his primitive style." ...

In a letter to Charles Dana the lectures were spoken of by Parke Godwin in this wise: "As to Dwight's lectures, let me say, that they have been the best things we have ever had here. All who heard them were delighted. He excelled himself, and for me they were 'a refreshing from the presence of the Lord.' If this city were not wholly given up to idolatry, it would have rushed in a body to hear such sound and beautiful doctrine."

In a letter to the Boston *Courier*, Mrs. Lydia Maria Child gave her estimate of the man and his lectures. "He possesses qualifications for such a task," she wrote, "rarely combined in one person,— a delicate musical organization, accurate scientific knowledge, and the far-reaching glance of a poet which enables him to perceive that music is the golden key to unlock all the analogies of the universe. But such a man must necessarily

always speak to a select few. The mechanical musician, occupied with counting the beats in a bar,
is by no means deeply interested when informed
that man, in his social progress, has arrived at the
dissonant Seventh, which clamors vociferously for
the coming octave. He who merely enjoys sweet
sounds, as he would the gurgle of brooks in the
springtime, cares just as little about the spiritual
significance of three, seven, and twelve, without
which music could never have lived as an art or
taken form as a science. I was, in fact, surprised
that so many of the audience appeared excited by
his comprehensive thoughts and charmed with his
poetic fancies. I was myself especially pleased that
such an intense admirer of Beethoven was able to
do full justice to the graceful brilliancy of Rossini
and the sparkling fairy play of Auber. The same
mind has rarely a true appreciation of such diverse
forms of beauty.

" The great difficulty with Dwight is that he
always wants to say a great deal more than he can
say. Inwardly rich and outwardly unpractical, his
artless and beautiful soul is strangely out of place
in these bustling and pretending times. He always
seems to me like a little child who has lost his way
in the woods with an apron brimful of flowers,
which he don't know what to do with; but, if you
can take them, he will gladly give you all."

The *Tribune* said that " Mr. Dwight's lectures
mark an epoch in the musical history of New York;
for, although we have had the opportunity of hear-

ing so much fine music, it is perhaps the first time that we have had a clear and wise assertion of the dignity and compass of the art. Those who regard it as something too subtle to be discussed in lectures or in any other way will find that these are only expositions of the exact laws of infinite analogy and correspondence which govern music as a science, and, further, only a simple and sincere expression of the experience wrought by it upon a delicate and poetical mind to which music is the celestial expression of the sublimest hope. Mr. Dwight happily unites the characteristics of the three classes so well described in his first lecture, to which music is either sentiment, science, or recreation, so that he shows himself a wise lover and a sympathetic critic. His course is so short that he has been necessarily restricted to a bold sketching to convey his whole impression, but it lies so accurately outlined in his own mind that it is very beautifully presented to others."

From this time on the future of Brook Farm constantly engaged the interest of Dwight and his earnest colaborers. The number of members was reduced, each person was made responsible for his own personal support, and an effort was made to introduce the most remunerative employments. For a little time it seemed possible that the new methods might succeed. In September, while this adjustment was being made, Dwight wrote to Mrs. Child : —

"Your 'Poet's Dream of the Soul' I have read

with delight. I believe in its essential philosophy, and I was equally surprised with the result. Mendelssohn has been a great object of interest with me this summer. A friend gave me in the spring a set of his 'Lieder ohne Worte.' Hearing my sister play them, and working over them myself, has been the sweetest thing of this summer's life. I was just preparing to write down some fitting testimony to this pleasure in the *Harbinger*, when your story came. You will see I have made some use of it. But how to go on or keep a foothold in this element at all, just now, I scarcely see; for I am beset and preoccupied and exhausted with most perplexing and incessant cares.

"Brook Farm must either stop or change its form and operations most entirely. And I am in the midst of this,—everything to settle, nothing that is not altogether loose and unsettled, and meanwhile the *Harbinger* to edit, and ever so much of other work to which I had pledged myself. However, a week or two now will decide all, I trust. I think we shall go on, but on a much reduced scale, and every one who stays responsible for supporting his own business and his own material person.

"You date, I see, from the resolution of the flat Seventh into the Sixth, or composite. That is a very lovely region. Mendelssohn is there, it is true; and I sometimes effect a transition into it. But you may judge from what I have said above that I hail from the sphere of all distraction and discordance, perhaps I might say from the chord of the

Diminished Seventh, the type of universal transition, wild, impatient, tortured with uncertainty and suspense. As I can hardly expect to reach the octave, the sublime height of universal unity, I humbly hope I also may resolve into the lovely A."

Another year brought Brook Farm to its end. Ripley went to New York to struggle with the *Harbinger* for a year and a half longer. He wrote the bravest letters to Dwight through this period of bitter struggle and severest drudgery. Dwight went to Boston to find an opening as a literary worker, and had a struggle not less severe than that of his friend. Gradually the interest in association died out, though the most vigorous effort was made to keep it alive. The faith in it of both Ripley and Dwight lost no bit of its depth and force with the closing of Brook Farm; and they still hoped that new methods would bring larger results, or results more conducive to final success. Gradually they came to see that the struggle was in vain, at least for that time. They did not, however, lose faith in that for which they had labored so hard and sacrificed so much; and they were associationists at heart to the hour of death.

It has been assumed by many that Brook Farm came to an end in complete eclipse, and left no influence behind it except that it wrought upon individual lives. This is a mistake in every way, for it was in reality the forerunner of movements more important than itself. Out of the associationist movement of the later forties, of which Brook

Farm was the chief feature, came the efforts to organize the laboring men of the country. When W. H. Channing preached association in Boston, he drew about him a number of workingmen. One of these men said: " This is the first time I have found a church. Mr. Channing is the first preacher who has given me bread instead of a stone." When they found that they could not go to Brook Farm, they cast about for means of helping themselves in an associative way. A co-operative purchasing agency was established by them. The interest grew rapidly. Soon there were in Boston and vicinity a dozen such societies; and in ten years there were five hundred and fifty in New England, with an annual business of one and a half million dollars. In a considerable degree this result grew out of the lecturing done in behalf of Brook Farm and association by Rev. John Allen and John Orvis, who were kept in the lecturing field during the winter months after Brook Farm took up the teachings of Fourier. When Brook Farm came to an end, Orvis continued his labors in behalf of association, aiding in the formation of co-operative stores, lecturing in the interest of workingmen, and editing *The Voice of Industry*, a weekly paper which he published in Boston.

The lectures of Allen and Orvis throughout New England served everywhere to arouse the workingmen, and to lead them to agitate and organize. The efforts of these men, especially of Allen, led to systematic action for ten hours as the

length of the working day. A delegates' meeting
of workingmen, convened in Lowell at his call in
1844, resulted in the organization of the New England Workingmen's Association; and Louis K.
Ryckman, chief of the Brook Farm "Shoemaking
Series," was chosen the president. The object of
the association was to secure a persistent agitation
for a ten hours' day and the general social improvement of the laboring class. Allen was an
earnest and intelligent man, and exerted as a
speaker a marked influence over workingmen.
He had been a Universalist clergyman; but his
anti-slavery sermons gave offence to his denomina-
tion, and he withdrew from the ministry.

John Orvis, the brother-in-law of Dwight, was a
zealous believer in associative life. It was to him
an ideal and a religion, and for it he labored all his
life. His *Voice of Industry* he edited for about
two years in Boston as the organ of various workingmen's movements. It was spoken of by
Greeley as "one of the best weekly papers published in New England." During the panic of
1873, when the laboring class was in greater dis-
tress than it had ever known before, he was instrumental in the organization of the Sovereigns of Industry. As the national lecturer of that organization, he was for more than two years constantly in
the field, lecturing to workingmen upon the principles and methods of conducting co-operative stores
after the Rochdale plan, which he had studied on
the spot, and in organizing councils of the order in

ten States and in the District of Columbia. Large numbers of stores were started; and, while they mostly failed in New England on account of mismanagement, they were successful in the Middle and Western States, especially among the miners and workers in the large iron industries. He compiled from standard English authorities rules and regulations for the management of these stores, which were adopted both by the National Council of the Sovereigns of Industry and the National Grange of the Patrons of Husbandry, as authorized by these bodies respectively, for conducting co-operative stores.

There can be little doubt, as Mr. Orvis claimed, that Brook Farm was the chief instrument in setting on foot all the movements since 1840 for the betterment of the wage-earners and the toilers of every kind. Directly it may have done little; but it set the agitation under way, and pointed out the lines of effort which have so far been pursued, for the most part.

No one who was at Brook Farm has ever been willing to admit that the association was a failure in any but a financial sense. It is maintained by all who were there that the life was genial and happy in a larger degree than they have known elsewhere. This might be explained by saying that care and responsibility were removed from the individual, that a comfortable home was certain, and that there was no need of individual worry or discontent. However true this may have been of the majority, it certainly could not have been true of the leaders, upon whom fell the responsibility of providing ways and means under difficult conditions. The secret of the satisfaction that the community gave is to be found in another direction. Mr. Charles A. Dana described it in words which are as truthful as they are characteristic: "Each person chose what he wished to do, and none of the boys and girls tried to shirk. There was more entertainment in doing the duty than in getting away from it. Every one was not only ready for his work, but glad to do it. This brings me to a peculiar feature of the system: the person who did the most disagreeable work was the one to receive special honor and distinction, because he was the servant of the others, and was rendering to his brothers a service not pleasant in itself, but which under other circumstances they would render to him. That was a universal quality and characteristic of the society. Just as a sculptor, who is carving an Apollo, goes to his work with joy and passion, so among us every duty and every kind of labor ought to be performed with the same enthusiasm, zeal, and sense of artistic pride."

This kind of life had a charm of its own, and one that impressed itself deeply upon all who came within its influence. It was something idyllic, full of grace and beauty, and satisfying to the highest aspirations of the heart and mind. This charm consisted, as George P. Bradford testified, "in the free and natural intercourse for which it gave oppor-

tunity, and in the working of the elective affinities
which here had a full play, so that, although there
was a kindly feeling running through the family
generally, little groups of friends, drawn together
into closer relations by taste and sympathy, soon
declare themselves. The relief from the fetters and
burdensome forms of society was a constant delight
to those who had suffered from them in the artificial
arrangements of society, the inmates were brought
together in more natural relations, and thus realized
the charm of true and hearty intercourse, and at the
same time the relief and pleasures of solitude were
not wanting." Higginson adds to this testimony
by saying that, "whatever might be said of the
actual glebe at Brook Farm, the social structure
was of the richest. Those who ever lived there
usually account it to this day as the happiest period
of their lives."

It speaks well for Brook Farm that all the persons who were there for any considerable length of
time regretted its failure, and wished to have it go
on. They attributed its want of success to outside
causes, and not to any inherent defect in the association itself. The earlier years were undoubtedly the
most happy and the most idyllic, with a charm
superior to those which succeeded, when the pressure of industrial interests was greater, and when
the membership was more varied and less harmonious. If the members looked upon the outside
world as in some degree barbarian, and spoke of its
people with a tone of contempt as *civilizées*, it was

a justifiable expression of faith in their own form of life and its superior merits. Where peace reigned and good will was universal might be justly claimed as a place worthy of imitation.

The merits of Brook Farm were those of all similar societies wherever they have been successful. The clan life of primitive races and the house communities of more advanced peoples have shown forth conspicuously the same advantages. Brook Farm had the distinct merit of bringing together a large number of superior people who devoted themselves to an experiment in education of a unique and interesting character. In no other respect was their community different from those undertaken in considerable numbers at the same period, and on the same general principles in all times and countries. The advances in civilization have not been so made, and no superior form of social institution has ever been organized without free competition and individual struggle. Yet such an experiment shows clearly enough that life is finer and more beautiful, kinder and happier, where men are devoted to each other's good, and where the constant struggle for the mere means of subsistence is made less urgent and distracting. No one can find the real charm of life who is anxious each day that those dependent on him may have enough to eat and wear.

Such experiments, even in their failures, make it clearer that a natural and spontaneous community of interests is necessary to a true social and moral life. The method of the associationists was not large enough to secure the results they desired, but it hints of how men are helped by serving each other. Co-operation will secure what competition has never yet been able to attain,— a united and happy community,— whether tribe, state, or nation, —wherein the interests of all are the interests of each one, and wherein each member finds his own highest good in seeking that which will conduce to the good of the whole. The way to this happy issue will be found through the science of sociology rather than by means of any of the panaceas offered by communism and socialism.

CHAPTER V.

A TIME OF EXPERIMENTS.

AFTER leaving Brook Farm, Dwight took up his residence in Boston, and continued the literary employments which had largely engaged his attention for some years. He at first joined with a company of persons who had been residents of Brook Farm, or connected with the several associationist organizations in Boston, in trying an experiment of association in the management of a boarding-house. A house was taken in High Street, and the members applied the co-operative method in its management. The experiment was undertaken partly for the sake of economy and partly that as many of the Brook Farm members as possible might be kept together. This effort at association was continued for only about a year, when, some of the members failing to share their part of the burden, it came to an end.

A member of this co-operative family has given the following account of the occasion of its formation and of the arrangements by which it was held together: "There had often been talk of a 'combined household,' and in the fall of 1848 we decided to try the experiment for a year. It was with great reluctance we took the house in High Street, as it was too far out of the current to suit our purposes; but it was hard to find a house with rooms enough at a rent that we could meet. The rent of each room was appraised; and they were all quickly taken, mostly by members of the three unions of as-

130 JOHN SULLIVAN DWIGHT

sociationists,— the Boston, Religious, and Woman's Unions,— five of whom had been members of Brook Farm,— John S. Dwight, Jonathan Butterfield, Rebecca, John, and Charles Codman. I cannot think of any other. One party, who had been greatly interested in the movement, was obliged to give it up; and the vacant place was taken by strangers who had expressed great interest, but who had no part previously in the work. The Boston and Religious Unions held their regular meetings and social entertainments in the large parlors, and the Woman's Union had its little salesroom back. All the household was boarded satisfactorily by the Woman's Union, which cleared all expenses, the women being charged $1.50 and the men $1.75 a week. At the end of the year we separated in various directions, some retaining the house for another year. Mr. Dwight went with his friends, who took a house on Pinckney Street, and remained with them until after his marriage."

Dwight did not abandon in any degree his interest in association on leaving Brook Farm, and his efforts in its behalf continued for at least five years nearly as active as they had been at the community. One form of this activity was his connection with the Religious Union of Associationists, which grew out of the preaching of Rev. W. H. Channing at Brook Farm and a small religious society he there organized. The Religious Union was organized in Boston, Jan. 3, 1847, at the house of James T. Fisher, who was made the recording secretary, and was one of the most earnest and efficient members. Channing felt that association must be distinctly based on a religious foundation, hence the organization of the society. Its history has been fully told in Frothingham's biography of Channing. Dwight had charge of the music at the religious meetings held by the Union; and during the greater part of the existence of the society he was an earnest worker in its behalf, often presided in Channing's absence, and sometimes conducted the services. Among those who sang in the choir were Nathaniel Chapin, O. W. Withington, W. W. Story, Frances Dwight, Mary Bullard, Helen M. Parsons; and Harriet Grauptner was the pianist. At the first service, held January 3, 1847, the "Sanctus" from Mozart's Twelfth Mass was sung by the Misses Bullard and Helen M. Parsons, and by Messrs. Dwight, W. W. Story, and O. W. Withington. Most of these persons were warmly interested in association.

To the music of this society Dwight gave much attention, selecting the best, and that most truly adapted to religious purposes, whatever the source from which it was obtained. Mrs. Ednah D. Cheney says she first heard the *Kyrie eleison* at these meetings. Only the best music was sung, that which was classical in character and by the great composers. The grand old church music was frequently made use of, as were parts of the great masses of the Catholic Church. As Dwight had entire charge of selecting and directing the music,

he would have nothing which was not of the very
best æsthetic quality; and he especially aimed to
harmonize the music with the broad and catholic
spirit of the religious services as conducted by
Channing.

In the *American Review* for May, 1847, an account of these meetings was given, and the musical
part of the service was criticised. In the *Harbinger* for June 19 Dwight made reply, and gave
his reasons for selecting classical music. The critic
found fault that the singing was not such as he
could hear elsewhere, that the mass music was made
use of, and that the words were in Latin. "The
only aim of the singers," Dwight replied, "was to
have good and practicable music, whether they
found it in Catholic masses, in Protestant oratorios,
in Gregorian and Lutheran chants, or even in Yan-
kee psalmody. The taste and experience of the
choir led them for the time being to selections from
these masses, because the music seemed to them so
warm, so reverent, so beautifully expressive of the
heart's best aspirations, and of the true religion,
which is love and joy. The Latin words they did not
consider an objection, because they are so beautiful
and true in themselves, because they are consecrated
by long usage in a great part of the Christian
world, and because, being so simple and few, and
always the same for the same theme and sentiment,
they explain themselves in connection with the
music; while the ordinary practice of singing a long
didactic poem to a psalm tune is unmusical and in-

congruous in every point of view. But they have never bound themselves to this more than to any other music. It has reigned with them thus far because it proved convenient, and because the singers and the majority of the hearers felt a growing love for it. But the reviewer heard a common congregational psalm sung in the same place as a part of the same service on each day that he was present, which he does not mention; and let him not be surprised if on some other occasion he should hear there Protestant Händel instead of Catholic Mozart. For music is more catholic than all the churches,— the faithful, many-sided servant of the human heart; and whatsoever is good music is a harmony and help to what is most religious, loving, and profound in human souls, whether it was born on Catholic or heretic or even on a heathen soil.

"And this is all our answer to the charge of cutting a sublime thing out of its appropriate setting. Doubtless a whole mass would be better than a piece of one, a full choir and an organ would be better than a quartette and a pianoforte, and a cathedral, with its solemn lights and aisles, would be the fitting complement of such high strains. This none could feel more clearly than the persons who are drawn towards this music by its own intrinsic beauty and expressiveness. But because we cannot have all, may we not have a part? Is there no intrinsic meaning and beauty in the music by itself? If it inspires the singer and hearer, if it imparts a

warmth such as cold common psalmody cannot, if
it lifts the thoughts more nearly to the state which
we call worship, if it weaves a spell of holy communion round us, why reject it and put up with
duller things because we cannot have it in the full
glory of all its accompaniments?   As to its being
'sacrilegiously stolen,' we say this music came from
Mozart and from Haydn, and not from the Roman
Catholic Church; and it belongs to every soul
which can respond to it, which can appreciate it,
which has states answering to its solemn, cheerful
tones.   It belongs to humanity, to the one church
universal which is not yet, but which waits until
humanity be one.   For music is a universal language: it knows nothing of opinions, creeds, and
doctrines that divide.   It knows only the heart of
the whole matter, which is one.   It speaks to hearts,
to that which all men have in common, and in
cherishing which resides our only hope of unity, our
only hope of ever seeing a truly catholic and universal church.   In Christ we hear a kindred language; and by a natural and worthy correspondence
do associationists commune together in the thought
of Christ, and in the atmosphere of music, which is
both human and divine, as he was."

Immediately after leaving Brook Farm, Dwight
began to write on musical topics for the *Daily
Chronotype*, edited and published by Elizur Wright.
His work was that of giving an account of concerts
and other musical entertainments, reviewing new
music, and writing articles on special topics of

musical interest.   During the year 1849 he did the
same kind of work for the *Daily Advertiser*.

When the *Harbinger* came to an end, early in
1849, Dwight was ready to continue his efforts for
association, and made an arrangement for conducting a department in that interest in the *Daily
Chronotype* of Boston.   In the number of that paper
for Aug. 23, 1849, the editor of this one-cent daily
said, " By an arrangement with some friends of social reform we have given up to them the control
of three columns on the first page.   For the contents of them they alone are responsible.   Their
sentiments, we have every reason to believe, will
correspond with our own; but we' shall hold ourselves at perfect liberty to combat them when we
see fit."

Among those Dwight was able to gather about
him to assist him in this work were W. H. Channing, W. F. Channing, C. A. Dana, and Albert
Brisbane.   Poetry was furnished by C. P. Cranch
and others.   Dwight translated Victor Considerant's " Attractive Industry, or else the Slavery of
the Masses."   Among other topics on which he
wrote were workingmen as their own employers,
Fourier's writings, Hungary, systems of socialism,
protective unions for workingmen, and dilettante-
ism as opposed to the interests of the people.
The statement of purposes in the first number
was written by Dwight, and some parts of it are
worthy of notice as a summary of his opinions on
the subject of association.

"We mean that the great social problems of the times," he wrote, "the problem of labor and of a true society based upon labor rightly organized, shall have some justice done in these columns. . . . We propose to present a fair, kindly, and intelligent account of the great socialistic movement in all branches, to note all progress in the science and the practice of domestic and industrial association, to show the symptoms everywhere about us of the approach of the whole toiling and producing multitude to an era of complete and universal mutualism or guarantism, and, finally, to trace the several movements to the end in which they all converge; namely, to labor made attractive in complete association.

"We are disposed to take the name of socialist for better or for worse, and challenge all the world to prove that there can be a better Christian, a truer friend of order, a more sincere respecter of the rights of property and family, a more delicately careful guardian of every individuality and every sacred sphere of life, than is the genuine socialist who feels and understands his reconciling mission. He asks for guaranties of much more such protection to these principles than civilized society affords. He sees that, after all, there is no property secure, no union lasting, no family sacred, no individuality consulted, no true education possible, save by the happiest fortune of a few in a society whose spring is competition, and whose only order is the blind resultant of old anarchy that proves itself

even now too strong for its governing principle of
force. He feels that there is a common life which
sets through all humanity, and that humanity col-
lectively; in other words, society on this globe
must first be set in order before the individual can
be himself or know the meaning of the Christian
communion with his neighbor and with God. He
asks himself what it is that interests all men most
widely, that silently creeps under the political bar-
riers of nations, that understands itself in every language, and knits the widest and most complex
relations between the people of all countries, con-
trolling every legislature, cabinet, and throne. It
is the industry and commerce by which wealth is
created and distributed. This of itself can weave
a brotherhood of nations and transform any despot-
ism, but only on one grand condition,— only on
condition that the principle of *laissez-faire* or competition, by which it now tends to industrial Van-
dalism, shall be made to give place to association,
which shall reconcile all interests and open opportunities to all.

" We are associationists, but we are not 'promis-
cuous aggressionists.' We believe in an organic
solidarity, a harmony, and not in a confusion of interests. We believe a true society should guarantee
the 'right to labor,' without which every other right
is futile; but we do not believe in public bounties
upon idleness,— the right to labor, but not necessarily the duty of interference by the State, which
may be left to times and places. Meanwhile our

hope is strongest in the power of the laborers themselves by peacefully associating their industry to
guarantee to one another this right in its fulness.

"We believe in individual property. We are
not communists. Organization of labor will enrich
all, as no rash spoliation or division ever could.
We hold the laborer entitled to the fruits of his
own earnings, and that the employer will be the
gainer by making him a partner in the profits of
the production. We believe that labor, capital, and
skill, all three have rights, and must not be denied
remuneration. We are not for withholding interest
on capital, however it may bring us at issue with
some schools of socialism. We are of the party of
peace. Our watchword is the peaceful transforma-
tion of the subversive, false societies of competition
into the co-operative society of unity and harmony
under God's perfect code of love.

"We are not *red* republicans. We have no
sympathy with the red banner. Nor do we believe
that the spirit and tendency of socialism has been
anything but peaceful. Indeed, socialism altogether
is a peaceful protest against the red rule of force,
by which the privileged party of the past alone
maintains its sway. . . .

"Are we, then, masters of a social science, that
we are emboldened to address ourselves to such a
mighty task of reconciliation? . . . Frankly, we believe we hold the key to it. It is our privilege to
be born into a time when some of the great harmonies of such a reconciling law have been struck,

and our ears did not chance to be closed against them. A work of years, it may be, and of many minds united to show the full and fair proportions of the social science, to state in all its length and breadth, and all its infinite beauty of detail and special application, God's law of harmonic society on earth. But the only way — and to evade it would be treason to our souls — is to trust, and follow up such glimpses as we have. And we say that even now, in the confused whirl of noisy and impatient opinions which bears the name of socialism, there is mixed up some of the serenest wisdom which ever visited the human soul. There are clear outlines, benign intimations caught by some souls in the movement of a law, a science which shall reconcile all interests, all parties, do away all terrors, and effect a peaceful transition out of these ages of industrial competition, with its attendant train of poverty, ignorance, crime, war, slavery, and disease, into an age of universal co-operation, union, competence, refinement, peace, and Perfect Liberty with Perfect Order.

"J. S. D."

This venture did not prove a success, and the arrangement was continued only for a few months. The publishers of the *Chronotype* were not able or willing to carry out their part of the agreement. Various other plans were discussed by Dwight and his friends, but nothing came of them. In the mean time his interest in association did not abate, and he was one of the most active workers in the

Boston Union of Associationists.   He gave much
time to its meetings and to keeping the organization in a healthy condition.   He helped to provide
music, to organize entertainments, and to make the
meetings attractive.   He was a leader in celebrat-
ing the birthday of Fourier each year in April,
securing music, writing toasts, preparing the programme, and making the meetings a success.   Two
of the toasts prepared by him for the celebration
of 1849 may here be given as indicative of his attitude towards the social problems of the day : —

"To Joy! to Liberty! to Childhood's Mirth! to
Youth's Enthusiasm! to the warm life-thrill of Attraction felt through every fibre of existence!   The
times are coming — the Harmonic Times of Unity
and Love — when the Passions in their purity shall
prove themselves divine; when Liberty shall not
be license, nor amusement folly; when every faculty, the humblest as the highest, shall find supreme
delight in Uses; when Labor shall be Play; and
Joy and Beauty crown the works of men.   Let
rhythmic feasts and songs and dances still renew
the prophecy of the Harmonic Times!"

"The Wrongs and Hopes of Labor!   Long
has been its martyrdom.   A year ago the sounds
of its deliverance in the Old World pealed across
the ocean into the midst of our festival.   The
struggle outwardly has been in vain.   Still thousands starve in Ireland.   Still, goaded to madness,
the impatient crowds rising to claim their rights
have been shot down.   But not in vain has been

their martyrdom. A peaceful deliverance is nigh. The spirit of God is moving in this age in the instinct of association. Its ways are devious, fragmentary, many. But they will all unite, and industry be organized, and man be free and honored in his functions by his brother man."

During this period Dwight was in demand as a lecturer on musical subjects. In 1850 and in 1851 he furnished to *Sartain's Magazine* of Philadelphia a monthly article on some musical topic, and each article was accompanied by a popular piece of music selected by him. He wrote frequently for a musical journal published in New York, and called the *Messenger Bird.* He contributed to other publications on the great composers and their works, or on current subjects connected with music. During the first six months of 1851 he was the musical editor of the *Boston Commonwealth.* In this connection the following letter may find a place: —

West Newton, Nov. 23, '51.

My dear Sir,— I understand that you wish to ascertain, on Mr. Sartain's behalf, whether I could supply him with an article for his magazine. It so happens that I have recently written a story, and have it now on hand. As regards the important point of remuneration, Gresham made an offer a year since of one hundred dollars for an article; and I suppose (but am not quite certain) that his proposal would still hold good. Dr. Bailey, of the *National Era*, has likewise offered me the same sum. I should prefer to publish the story in a magazine rather than a newspaper; and on this account, and because I do not know whether Gresham wants the article now, I would let Mr. Sartain have it at the above-named price.

If it will increase the value of the article, Mr. Sartain may be assured that I shall not write anything else for the magazines at present, being about to engage in a large work.

Very truly yours,

NATHANIEL HAWTHORNE.

P.S.— I am established here for the winter, and it would give Mrs. Hawthorne and myself much pleasure to see you.

During the years 1850 and 1851 Dwight seriously discussed a removal to New York, and the connection of himself with the *Tribune*. His friends Ripley and Dana had secured for themselves places on that newspaper, and they wished to have his aid as a coworker. Ripley urged his making the venture of joining the staff of the paper, and making for himself a permanent place there. In February, 1850, Ripley wrote to him: " We stand in the greatest need of you here, however little you may need New York or anything that therein is. You can not come too soon."

In September, Ripley wrote, urging his friend to come to New York at once and begin work; but no definite remuneration was guaranteed. A little later he and Dana made an effort to secure a place for Dwight on the *Herald*, and Parke Godwin the next year endeavored to connect him with the *Evening Post*. Dwight seems to have tried the work on the *Tribune* for a short period, but it evidently was not wholly to his liking. During the year 1851 Ripley secured the promise of publication, by J. S. Redfield, of New York, of a biography of Mozart which Dwight was then preparing. In October of that year Dwight wrote from New York to his brother: "As to the Mozart book, I have almost decided to let Mason & Law publish it. They offer me ten per cent. on all sales, and wish to stereotype and bring out the whole at once in two volumes, say in July or August." This work was not published, probably owing to the fact that Dwight soon gave his attention to the publication of a musical journal in Boston.

John S. Dwight and Mary Bullard were married Feb. 12, 1851, by Rev. W. H. Channing. Miss Bullard was a frequent visitor at Brook Farm. She was a member of the choir of the Religious Union of Associationists, and she was an active worker with Dwight in all his efforts to keep alive the Boston Union of Associationists. From 1849 he had been living in Pinckney Street, an inmate of the house of Mrs. Parsons, who, with her daughters, was a member of the Union of Associationists. Here Miss Bullard also had her home, here they were married, and in the same house they remained for several months after this event. In

1853 they rented a house in Charles Street, near Cambridge Street; and here they resided for several years.

Mary Bullard was a beautiful, winning, unselfish woman, a fine singer, and a person of many attractions of body and mind. She had a serene and charming face, was a fine talker, and had a most gracious and attractive manner. At Brook Farm her coming was hailed with delight by all; for she was a superior singer, and she lent herself pleasantly to all the interests of the place. A Brook Farmer says that "she was vivacious, quick, and sprightly; was fond of conversation, but, no matter how trivial the subject of discourse, it grew into earnestness in her mind, unless she was wholly playful. But her chief distinction was her love and talent for music, and in the capacity of beautiful singer she was first introduced to us." At the farm she was known as "the Nightingale," because of her gifts as a singer. By this name Ripley mentions her in his letters to Dwight, and by that of "die lieblichste." One of her intimate friends has written of her: "Mary was a lovely person for a housemate. She was frank, outspoken, but always just and harmonious." William H. Channing said that, without being morbid, she was the most thoroughly conscientious person he ever knew.

The five years which had now passed since Brook Farm closed had been years of struggle and disappointment for Dwight. They had also been years of poverty and failure. He had tried many things, had struggled hard to find a permanent place, and all had ended with small results. His marriage had been delayed through four or five years for these reasons, and was entered upon with few prospects for the immediate future. At last he was to find the place for which he was fitted ; and, though it did not give him much money, it did give him congenial employment and a task suited to his genius.

CHAPTER VI.

"DWIGHT'S JOURNAL OF MUSIC."

THE reason why Dwight did not connect himself with the *Tribune* was doubtless because he had an ambition for a periodical of his own, to be devoted exclusively to music and to be entirely under his own control. Early in the year 1851 that project had taken definite shape in his own mind, and he wrote to Ripley in detail of his plan. He proposed to secure a guarantee fund that would enable him to carry the paper on for one year without loss, to become both publisher and editor, and to devote his paper entirely to music and the kindred arts. Ripley objected to his undertaking to act as his own publisher, and the taking any responsibility of a personal character which would involve financial loss to himself. "You will not bother yourself, I hope," Ripley wrote, "by incurring any personal responsibilities on the strength of anticipated sub-scriptions. The friends of music should shoulder the burden, raise the money, while you give to it the aid of your talents and taste."

This advice was taken so far as securing a guar-antee fund was concerned, and the next year was devoted to obtaining the aid of those interested in the project. In February, 1852, the plan was so far matured that a circular was prepared by Dwight, setting forth his purposes in establishing a musical journal of a superior character. How he proposed to conduct it he stated in these words: —

" The *tone* to be impartial, independent, catholic, conciliatory, aloof from musical clique and controversy, cordial to all good things, but not eager to chime in with any powerful private interest of publisher, professor, concert-giver, manager, society, or party. This paper would make itself the 'organ' of no school or class, but simply an organ of what may be called the Musical *Movement* in our country, of the growing love of deep and genuine music, of the growing consciousness that music, first amid other forms of Art, is intimately connected with Man's truest life and destiny. It will insist much on the claims of 'Classical' music, and point out its beauties and its meanings, not with a pedantic partiality, but because the *enduring* needs always to be held up in contrast with the ephemeral. But it will also aim to recognize what good there is in styles more simple, popular, or modern, will give him who is Italian in his tastes an equal hearing with the German, and will even print the articles of those opposed to the partialities or the opinions of the editor, provided they be written briefly, decently, and to the point."

In this effort to establish an independent journal, devoted to the interests of music, Dwight had the active support and co-operation of the Harvard Musical Association. He brought his project before that society at the annual meeting of 1852, which was held in January; and, at a special meeting held in February, measures were taken to afford him such aid as he needed. The securing of the guarantee fund was in considerable degree due to the co-operation of the members; and he had their efficient help in procuring subscribers, as well as in getting the business details of the paper into working order.   So long as the paper was published, the association stood by him, and gave him its active support.

"Be not startled at my prospectus," Dwight wrote to Cranch, "but try to get me ten names upon it, and mail it back to me in a few days.   You see I am bent on establishing a journal of music and æsthetic matters, which shall be my own.   I am sick of writing off and on for other people, for unreliable publishers, etc.   I propose to print a small weekly paper,— say eight quarto pages,— without printed music, but filled with notices of concerts, composers, musical publications, etc., essays on styles, analyses of compositions, with some brief notices of other arts, and a small sprinkling of original poems, songs, tales, etc.   Now in this last you perhaps can help me.   Send me a little poem or two of yours.   I should like one for the first number.   I shall have to rely on friendship for all my variety, since it will take a year or more to make the paper pay for itself.   But I shall not start until I am guaranteed for one year against debt, partly by a guarantee fund of fifteen hundred to two thousand dollars (which some moneyed friends of music here are organizing), and partly by such subscription list as I can raise in a couple of weeks by these papers.   The Harvard Musical Association took the plan up warmly at the annual supper (when your note was read), and are to have another meeting about it next week. If each member will get me ten subscribers, it will make five hundred at once. I shall want some letters, too, from New York about the concerts and operas there. Will not the spirit move you occasionally?

" If you see the Howadji, can you not enlist his active sympathies a little in my cause? A letter now and then from him on music or other art would be a feather in the cap of my enterprise. It is my last, desperate (no very confident) grand *coup d'etat* to try and get a living; and I call on all good powers to help me launch the ship, or, rather, little boat."

The name to be given the new journal called for much of consideration. Dwight objected to the use of his own name as a part of that of the paper, not liking to hear persons say that " *Harper's* has come," and decidedly objected to the statement that " *Dwight's* has come." Curtis wrote him that he had submitted the problem to the editorial council of the *Tribune*, and that the conclusion was he should call the paper " Dwight's Musical Journal," with the sub-title, " A paper of Art and Literature." To Longfellow, Dwight wrote for contributions and for suggestions as to the name.

Cambridge, March 25, 1852.

Dear Dwight,— I should have been more rapid in my reply to your friendly note if I had had anything

to send you which would make my answer agreeable. But, since I have taken to writing long
poems, I have given up writing short ones; and I
find I have nothing which I should be willing to
publish.

But much more important is the name you may fix
upon. " Pon lo tuyo en consejo, uno te dirá que es
blanco, otro que es bermejo," says the Spanish prov-
erb, and I have always found it true. I agree with
you in thinking the simpler the better. Why not,
then, say " Musical Journal," and no more, without
troubling yourself about a second title? No one
can object to that, I fancy.

Speaking about this with Batchelder the other
day, I made the same suggestion that the Howadji
made. But I feel your personal objections, and
now make the proposition to retain only two words
out of three.   Yours truly,

HENRY W. LONGFELLOW.

Finally, the name settled upon was " Dwight's
Journal of Music: A Paper of Art and Literature."
The first number was dated April 10, 1852, but was
issued several weeks earlier. This number began
with the prospectus, and was followed by a " Son-
net to my Piano," by C. P. Cranch; a short article
on Jenny Lind's devotion to her art; a letter about
music in New York, signed by " Hafiz,"— in other
words, George W. Curtis; a letter on the Music
Hall then being erected in Boston; and reviews of

books. Much space was given to music in Boston; and the musical news of Paris, Italy, England, and Germany, was reported. The "Introductory" was an earnest and explicit statement of the purposes of the new journal, in part restating what has already been given, and adding some personal considerations which may be given here, because of its honest recognition of his own strong interest in music, and the limitations under which he labored in desiring to promote its interests.

"Without being in any sense a thoroughly educated musician either in theory or practice, we have found ourselves, as long as we could remember, full of the appeal which this most mystical and yet most human art — so perfectly intelligible to feeling, if not to the understanding — has never ceased to make to us. From childhood there was an intense interest and charm to us in all things musical. The rudest instrument and most hackneyed player thereof seemed invested with a certain halo and saving grace, as it were, from a higher, purer, and more genial atmosphere than this of our cold, selfish, humdrum world. We could not sport with this, and throw it down like common recreation. It spoke a *serious* language to us, and seemed to challenge study of its strange, important meanings, like some central oracle of oldest and still newest wisdom. And this at a time when the actual world of music lay in the main remote from us, shooting only now and then some stray vibrations over into this western hemisphere. We felt that music must

have some most intimate connection with the social destiny of Man, and that, if we but knew it,
it concerns us all.

"A few years have passed, and now this is a
general feeling.   Music is a feature in the earnest
life and culture of advanced American society.
It enters into all our schemes of education.   It
has taken the initiative as the popular art *par ex-
cellence* in gradually attempering this whole people
to the sentiment of Art.   And whoever reflects
upon it must regard it as a most important saving
influence in this rapid expansion of our democratic
life.   Art, and especially Music, is a true conservative element, in which Liberty and Order are both
fully typed and made beautifully perfect in each
other.   A free people must be rhythmically educated in the whole tone and temper of their daily
life; must be taught the instinct of rhythm and
harmony in all things, in order to be fit for freedom.
And it is encouraging, amid so many dark and
wild signs of the times, that this artistic sentiment
is beginning to ally itself with our progressive energies, and make our homes too beautiful for ruth-
less change."

At the end of the year the editor made a hopeful report, saying that he had not accomplished
as much as he desired, but all that seemed possible under the circumstances.   He said that the
paper paid its own way, but that "the editor's
remuneration, beyond the barest minimum, is in
the future."   "When we commenced," he said,

"there were not a few to warn us that we undertook a perilous and almost impossible voyage; but there were believing friends that helped to provision and insure the ship. Our success has not been brilliant; but we have got decently through, and with such encouraging response from those whose good opinion we most valued that we feel small fear for the future."

The contents of the paper during this first year were notable, as they continued to be to the end of the last volume published. The editor himself carefully, sympathetically, and yet fearlessly reviewed the music of Boston during the year. His reports were not mere newspaper chroniclings, but intelligent and appreciative studies of the music of the day and the way in which it was presented to the public. Next in importance was the presentation of the art of music through translations from leading writers and journals. In the third number began a series of articles by Franz Liszt on Frederic Chopin, translated by the editor from the German. A study of Weber's "Der Freischütz," by Hector Berlioz, was also translated, as well as critical accounts of Berlioz's latest musical work. In an early number was begun the publication of A. Oulibicheff's "Life and Times of Mozart," a work of great merit by a Russian. This was the book on Mozart about which Dwight was negotiating with publishers the year before. The greater part of it appeared in the *Journal of Music*, being continued through several years.

Numerous other translations appeared from German, French, and Italian writers on music. In this connection it may be stated that Wagner was mentioned in the first volume,— six months,— and that much notice was taken of him in the second. Three long articles were devoted to a statement of what was then known of him,— his life, theories, and music. No less than three translations from his own writings were given, and four or five articles by leading German or English writers on musical subjects. The same breadth and generosity of treatment appeared in his other selections and translations. In all the matter of this kind which he published, his aim was educative and catholic; and it was of a sort calculated to bring the reader into closest sympathy with the best in music, and with the aims and spirit of the great masters who most truly represented this most emotional and spiritual of the arts.

The list of contributors to the *Journal of Music* was not a long one, for the editor was not able to pay more than a mere pittance for even the best articles. For two or three years George W. Curtis wrote occasionally from New York. So long as the paper was published, Cranch was an occasional contributor of poems; and here for the first time appeared many of the best of his shorter pieces. Rev. Charles T. Brooks was also wont to send to Dwight his lyrical outpourings, many of which found the public in the *Journal*. It may be said that this paper was notable for its poetical selections, every number usually having two or three of the best short poems of the day. Another feature of the paper was its correspondence from all the music centres of Europe, and its careful selection of the musical intelligence of the day. From all American cities where there was any interest in music came full reports, and several able writers on music were in this way trained to their work as music interpreters and critics. One of the most frequent contributors to the *Journal* in this way was Alexander W. Thayer, who began by sending news notes from New York. For several years he contributed his thoughts on musical topics under the title of "From my Diary," which attracted much attention; and he came to be known as "The Diarist." A later series of his contributions were reprinted in book form. He spent several years in Europe,— was the United States consul at Trieste, and published the most important life of Beethoven which has appeared. He contributed to the *Journal* more largely, and for a longer period, than any other person except the editor.

Another frequent writer was Frances Malone Raymond, who afterwards became Mrs. Frederic Ritter. To early volumes of the *Journal* she sent poems, music criticisms, and translations; and her connection with it continued to the end. She has published many volumes on music, including a translation of Robert Schumann's "Music and Musicians," and original works on "Some Famous Songs" and "Troubadours and Minnesingers."

Her volumes of poetry include " Madrigals " and
"Songs and Ballads." Dr. Frederic L. Ritter was
a contributor to some of the later volumes. Mr.
W. S. B. Matthews, now the editor of *Music*, an
able monthly published in Chicago, wrote often
during the later years of the *Journal's* history.

In turning over the volumes of the *Journal of
Music* to-day, one is impressed with the variety and
high character of its contents. Its excellent literary
quality appears on every page, as well as the profound love of art in its musical form everywhere
manifested by the editor. The twenty volumes in
which it is bound make an almost complete ency-
clopædia of music, so wide is the range of interest
shown, and so catholic are the appreciations displayed. This statement will seem to be quite out
of harmony with the criticism often made, that
Dwight cared only for German music, and that of
the older schools. It may be granted that his taste
was formed before the newer schools came into
vogue, and that he was intensely German in his
preferences. It is thoroughly true, however, that in
his selections and translations he took the widest
range, and that he thus gave every school an opportunity to speak for itself to his readers. No one
could have been more generous towards Wagner, for
instance, who occupies a large space in the *Journal*,
not only with extensive translations from his own
writings, but with the commendations of his admirers. It is true that the other side is presented,
and that the editor gives his own opinions honestly

and without reserve; but let it be noted that he is most generous in his recognition of the music of Wagner and of his theories. He did not like the music; and he did not agree with the theories, and he said so plainly, giving good reasons for his dislikings. He was a candid critic, speaking his own mind freely; but he was an appreciative and a sympathetic critic, as well.

There can be no doubt that the *Journal of Music* would have been a much greater financial success if its literary and musical standards had not been so high. The editor had no gift for appealing to merely popular tastes. His standard was of the highest kind, and he had no wish or capacity for lowering it for the sake of outward success. He took the course, undoubtedly, which was of the largest benefit to music, most truly educative of public taste; but he appealed to only a limited circle of readers. The paper fixed the musical standard, not only of Boston, but of the whole country; and genuine lovers of music turned to its pages as to a supreme authority.

At no time did the *Journal of Music* give Dwight more than the scantiest remuneration for his labor bestowed upon it. It tied him down to a life of the severest drudgery, to work he did not love, and kept him from that kind of work for music which would have been to him a delight. So scanty was the remuneration which came to the editor that on two occasions, at the end of the second year of the *Journal* and again at the end of the fourth year,

the musicians of Boston gave complimentary benefits to the paper.   These were cheering indications
of the interest taken in it by those best able to
appreciate its work.   On the first occasion the
musicians of Boston said to the editor: "We look
upon the *Journal of Music* as an institution which
it is the interest and duty of all artists to sustain.
We owe it a debt for mediating between us and the
public, and laboring to raise that public to a fuller
appreciation of the things we do from our own
hearts and for the love of art rather than for the
praise and money of the crowd.   We know enough,
too, of the world to know that, in the nature of
things, a musical journal, conducted on such high
principles as yours, though sure of fair success in
the long run, and not without encouragement thus
far, cannot in times like these remunerate its editor
according to his labors.   We artists would sustain
it, as in some sense our common organ, as we
would a temple or an academy of music, as one of
the public instrumentalities for the due furtherance
of our art."

How keenly Dwight felt the drudgery of much of
the work he was compelled to perform as best he
could may be seen from some bits of his correspondence.   In March, 1856, he wrote to Charles T.
Brooks, in answer to that friend's request for aid in
buying a piano: "Do not despair of me as a corre-
spondent.   I have not forgotten about the piano,
although I have taken the benefit of your Uhland
poem.   A capital translation it is, too.   I must take

a little more time to look about among the pianos. For the last two or three weeks I have been so beset and harassed by my miserable *Journal* — especially the many matters thereto pertaining — that I could think of nothing else. Besides lack of time, too, I have lack of quiet, lack of clearness and effective movement, lack of brains. These latter seem to be getting 'muddled' in the old cocoanut; but the warm spring sun and running rivulets (of melting snow in the gutters) promise peace and sense of freedom.

" I was surprised and greatly interested to hear of your 'Faust' labor. Verily, it must have been a great work; and I trust it will be rewarded. I am anxious to see it, and shall hint to some of our publishers. If Ticknor relucts, I think it quite possible that Phillips & Sampson would like the glory of such an enterprise, and turn it to profit, too, as readily as anybody. I will speak to their literary partner, with whom I am well acquainted. Will you pardon, and yet have patience with, yours truly ? "

At the very end of the same year Christopher P. Cranch, in a letter written from Paris, said to Dwight: " As to yourself, my dear fellow, I grieve that you must grind and grind, and still be poor; for you haven't even a poor painter's eternal satisfaction of attractive labor to put in the other scale against poverty. It is a hard thing, if a man must make a machine of himself, that he can't accomplish a machine's work, and coin money with his

cranks, wheels, and pistons; for dollars stand in
the relation to this incessant intellectual grinding
that the future life does to this.   What's it all for,
unless there's a crown of glory waiting for us?   I
wish to heavens you could step out of your 'tread-
mill,' as you call it.   Isn't there a fat professorship
somewhere in reserve for you?   That would be the
thing for you.   I find it a devilish hard case that
a man of your powers and acquirements shouldn't
be seized upon and chaired with huzzas, and floated
over the people's heads into some academic or other
throne.   You ought to have a larger sweep than
you have with your musical, critical, literary broom;
and I don't see why Boston and Cambridge don't
open its eyes and its purse to the fact."

In October, 1856, Alexander W. Thayer wrote in
this wise: " It will wear you all out to go on this
way; and I want you, at all events, to get so situated that you can think out your thoughts and give
them to us fresh and full.   Take up with almost
any terms, I should say, at least for a certain length
of time.   Courage, if possible."

This refers to negotiations with Oliver Ditson &
Co. for them to become the publishers of the
Journal of Music.   Such arrangement was soon
made; and with the beginning of the sixth year, in
April, 1859, that firm relieved Dwight of the drudgery of being his own publisher and office clerk.
This enterprising and well-established firm of
music-sellers and publishers took the entire responsibility of the publication of the paper, giving to

Dwight the full control of its editorial management,
leaving him free to conduct it in his own way.
The paper was to remain the same in size, price,
and in other details, the publishers adding such advertising pages as they desired; and they paid
Dwight twelve hundred dollars a year as salary.
Such compensation was miserably small; but it gave
a regular income, paid weekly, and the arrangement enabled Dwight to devote himself more un-
reservedly to the higher interests of his journal.

In announcing the new arrangement in the
Journal of Music, the editor said: " Ever since we
started it we have united all the functions of editor,
business manager, clerk, collector, and paymaster
in our own person. This has been a heavy weight,
full of untold annoyances, and sadly interfering
with the full and free carrying out of those very
editorial ideals which we had most at heart.
Neither in the high sense nor in the popular sense,
neither to the exacting few nor to the many who
require ' milk for babes' in art, has our paper been
all it would have been, had cares of business left us
more free hours for thinking out and serving up all
the right varieties of matter. Of this shortcoming
no one has been more conscious than ourselves.
Our main reliance, meanwhile, has been in the evi-
dence of true intention, in the spirit of impartial
loyalty to art which, we are assured, has first and
last shone clearly through the columns, and in such
not altogether hopeless approximation to our design as, with the aid of noble helpers and con-

tributors, we have, in spite of all, been enabled to make.   Now we shake off the business chains, and shall be more free to think and feel and write and seek welcome and instructive access to the sympathies of a much larger circle of friends."

The paper went on much as it had done before, but the work of the editor was easier and much more satisfactory.   He found in some degree the leisure he had desired, and the improved quality of the paper showed this result.   The paper was more widely circulated, and became more truly an authority in everything musical.   One new feature was the addition of music to each number.   This was printed by itself, and had no distinct connection with the paper.   In selecting this music, Dwight exercised his superior taste, so far as possible, and sent out nothing which was not of the highest merit.   During the first year the selections were taken from Mendelssohn, Schubert, Bach, Bellini, Wagner, Gluck, Donizetti, Mozart, and Alfred Jaell.   Compositions of length were published in parts, " Don Giovanni " being issued in this way during 1859, and " Der Freischütz " during 1860.   A considerable number of the great works were in this way sent to the subscribers to the *Journal of Music.*

A few personal letters will more clearly indicate how busy was Dwight's life at this period, and how greatly he enjoyed the few days of leisure which he was able to secure during each year.   In the summer he was able to get away for a few days to

North Conway, where his friend, Mr. F. W. Channing, placed a charmingly located house at his disposal, or he went to visit friends other few days in Newport.

In June, 1854, Dwight received this rather surprising letter from Lowell, who said: " It has occurred to some of your friends that you might find your account in establishing something of this sort,— a bureau for governesses. Don't you see? There is a great and constant demand for them, and they as constantly are asking to be taken; but neither wanter nor wantee get to hear of each other. Now the kindly office I propose for you is to take these wandering hooks and unite them with the forlorn eyes that somewhere await them.

" Applications are constantly made to teachers by both hooks and eyes; but, owing to want of responsibility and system, everything is at loose ends. You could have a book in which the name of the applicant, the date of application, and the names of references, etc., could be entered, and then act as hooker, receiving a proper commission. You could advertise at first in other journals, but by degrees could make your own paper the exclusive bulletin for such matters.

" I am certain from what I hear and know that, with no great trouble to yourself, you might make a profitable business, and be thanked all round into the bargain. I am in an immense hurry just now, but I will only add that character and everything of that sort make you just the man."

This letter evidently puzzled Dwight, as it will any one reading it now, as to how much or how little it meant. Probably it was Lowell's purpose to suggest something like a "teachers' agency," and that he was quite sincere in the advice he gave. No one could have been less fitted for such a task than Dwight, and he was already too much occupied with similar labors to give him peace of mind or body.

"I really am unable," was Dwight's reply, "to see that I have any calling in the direction you suggest, — or that has been suggested to you,— unless it be a call to earn money by any honest means whatever, and that with the least possible squeamishness. What should have led anybody to think of me in such a connection, I can hardly imagine. I am altogether too easily bored (sensitive, selfish, touch-me-not that I am) to wish to be any more of an intelligence office than I already involuntarily am, as part of the penalty of editing a musical paper. I hate so much of the personal go-betweenism even of the musical world, and would like (if possible) to deal with that world more at arm's length instead of having to personally meet so many of the music-teachers and the applicants for such. If it came to governesses, what should I do?

"I am surprised to learn, too, that there can be any lack of such a medium. How can it be that the wants of society have not already organized the matter? I should think some lady would be most competent and suitable for such an office. Why would not our sister E. P. P.'s back room in West Street be just the place?

" I should have written and said all this, in answer to your kind note, before. But first I was puzzled, and therefore dumb; and then I was busy, and time flew unawares. Pardon me, will you not? I wish I might see you in Boston, and our Howadji with you."

In November of the next year there came to Dwight this note from George W. Curtis: " I am engaged to Anna Shaw, daughter to Mr. and Mrs. Frank. Do you remember her in Brook Farm days? She was a child then: she is twenty years old now. There was never anything that made parents and children happier. She is so inexpressibly dear and beautiful to me that I cannot conceive you should not love her dearly. To outsiders she is a superb and silent Shaw: but her heart is so true and tender, she is so noble and pure and affectionate, that you will be afraid to be the friend of such a Polycrates as I. When do you come to New York? I so want you to see her and know her: then, of course, you will love her. Give my love to your wife.— think that love is not for this world, but forever, — and remember your friend who remembers you."

To this most confidential note Dwight made reply: " Happy friend! Your little note was the ray of sunshine in a miserable, hurried week. All of us, your friends here, thought it the best of good news, especially I. Believe me, my dear friend, it is

an event upon which I can heartily congratulate
you, and on which I somehow unmisgivingly found
the fairest hopes for you. This time I am sure
there can be no mistake. I hope you will be married soon.

"You are right, George. Link your destinies
with *youth*. I scarcely believe in anything else —
except Spring and Morning. But, then, there is
a way of making these — the soul of them — perpetual; and you have the secret of it, I am sure,
better than most of us.

"To think of that child, who used to play about
Brook Farm, and make young master Ally K.
'stand round,' as the boys say, and go through
finger drudgery under my piano - professorship, —
Heaven save the mark! — the child of our young
friends Mr. and Mrs. F. S., — how can you think of
them as parents? — being the future Mrs. Howadji!
or I a dull drudge of an editor. I do wish, indeed,
to see and know her, and doubt not I shall find
your glowing statements all confirmed, and that in
your height of joy you need not be ashamed to
'blush it East and blush it West.' There is a certain 'Maud'-like ecstasy in your note that makes
me think of that.

"A small bird had already sung the news in my
ear. But it was doubly pleasant to have it straight
from you. It was good in you to remember me
so. I should have written you immediately my
thanks for that, as well as congratulations on the
general issue, had I not been overwhelmed with

cares just then, as I have been since, and sick, besides. But you know I never did catch up with the world's flight, and you can pardon slowness to the account of constancy. You were always so good in trusting me through all my silence. It will be very pleasant to associate 'our George' with our friends the Shaws, whom I have not seen since their return. Pray commend me cordially to them, not omitting *la belle* Anna. Would that I might see you in New York! but I must content myself with the not very remote prospect of having you by the hand here. Till then believe me happy in your happiness, and faithfully as ever your friend."

One of Dwight's literary friends of this period was Henry James, with whose religious opinions he was much in sympathy. Mrs. Dwight was especially interested in the thought of this mystic thinker, so that Dwight said of her, " James has a church of one member, and I am the unbelieving sexton." A few years later Dwight invited James to his room to meet a few friends, and received the following request: "Don't, I beg of you, put yourself out to invite any one to meet me to-morrow night. Especially, don't invite any literary men purely, like Holmes or Woodman, who would keep me from talking, as they have no beliefs in God or man; while you and I live only by such belief. If any publican or sinner of your acquaintance would like to come, invite them; but no saint."

CHAPTER VII.

A YEAR IN EUROPE.

EARLY in July, 1860, Dwight set out for Europe, to spend a year in the study of music and in travel. He left the *Journal* in charge of Henry Ware, a young journalist of musical and literary tastes; and he sent to it editorial correspondence during the greater part of his absence. He made but a brief stay in England, spent seventeen days in Paris, rambled for several days over Switzerland, and then pushed on to Germany. At Frankfort, October 7, there reached him the startling news of the death of his wife, who had been ill almost from the time of his leaving Boston, but who had been reported to him as nearly well, when he last heard from home.

He wrote at once to his brother: "Your two letters, September 6 and 11, with many other kind letters of dear friends, came upon me all at once to-day. I have waited in Munich, in Heidelberg, and here for letters until now. The Paris banker must have been at fault. And, oh, what news! I know not what to say or do. I must break away from this loneliness. I must get to Bonn, and see Thayer, and there rest and realize and decide. I take the steamer direct down the Rhine to-morrow. Oh, with what eyes I shall pass that lovely scenery! The Rhine! Dear Frank, how in my heart I thank you for your letter! It was a true brother's letter, and all you say most wise and tender.

" My life is gone from me ! Oh, may God send her sweet spirit to visit mine daily, and help me to bear the blow, and become more worthy to have had that beautiful life so long bestowed on me. No more now. Thank all my dear friends for their kind words and their kind acts to Mary. I shall write to them in time, but now my eyes are dim and my hand trembles."

The story of the wife's illness and death may be told in the words of a letter written by Dr. O. W. Holmes, who lived only a few doors away in Charles Street, to the bereaved husband, and dated from Boston, November 11 : " I have been wishing for many weeks to write to you, but felt it more fitting to wait until I heard from you through your friends. I have shed many tears over those letters of yours ; and I am sure by the feelings they express that I cannot intrude upon you by sending you first of all my tenderest sympathy, and then such few recollections as I can add to the story you have heard so fully from those who are now nearest to your heart. I never knew in my life a more genuine feeling of brotherly love and interest than this affliction called forth from all who spoke of it. Be sure that, with the message of grief which took so long to reach you, there went many prayers that God would give you strength to bear your great trial, that your kind and gentle soul might bend without breaking under the blow. I think all your friends feel that their prayers have been answered, that you have a faith and a hope which can support you even in this extremity. May God still continue to bless and comfort you with his presence, and may the recollection of the sweet life you have shared so long be a light in the midst of this darkening sorrow!

"I was walking by to Cambridge Street one morning, perhaps a week or two after you had gone, when I noticed that the street for some distance was covered with tan. On inquiring, I found that Mrs. Dwight was ill, threatened with a fever, if not suffering from one. At the house I learned that she had been gradually growing weak for some time, with feverish turns, and much nausea, but no other very marked symptom that I could hear of, though I asked particularly for those which I most apprehended. The disease did not seem to excite much apprehension, except for that one symptom of nausea. Perhaps I ought rather to say that not much apprehension was expressed by those I saw, but a cheerful expectation of recovery appeared to be entertained. After this I called frequently, sometimes alone, sometimes with Mrs. Holmes, to inquire after Mrs. Dwight. The accounts were mostly, as I have said, encouraging. Sometimes we saw the servant-girl only, sometimes Miss Jenny or her mother. I did not for a while think it best to ask to see Mrs. Dwight, doubting whether it would be well for her to see any company.

"At last, finding that she continued languishing and suffering from nausea, I got uneasy, and left word at the house that I should be very glad if her physician (whom I did not know, and who was, as I was led to think, a homœopathic practitioner) would call at my house after his visit, and talk over her case with me. The physician, Dr. Newell, accordingly came, and gave me a full history of all the principal facts of the case. He told me all that he had done, which, as far as I could see, was essentially the right thing. It did not seem to me a case for heroic treatment, but for cautious palliations and patience; and that was the way it had seemed to him. I made every suggestion I could think of,— not at all as having any claim to meddle with the treatment, but knowing that a hint oftentimes proves useful when a physician's attention has become fatigued by long attendance. Dr. Newell behaved very well about it, seemed to be glad that I had taken it upon me to make suggestions to him, and proposed, I think, that I should see Mrs. Dwight. At any rate, he favored my seeing her; and the next day I sat by her bedside ten or fifteen minutes. This was the last time I saw her, and I know you will treasure this last glimpse I had of her living face as a fond recollection.

" Mary — for so I must call her, speaking to you now — was lying with her head raised upon her pillow, looking not like herself as you remember her, and yet less changed than I had feared. She was much wasted; but her look was natural and bright, and the tones of her voice were cheerful. Her beautiful hair lay loosely upon the pillow (she was too weak for all those nice arrangements she might have cared for in health), but she looked so sweetly that I would not have that last image changed. It was of perfect serenity and all herself, only shadowy and fáint as compared with her natural luxuriance of life. I did not wish her to talk much, spoke to her as cheerfully as I could, encouraged her to hope that she would be well when the cool autumn days had come, and left her, feeling that she might probably do well, but that she must not be excited by too much visiting or talking. After this I commonly got favorable accounts. She had begun to take food, they said; and at last every day I was told she was better. I began to feel quite easy about her. One morning my daughter Amelia brought a bunch of fresh flowers from the Public Garden. 'Go carry them to Mrs. Dwight,' I said. 'She is getting better, and they will please her.' Amelia went over, and brought back word that she was in a very critical situation,— that they had thought she was dying that morning. It was a surprise and a shock to me, utterly unexpected. I had become easy about her, and expected soon to see her riding out. That forenoon I met Dr. Newell, who told me of alarming symptoms which had appeared. He had called Dr. John Ware in consultation, a wise and good man, who doubtless counselled whatever medical art could do. But it was in vain. Towards evening I called. The servant-girl, who had always seemed truly devoted and interested, came to the door. Her look told me that I need not question her; but I said, with a hesitating voice, ' How is

Mrs. Dwight?' The poor girl said never a word; but she slowly shook her head, and on her face there was a look that said as plainly as words could say it, ' She is in heaven.'

"I listened to the sweet music which was sung over her as she lay, covered with flowers, in the pleasant parlor of her house, by the voices of those that loved her,— I and my wife with me,— and then we followed her to Mount Auburn, and saw her laid in the earth, and the blossoms showered down upon her with such tokens of affection and sorrow that the rough men, whose business makes them callous to common impressions, were moved as none of us ever saw them moved before. Our good James Clarke, as you know, conducted the simple service. It was one which none of us who were present can ever forget; and in every heart there was one feeling over all others,— that for the far-distant husband, brother, friend, as yet unconscious of the bereavement he was too soon to learn.

"I cannot help speaking of the affectionate care with which your Mary was encompassed during all those weeks of illness. Her mother was tenderly devoted to her; and, as to her sister, I do not know when I have ever seen devotion and love carried further, and that with a gentle firmness and placidity which filled me with admiration. At the very last moment at Mount Auburn I saw Miss Jenny standing and looking down upon the last resting-place with a face as of an angel, as she threw the last wreath upon her.

" I hope all these details, while they seem to open the wounds of grief afresh, may yet be, on the whole, a sad kind of relief. Your great affliction has touched all our hearts; and there is not one of us who does not long in some way to help you to bear it, and to endure through that period of absence which must separate you from your many friends. My wife desires to be most kindly remembered to you, and I need not again assure you that you are continually in my affectionate remembrance. Thank you for thinking of Wendell in the midst of all your distractions. It was like your kind self. God bless you and comfort you."

Four days later Dwight wrote from Bonn, having found his friend: " I wrote you last Sunday, in Frankfort, a few hurried lines to let you know that I had at last received your agonizing but most brotherly and tender letter. I hardly know what I wrote. It was growing dark: I wrote in tears, in a little dark, cold room,— a rainy, gloomy, cold day, with but an interval of Novemberish sunshine in the middle of the day, during which I had rushed out (after reading all those kind letters, as well as tears would let me) and walked entirely round the outside of the city, under the trees that dropped their brown leaves and their nuts upon me; for the cold, autumn days had come,—'the melancholy days, the saddest of the year.' I was bewildered, stunned almost. I could not realize the terrible fact. At moments in the walk my thoughts turned to Mary as naturally as they did in Switzerland, and wherever I saw that which in my mind I always shared with her. Indeed, she did seem *with* me; and the kind words of your own and of the other letters were not without their soothing, cheering influence even then,— that first bitter day.

"The heavy news had been long in coming. The letters seemed to have lingered on the way, as if conscious of what they bore, and shrinking from their duty. So they all came at once,— seven envelopes: your two, for which I thank and love you more than ever; a most full, minute, kind, beautiful, and comforting account of all from Anna Parsons (to whom give my love and thank her,— I shall write her soon); a true, manly, tender, strengthening, wise word from Woodman; also from Fisher and from Apthorp; and a most beautiful and touching one from Henry Ware,— all beautiful letters, making me feel rich in friendship, and as if dear Mary, *our* dear Mary, were indeed still present, very near in the love that unites us all. Dear Jenny's letter, too, though brief, was full of heart and high and tranquil sentiment, full of cheering, strong belief; and every word meant much to me. How is it with me? What have I done? What shall I do? you ask.

"First, Frankfort was a gloomy, intolerable place to me. I had only waited there for letters; and, though I was sustained and calm that day to a degree that made me wonder at myself, and seem almost like heavenly or Mary's influence, when the short autumn day waned into night, there was

only grief and sleep to occupy its long watches,—
no human soul to talk or sit with; no light; no
eyes to read or write with. I got through as I
could, God helping, and in the dull and cloudy
morning started by rail and boat to go down the
Rhine to Bonn, where Thayer had several days
awaited me.

"All sense of cold and rain vanished when the
good Thayer welcomed me in the little dark hotel
(the 'Swan'). How soon he felt my feeling! and
so sympathetically met me that it was a relief to
tell him all. I have really been quite cheerful with
him; and without him, when he is at work, I find
a sweet, sad pleasure in reading over and over the
dear letters from home. They are a real treasure
to me. Yesterday I got more of them. . . .

"You see, the second question is already answered. That is, I shall try to stay in Europe. I
felt at once the wisdom of the advice of you all;
but the first impulse was, the present yearning is,
— how strong you hardly can imagine,— to come
back and be among my friends,— those who loved
Mary, those who, with her, have formed my human
sphere and home of life. I am terribly isolated
here. The difficulty of language cuts me off from
all but necessary intercourse with others; and, even
if it were not so, I am so wedded, rooted, in all my
feelings and affections, in the familiar circle there
at home, that it is all exile while I am away from it.
I felt it very much so before this sad news: how
much more so now! My only comfort is to peruse

the letters I get; but it takes many weeks to answer and exchange words. I want you all near me. Spiritual nearness I shall learn, perhaps — God grant it! — through this very trial. But home, home,— where shall I again find home?

"As you say, there appears no actual need — outward need — of my coming home. The dear home in Charles Street is already broken up, and all have scattered. This is very, very sad to me. It would have been a great comfort still to revert in feeling to that spot, and to know that Jenny and Harriet and other dear friends still kept a gentle, homelike sphere there; but I know it was impossible. Jenny must and should be with her mother, and the old house would be a sad place henceforth to them. We will trust to God; and all that is good and true in past affinities and harmonies will certainly be saved and reappear and recombine in new forms (still the same life), if not here, in another and a better world.

"I have entire confidence in all that you have done or will do in regard to my affairs. . . . I have scarcely thought of these things. But one disposal occurs to me which I desire to have made. I wish you to send the piano to Grace Hooper, to use as long as I am away. She needs an instrument on which she can practise; and I am too happy to be able to offer her this, such as it is. Any of my music, too, which she may like, is at her service. Pray do this. I certainly must keep the instrument,— it is sacred; and I know there is no one with whom Mary would more like to have it left in charge and in use than Grace.

"Thank you, dear brother, for all the kind care you are taking for me; and, believe me, I am, on the whole, more cheerful and composed — at all events, resigned — than I could have supposed possible under such a blow. But perhaps I do not yet feel its full weight. I am desolate enough. The coming days and months and years look dark, to be sure; but I feel that it is all for the best. I know that it is a blessed change for Mary, and that she was ripe and fit for it, and lives now in joy and peace; and this alone ought to lend a deeper, richer, though a sad, joy to my life. When all of you, who are all afflicted, take such high and cheerful views, and find her death so beautiful, I should feel that I was a hopeless sinner, did I not partake some of the same cheerfulness." . . .

A few selections only from his correspondence can be given here, and these from his own inward experiences and his music studies rather than from his delightful accounts of travel.

"I think I omitted in my last to mention one pretty little adventure which I had on my foot-tour in the Oberiand. Walking from the Grimsel down the wild and exquisite Hasli Thal, one perfect morning, I stopped just below Guttanen, in a lovely pastoral meadow or *Matten*, at a little hut, to drink some milk, which was as sweet as the smiling promise of the good woman's face. I sat at a bench outside the cottage, resting myself and enjoying

the beauty of the scene. Meanwhile my guide
had gone into the house, and, I suppose, had told
the woman that I was an American; for, when she
returned, she asked me if I was, and then with
beaming face said, 'Und kennen Sie vielleicht den
Herrn Agassiz?' On my reply in the affirmative,
she seemed quite delighted. 'Komm hier, hier,' she
said, and pulled me into the house, took down a
large and curious silver watch containing the inscription, 'L. Agassiz to —— Leuthold,' and said
it was a gift to her good man, now dead, who seven
years ago built the hut in which Agassiz lived upon
the Aar glacier. She cherishes the professor's
memory with the utmost enthusiasm, called him
the 'best man in the world,' asked me all manner
of questions about him, whether he was rich, etc.,
and made me write down his address carefully in
English and German, and promise her I would tell
him I had seen *die Witwe Leuthold.* As I rose to
go, she called me back again, and ran to get the
freshest bunch of Alpenrosli (rhododendron) she
could find, and stuck it in my hat; and with a
warm pressure of the hand, and many blessings,
sent me off rejoicing. Was not that a pretty addition to the charming memoirs of the day?"

From Berlin he wrote:—

"With leading musicians here it is hard to have
much intercourse. They have very little with each
other. No one seems to know what another is
about or how to find him. Of course, it would be
easier to me if I could talk German better. I like

Haupt the best,— the best organist, perhaps, in
Germany; a thinking, high-toned, learned, non-
friendly, wise, and cheerful man, but hardly heard
of abroad, because he sticks to his place without
ambition.   It is just so with Franz.   You would be
surprised to find how few Germans know anything
about him.   I have not heard a song of his since I
have been in Germany.   Yet Haupt, Franz, Dresel,
are the men who ought to be gathered together
somewhere, and radiate an influence, as smaller men
do in Leipzig, simply by virtué of their combined
position.

"One of the kindliest to me here is jolly old
Wieprecht, grandmaster of all the military band
music of Prussia, who probably knows more about
instruments than any man living, and to whom
Berlioz, Liszt, and others owe not a little of their
fame as masters of instrumentation.   Taubert I
hope to know,— I admire his face and appearance,
— the most perfect model of manner as an orchestra
conductor.   Bülow, Liszt's son-in-law and chief representative, almost as good a pianist as himself (in
execution), who plays whole programmes of Bach,
Beethoven, Chopin, Schumann, Liszt, and everything without looking at a note (he has a concert
to-night), I was once introduced to by Liszt.   That
famous personage stopped at this hotel the other
day; and I had a half-hour's interview with him, of
which I will tell another time.   I must now fly to
Leipzig,— a concert all of Mozart."

After a stay of four months in Berlin, Dwight

spent a few days in Leipzig the first of March, and
then passed on to Italy.   He went by the way of
Vienna and Venice, in each of which cities he spent
a few days.   Then he visited Padua, Florence,
Turin, Genoa, Leghorn, went back to Florence, and
then on to Rome, which city he reached the middle
of May.

Rome, June 2.   "I couldn't help going in to
Story's studio, who was out; and I was led from
room to room, looking at statues while I waited for
Story.   And I sat a half-hour there amid his white
ideals,— his 'Cleopatra,' 'Hero,' 'Gretchen,' 'Beethoven,' and last of all, and really great, his 'African
Sibyl.'   It was a fine introduction; and it had
the feeling of Rome and of home in it to me, so
long accustomed to entire strangers only.   Then I
sought him at his house, and was most warmly
welcomed.   Mrs. Story took me out to drive with
her two dear little boys, to Trevi fountain and to
St. Peter's, and then bore me bodily, bag and bag-
gage, up to their Quirinal Hill, to their home in
the Barberini Palace (spacious, grand old place,
containing the original Beatrice Cenci portrait,
etc.); and here from that time I have been most
comfortably and cheerfully domiciled, in a spacious
room, overlooking all Rome, with St. Peter's loom-
ing in the background.   Nothing could be more
cordial nor complete than the hospitality of these
good friends.   They have made me perfectly at
home; and I have passed daily several hours in the
society of Robert Browning, and have had several

pleasant interviews with Mrs. Browning, both of whom I like very much.   They have given me their photographs.   The first evening I was taken to a little company, to hear Hans Christian Andersen read some of his little stories; and a day or two after he came to a children's party of the little Storys, and read to them.   And Browning read them his 'Piper of Hamelin,' and then a whole troop of beautiful children acted it out.   Sam. Longfellow, too, appeared on that occasion; and he and I have hunted in couples, seeing the sights of Rome.   Of these and my many great enjoyments here, I must tell you another time."

June 5, on steamer to Marseilles, to his little niece.   " Did you ever read any of Hans Christian Andersen's charming little stories?   The other day he came to a children's party where I was, and read some of them to a pretty little group, the little Storys and their friends.   How happy they all were!   The two sweet little boys, ' Bobo ' and ' Gudie ' (Waldo and Julian are their real names) were very eager to see Mr. Andersen, and to ask him if his story of the ' Ugly Duckling ' was true. So the party was made, and the tall man came,— the tall, homely Dane, the friend of little folks ; and a nice time they had of it, I assure you.   It was in the upper story of a great splendid palace (Palazzo Barberini), which looks off over all Rome.   This palace is very large, all built of gray-white stone; and very broad marble stairs lead from the ground to the topmost story, five or six flights.   And on the stairs you meet a great marble lion (an old Roman work) and many statues; and in the palace live a cardinal and a duke of the Barberini family. My friends hire and occupy one-half of the upper story, which contains forty great square rooms. What a grand range for the children to run and play in! There was a poet, too, in the party,— Robert Browning; and he sat down on the carpet, in the centre of the ring of boys and girls, and read them his 'Piper of Hamelin,' whose pipe drew all the rats out of the town, and the children after them. And. then Mr. Story dressed himself up like the piper, and tooted on a flute; and all the children followed him, shouting and screaming, up and down the long, long range of rooms."

After spending a few days in Paris, Dwight went to London, from which place he wrote July 6: "I was very glad to get the photograph, and liked it in many respects much better than the first one, although that has perhaps more of her living expression; but this one gives her beautiful head, and is besides a finer picture. William Story, who seems to retain a lively impression of her, thought neither of them did her justice. Oh that a mould had been taken from her head after death! Story was so kind as to say that, if he only had that for a guide, he would gladly model me a bust of Mary. And his portrait busts are admirable. One which he made of Robert Browning (begun and finished in one week, while I was there) is wonderfully true and lifelike. Poor Mrs. Browning was delighted

with it. Yesterday I was shocked to read of her
death, in Florence. Just as they were leaving
Rome, she had her photograph taken; and she
promised to send me one. I saw Cavour, too, only
a month before his death,— saw him in full health
and life." . . .

He sailed for home on the " Great Eastern "
September 10; but the steamer encountered a fear-
ful storm, and after desperate efforts succeeded in
reaching the coast of Ireland, having been almost
wholly crippled for several days. Dwight landed
on the Irish coast, and found his way back to London, where he wrote a long account of his experiences, which was published in his *Journal.*

London, October 30. " I feel strangely confused
about it [returning home], but presume it will be
for the best. I had, while waiting in vain for advices from home, almost settled down in the feeling that I was to stay in Europe. I have had the
impression all along that my friends rather favored
the course, in view of the war, the want of all music,
and of my desolated home, and poorer chance of
health, bodily and mental or moral, there than here.
I confess my fear of all this has been growing on
me, and I have been almost superstitious about
my being driven back so. But tell Fanny that I
cannot think God would have so inconvenienced
and perilled eight hundred people, just to turn me
back from a course I was pursuing."

November 1, to C. P. Cranch. " I have but a
minute to say good-by! I sail in 'Niagara' to-

morrow for Boston. I had been waiting long for advices from home, and had about made up my mind that I should stay in Europe, and was pleasing myself with the thought that I should now see you in Paris; but last Tuesday came letters from home, making my return imperative. My publisher thinks the paper suffers by my absence, and even disinclines to continue the arrangement unless I come back. So I must hurry home before the bottom falls out."

Writing from London August 10, Dwight expressed his pain and depression on hearing of the battle of Bull Run and the defeat of the Northern army. 'The real feeling of the English people is sympathy for the North, and profound sorrow for the war. They think anything would be better than to fight one another. . . . Since the defeat, too, the general opinion seems to be (and a very obstinate one) that the North will not succeed in subduing the South. They do not understand us, that is plain. Pretty hard, is it not, to have to read and to hear all this continually?" On his return to his editorial labors, in reporting a chamber concert of the Mendelssohn Quintette Club in the paper dated November 30, Dwight took occasion to speak of the war, his hatred of slavery, his faith in the Union cause, and his conviction that success was certain to come in the end.

CHAPTER VIII.

YEARS OF TOIL FOR MUSIC.

On his return from Europe, Dwight was without a home. He went to his mother's house in Jamaica Plain for a few days, and then, Dec. 4, 1861, took up his residence in the Studio Building, Tremont Street, only a few steps away from the office where his paper was printed, in School Street. In this building he secured a study and sleeping-room; and he took his meals at some hotel or restaurant, usually at the Parker House. After this he spent two winters in Boylston and Derne Streets, with his mother, brother, and sister Frances. On June 15, 1873, he removed to the rooms of the Harvard Musical Association, at 12 Pemberton Square. From his removal to this place to the end of his life he had no domestic establishment of his own, no immediate family circle around which gathered the tender sympathies of his warm heart-life.

Dwight's father had died in 1853, but his mother lived until 1876. After the breaking up of Brook Farm, the Dwight and Orvis families found a home in Forest Hill Street, Jamaica Plain. Dwight and his brother Frank, who established himself in Boston as an architect, were very fond of each other, and faithful to each other's interests. Frances E. Dwight was also a member of the family, and devoted herself to the teaching of music with marked success. Here Dwight spent whatever time he could take from his work, and was always welcomed with delight. His family were fond of him, and took great pride in his success.

If Dwight had no fireside of his own, he found a welcome place by that of many of his friends. Some hints of his personal life contained in his letters may here be given, and these mostly related to his summer outings or to his own monotonous life in the city. The first is a letter to his intimate friend, Otto Dresel, written July 12, 1863, which gives suggestion of how he often rebelled against the drudgery of his editorial task: —

"It is simply impossible for me now to decide about going anywhere. If I go to the mountains, I shall wish to stay away three weeks or so; and, therefore, I should have to get all the matter cut and dried for two numbers of the 'old paper,' which I would too willingly 'stop' if I could, without stopping at the same time the bread and butter and the means of travel. I wish I could start off to-morrow, for it is insufferably *schwül* and sultry here to-day, and I creep round sick and miserable,— in fact, not in a condition to make a journey; but I shall soon be better."

He went to Newport more often than to any other place for summer recreation, and found there the human companionship and the nearness to nature which he loved with strong affection. A letter to one of his sisters, written Aug. 25, 1871, shows something of what this brief period of recreation was to him: —

"I came home on Wednesday, having had a de-

lightful week with the Tweedys.   Newport is love-
lier, fresher, sweeter, than ever.   Every day Tweedy
took us to drive,— Willie James and me: he is a
rare youth,— and I saw so many old friends from
New York and elsewhere that it seemed as if one
had only to go to Newport to meet everybody he
ever knew.   I had a very pleasant half-hour with
Nilsson.   Parke Godwin and his daughter, too, I
saw much of.   They have had Nilsson a month
with them at Roslyn.

"One occasion of the rarest interest was hearing
M. Athanase Coquerel, the eloquent Unitarian
preacher of Paris, preach in Brooks's church.   He
reached New York unannounced; sought eight or
ten of his old friends who had known him in Paris,
but found not one except Horace Greeley.   Greeley advised him to come to Newport, so associated
with the names of Channing and Roger Williams;
and only on Saturday morning Brooks received a
telegram, 'The Rev. Mr. Coquette will be in Newport to-night, and will preach if desired,'— Greeley's bad writing.   But Brooks guessed it out, and
had him domesticated at Gardner Brewer's beautiful residence; and the little church for once was
crowded.   Scarcely ever have I been so interested
in a preacher.

"We drove out once to the Howes, and met them
once at a picnic of the new literary club in Paradise and Purgatory.   James Sturgis, who is living
near Tweedy, went down with me and came up
with me.   But, ah! the change from that pure,

sweet air to Boston streets and dog-day heat.   I
was sick as soon as I got back, so that I could do
nothing, and had to huddle my *Journal* out anyhow.   I am better, but still not right."

Music had now become for Dwight the chief interest of his life, and almost its sole interest.   It
was ever in his mind, and for it he was toiling almost constantly.   Besides the work of editing his
paper, which involved a regular attendance upon
most of the musical entertainments of the city, he
gave much time to other phases of the advancement of music, was constantly appealed to for advice and assistance, and so thoroughly mastered
his subject that he came to be known as the chief
musical authority in the country.

At this period Dwight devoted much time to
translation.   In 1859 there was published in Boston his translation of H. Wohlfahrt's " Guide to
Musical Composition."   The same year Ditson published Bach's " Saint Matthew Passion Music," with
a translation of the words by Dwight.   He also
translated a large number of German songs and
poems for Ditson, which were published with
music.   In 1865 several of the songs in Heine's
" Buch der Lieder " were adapted to selections from
Schumann's " Dichterliebe."   The same year he
translated a number of German songs to accompany
an edition of the song music of Robert Franz,
which was published by Ditson.

On the first day of January, 1863, a Jubilee Concert was held in Music Hall, Boston, in recognition

of the Proclamation of Emancipation issued by
President Lincoln.   The public announcement of
the concert was signed by H. W. Longfellow, Edward E. Hale, James T. Fields, O. W. Holmes,
R. W. Emerson, John G. Whittier, E. P. Whipple,
F. H. Underwood, John S. Dwight, and others.
Dwight had much to do with planning this occasion of rejoicing, and much of the work necessary
to make it a success was done by him.   He invited
Emerson to prepare and read a poem suitable for
the occasion, in reply to which he received the following : —

Concord, 19 *Decr.*, 1862.

My dear Dwight,— I am sorry not to have be-
thought myself at once of the obstacle when your
fine project dazzled my eyes.   But, when I came
home last night and made some rude experiments
at verses, I saw at once that, however alluring and
most inspiring was your invitation to insert my
contribution — if I shall have one — in your noble
atmosphere of music, yet this was wholly to break
faith with my first inviters, the Fraternity, to whom
I had signified no dissent from their desire that I
should join them.   I could heartily wish the two
celebrations could be combined ; but, if that is out
of question, I fear I owe all my duty to the Fraternity.   This is a long note to write about only a possible copy of verses.   Ever yours,

R. W. EMERSON.

Emerson was persuaded to make the effort to give a poem on the occasion, although he gave an address before the Parker Fraternity on the same day. His muse would not be inspired at his bidding, however; and two days before the time for the concert Dwight received this note from him : —

My dear Dwight,— At this hour you must certainly print the programme without my name, as I have had little or no good fortune. Still, I flatter myself that, if I should have a good sleep to-night, —for I am a bad sleeper lately,— I may even yet, at the eleventh hour, pray to be admitted. But it is too slight a chance to be at all waited for; and I am heartily grieved I did not find the fact sooner.

Yours,
                                R. W. EMERSON.
Parker House, Tuesday P.M.

The programme was printed without Emerson's name; but he got a good night's sleep, and the concert opened with his " Boston Hymn," one of his most inspired utterances. Noble music from Beethoven, Mendelssohn, Händel, and Rossini, was included in the programme, and some of the best singers and musicians of Boston joined their gifts to make a most inspiring occasion. One special feature was the singing, by solo and chorus, of O. W. Holmes's " Army Hymn," with the fifth verse specially written for the occasion, to music furnished by Otto Dresel.

The concert was a great success in the largeness

of the attendance, the enthusiastic response of the
audience to the expressions of patriotism, and the
delight with which the final announcement of emancipation was welcomed. The music was fitting,
and rendered in a manner worthy of the occasion.
Dwight said of Emerson's poem: " It was a hymn
of Liberty and Justice, wild and strong, and musical and very short, and in his rich tones spellbound
the great assembly." " This concert will be long
remembered," was his final comment upon it. " It
will become an anniversary. Whether regarded as
a patriotic celebration or as a strictly musical occasion, it has called forth more spontaneous expressions of delight than any festival that most of us
remember."

These details in regard to the Jubilee Concert
may be justified, in view of Dwight's attitude
towards the " National Peace Jubilee," held in
Boston, 1869, under the direction of Mr. P. S. Gilmore. Dwight's attitude towards this great musical festival was one of suspicion from the first, and
of criticism to the end. In this he was thoroughly
consistent, and fully justified by his own standard.
A monster celebration, such as the " Peace Jubilee,"
however noble the primary motive and purpose, was
to him objectionable in every way. In the excess
of noisy triumph and shouting patriotism, he saw no
real advantage to art, no fit expression of its nobler
motives, and no just interpretation of its relations to
a nation's victories for freedom and peace.

He could not conscientiously give Mr. Gilmore

the assistance for which he asked; but it was from
no lack of patriotism, no failure to rejoice in the
triumph of freedom and union, and no want of conviction that music was the fit instrument for giving expression to the rejoicings of the nation. He
had already expressed his strong "conviction that
the great thoughts of Humanity and Freedom, the
progressive moral instincts of the age, although to
this day spit upon and crucified, are yet in most
intimate alliance with the loftiest inspirations and
utmost refinements of creative genius and art,—
musical art especially." His objection to the Gilmore celebration was that it was not truly artistic,
that it gave no genuine recognition to music as an
expression of the deeper sentiments of mankind,
and that the whole spirit of it was dominated by
show and self-gratulation. Instead of being used
to lift music to its highest level, and to lift the
people to the same high elevation of patriotism and
humanitarian sentiment, it was conceived in the
spirit of the cheapest patriotic boasting and the
most noisy musical demonstration. It aimed to
please the groundlings, and sought for nothing
more. It may be said that many truly artistic and
patriotic people gave it their support, but considerations of a selfish and narrow character largely pre-
dominated in its conception and execution.

In his "History of the National Peace Jubilee,"
Mr. Gilmore saw fit to treat Mr. Dwight as his
enemy, and to speak of him in a most jaunty and
insulting manner. It is not necessary to dwell

upon their relations to each other, or to point out
the fact that the one was a showman and that the
other was a lover of music for its genuine artistic
values.   It may be said, however, that Dwight was
as fair-minded as he was honest and sincere, and
that, though he opposed the Jubilee from the start,
yet he recognized its good features, and spoke of it
in a friendly manner.   Of the first day he made
this report in his paper, immediately after: " Much
as we disliked the extravagance of the plan originally, and shrank from the boastful style of the announcement of this ' greatest musical festival ever
held in any part of the world ' (as if greatness were
to be measured by mere magnitude and numbers),
we cheerfully make haste to own that the result so
far has in many respects agreeably disappointed us.
Upon the whole, a better thing has been wrought
out of it than a plan so vainglorious in the conception, so unscrupulously advertised and glorified
before it had begun to be, and having so much of
claptrap mixed up with what was good in its programme, gave one any reasonable right to expect.
But the wide, stupendous advertising filled thousands of minds with an enthusiasm which, if igno-
rant, was entirely honest. . . . We can only say that
the success of Tuesday was in the main glorious
and inspiring.   The vast audience was greatly
stirred, delighted.   The best effects were achieved
by the great chorus."

The editors of the New York *Tribune* asked
Dwight to write for them a " careful, critical sum-

mary of the net result " of the concert; and he sent them an extended study of its various features. He fully recognized its pretentious and grotesque elements, the ordinary musical capacity of its projector, and the bombastic manner in which he advertised himself and his undertaking. He showed how all this repelled genuine lovers of music and those with cultivated artistic perceptions. He frankly admitted the good in the concert, however, and gave it much enthusiastic praise. He pointed out the incongruous elements in the programme, as well as its ambiguous and pretentious features; but he gave praise to everything which could be praised, and approved the final outcome of the gigantic undertaking. He said that "as an occasion, of a new kind, of unexampled magnitude,— whatever it may have been musically,— the Jubilee was a success. It has become a splendid fact, which has to be accepted." On the side of the execution of the music, he said "there was very much to praise. In the great chorus there was far more unity, precision, light and shade in rendering, than almost any one of musical experience could have believed possible. And it grew better as the thing went on. It gave one a proud joy to know that so many thousands of singers, with only one rehearsal of the whole, could sing so well together. It told of musical enthusiasm, of *esprit du corps*, of good native average of voices, and of talent, good instruction, and inspiring drill in separate bodies."

Of the World's Peace Jubilee, held in the sum-

mer of 1872, and under the auspices of the same
director, Dwight wrote with the same honest recognition of the good and the bad which it presented.
He saw clearly the personal ambition which directed it, and the excess of zeal which presided
over its development. He pointed out with un-
flinching courage and keen musical insight the
reasons of its failure from a high musical point of
view, and yet he was as sincere in recognizing its
good features. He devoted three long articles to
a review of its work, and they afford a remarkable
instance of what a critic can accomplish in the way
of correcting the follies of men of large projects
and small artistic ability.

With the beginning of the twelfth year of the
Journal of Music, April, 1864, it was changed from
a weekly to a fortnightly publication, the price
being continued at one dollar a year, though it was
soon after changed to two. These changes were
the result of the Civil War, its absorbing interest,
and the consequent depression in the artistic life of
the nation. None could rejoice more heartily than
Dwight when the war came to an end, with the
triumph of freedom and with a united country. On
Commencement Day of 1865, Harvard University
did honor to those of its members who had taken part
in the war, and especially to those who had fallen
in the strife. The speeches of the occasion were
made by General Devens, Governor Andrew, President Hill, General Meade, Admiral Davis, and
Emerson. Poems were read by Holmes, Lowell,

Mrs. Howe, and Charles T. Brooks. The music
was in charge of Mr. J. K. Paine, then the musical
director of the university; and he was assisted by
a chorus from the Harvard Musical Association.
Among the other pieces was a " Horatian Ode "
written by Dwight, sung to Flemming's "part-song,
a strain of simple, solemn, noble harmony," as
follows : —

"INTEGER VITÆ SCELERISQUE PURUS."

Manly and gentle, pure and noble-hearted,
Sweet were their days of peaceful use and beauty.
Sweeter than peace or days or years is freedom,
    Thought our young heroes.

War's wild alarm drove sleep from every pillow;
Slavery, rampant, stalked athwart the broad land.
Prompt at the call of Country and of Duty,
    Flew the young heroes.

Darkly the clouds hung o'er a doubtful conflict:
Out shone the rainbow,— LIBERTY TO ALL MEN !
Lo! now a Country grand enough to die for !
    Peace to our heroes !

Rear we for them no cold sepulchral marble :
Fresh in our hearts their very selves are living,
Dearer and nearer now,— e'en as God is nearest,—
    Risen in glory !

Cease from thy weeping, rise, O Alma Mater !
Count thy young heroes tenderly and proudly;
Beaming thine eyes, with holy joy confess them :
    These are thy children !

On March 26, 1870, Dwight gave a lecture on "Music in Relation to Culture and the Religious Sentiment," in the "Horticultural Hall Sunday Afternoon Lectures." Among the other lecturers in the course were John Weiss, O. B. Frothingham, T. W. Higginson, Samuel Longfellow, Julia Ward Howe, Ednah D. Cheney, David A. Wasson, William H. Channing, and Wendell Phillips. A few days later the secretary of the lecture course wrote him, " The reports of your lecture on music have awakened so general an interest in it that we are thinking of inviting you to repeat it some weekday afternoon, at such time as shall suit your convenience." A request for its repetition, in behalf of those who were not able to hear it, was sent to him, signed by O. W. Holmes, J. R. Lowell, James B. Thayer, William I. Thorndike, G. S. Hillard, Samuel Longfellow, F. H. Underwood, and others. In response to these requests the lecture was repeated on May 6. The next day Dwight received the following letter from one of the leaders of musical interest in Boston : —

" I listened to your lecture with an interest that would not have flagged if you had given us three hours instead of one. It is so far the best thing that one might say it is the only thing that has been said about music on this side of the water. My only complaint is that you turned over too many pages. You had there material for at least three lectures. Now why cannot you give it all to us, without abridgement, in the *Atlantic*? They would pay you for three articles as readily as for one. Divide thus, for instance: I. The story of the coming-in among us of the true thing, its relations to the new growth of culture and religion, a fuller sketch of the old Odeon days, before the musical recollections of many of us, with perhaps a reference to what George Curtis has also said about them, already made in the *Journal.* And so on down to the present, with its great smoke without, and its hot fire at the heart,—its display, egotism, vanity, and mercenary sordidness, but, by contrast, the real feeling at the bottom. II. The scope and importance of music as culture and religion, which would comprise the bulk of what you read last night. III. The intrinsic qualities which make it so important, which would give an opportunity for all that you desire to say about the structure of fugue and symphony and other forms, as well as for the analysis which you did not give us of representative works, such as the 'Passion Music' and the 'Choral Symphony.' It is time for you to go to Fields with a manuscript of 'Musical Essays, 1st series'; but meanwhile the three *Atlantic* articles will not be amiss."

The lecture was published in the *Atlantic Monthly* during 1870, the first part appearing in September, under the title of "Music a Means of Culture," and the second part in December, as "The Intellectual Influence of Music."

In 1879 came another change in the career of the *Journal of Music.* From the first the publisher and the editor were not wholly in harmony as to the best method of conducting the paper. It was the publisher's wish to make it popular and a help to his business interests. The editor was strictly concerned for the good of music as an art, his literary aim was high, and he was not in sympathy with the popular tendencies of the musical profession. With the trade interests of the publisher he had no sympathy, and he was not willing to make any concessions in that behalf. It must be remembered, however, that he had made many sacrifices for the sake of pushing the claims of music as an art, that he had a salary of only one thousand dollars a year after the paper became a fortnightly, and that he had steadily held to his high aims against many discouragements. The cost of fidelity to his ideals was borne by himself without complaint.

In July, 1878, Dwight received from Oliver Ditson & Co., his publishers, a letter in which they notified him of their wish to change the character of the *Journal of Music*, making it more popular, and using it to further their publishing interests. Upon consultation with several of his friends, they advised against the proposed change; and Longfellow took the lead in finding another publisher and securing a guarantee fund that would enable the paper to go on under better auspices. It was arranged that Houghton, Osgood & Co. should undertake the publication.

After twenty years of connection with a great music-publishing house the *Journal* severed its relations therewith at the end of the year 1878.   The new arrangement was announced in the number for August 31, in which the editor said, " We make few promises,— only this one in fact, that we shall do all in our power to keep the *Journal* true to the character and name it has so long maintained both in this country and abroad.   In renouncing all connection, all appearance even of identity of interests, with the music *trade* in any of its representatives or branches, our *Journal* offers a new guarantee — were any needed —of fearless honesty and independence in its views and criticisms.   We wish to add to its contents new elements,— the contributions of younger minds, as well as of mature experience,— and this we shall do just so far as we shall be enabled by the prompt support and patronage for which we look to friends of Art and lovers of the best in Music."

The paper was now a fortnightly of eight pages, published at two and a half dollars a year; but it presented an attractive appearance, and the contents were much improved.   The old contributors remained, and new ones were secured.   It was the plan to secure articles of first-class value and interest from leading writers on literary and artistic subjects.   The first number opened with a poem by C. P. Cranch, which was followed by a musical article from the pen of William F. Apthorp.   This was succeeded by a study of Chopin from the pen of Fanny Raymond Ritter, and to the book reviews Francis H. Underwood was a contributor.   In succeeding numbers there were articles, poems, or book reviews by Julia Ward Howe, T. G. Appleton, Stuart Sterne, Frederic Louis Ritter, and William M. Hunt.   The paper was now abler in its management, had a greater variety of contents, and was better calculated to serve the higher interests of music than ever before.

It was soon evident, however, that the public was not ready to support such a paper as the editor was trying to make.   The plan of paid contributors had to be given up, and the editor had to fall back upon his own resources.   There was a considerable loss the first year, but this was greatly reduced the second.   In December, 1880, the friends of the editor and the paper gave them a testimonial concert.   A testimonial committee was organized, of which John P. Putnam was chairman, Francis H. Underwood secretary, and A. Parker Browne treasurer.   This committee addressed Dwight the following letter : —

Boston, Nov. 15, 1880.

Mr. JOHN S. DWIGHT :

Dear Sir,— A number of your friends, who remember your long and faithful services in behalf of the cause of music, and who are deeply grateful that it has been permitted to you to accomplish so much in elevating the standard of public performances and in refining the public taste, have determined to offer you a Testimonial Concert to be given on a fitting scale, early in the coming month, at the Boston Music Hall.   They respectfully ask your acceptance of the compliment, with their united good will and affection, and with best wishes for your continued health and usefulness : —

R. E. Apthorp, W. F. Apthorp, L. B. Barnes, F. P. Bacon, W. P. Blake, J. Bradlee, A. P. Browne, G. H. Chickering, E. H. Clement, C. P. Curtis, Oliver Ditson, E. S. Dodge, L. C. Elson, Julius Eichberg, Augustus Flagg, John Fiske, Arthur W. Foote, L. L. Holden, H. L. Higginson, F. H. Jenks, G. P. King, H. W. Longfellow, B. J. Lang, S. W. Langmaid, H. K. Oliver, Carl Prüfer, George L. Osgood, H. W. Pickering, John P. Putnam, J. C. D. Parker, Ernst Perabo, Charles C. Perkins, John K. Paine, LeBaron Russell, Arthur Reed, Henry M. Rogers, S. B. Schlesinger, W. H. Sherwood, James Sturgis, A. J. C. Sowdon, S. L. Thorndike, F. H. Underwood, R. C. Waterston, Henry B. Williams, B. E. Woolf, Henry Ware, L. Weissbein, Robert C. Winthrop, Erving Winslow, Carl Zerrahn.

Dwight's reply was in these words, his letter being given in full, and not in the abbreviated form as printed on the circular of the committee : —

Boston, Nov. 16, 1880.

TO THE HON. J. P. PUTNAM, *Chairman, etc.:*

Gentlemen,— Your kind and courteous offer touches me deeply, and demands fitter answer than I know how to make. Such a recognition — entirely spontaneous, unexpected, and undreamed of

on my own part — of my poor persistent labors to
convince others of the beauty and the holiness of
the Art which I have always loved, and always shall
love, comes upon me as an exquisite surprise.
After many periods of misgiving, many fears that
the old tree had proved fruitless after all, this comes
to revive hope and motive, and give me, as it were,
the sense of a new life,— at all events, to encourage
me to attempt yet further and — let us hope — better work.

I am sure I understand you, gentlemen.   What
you would honor in me is simply the high purpose,
the honesty, and the consistent perseverance of my
course.   To this, and to nothing more, can I lay
claim.   When my work began, music was esteemed
at its true worth by very few among us.   I simply
preached the faith that was in me.   Now we are
almost a musical people.   Those who come forward
now learn music as it should be learned, learn to
speak of it with knowledge,— the knowledge that
comes of practice,— and will readily outstrip me.
What more could I desire?   There is a lesson in
all this which every young man should take to
heart: it is that every worthy, independent, honest,
work, persisted in, in spite of neglect and abuse
and years of seeming failure, is sure of recognition
all the sweeter in the end.

To a committee so largely representative of the
best elements of the musical profession, of the best
and wisest friends of music, as well as of the honored names of dear old Boston, and for the prof-

fered Concert, which in such hands is sure to be a noble one, I can never be too grateful. But let me come to the point at once, and simply say that I most thankfully accept the compliment you offer.

I am respectfully and cordially yours,

JOHN S. DWIGHT.

This concert was held in Music Hall on Thursday afternoon, Dec. 9, 1880, and was in every way a success. A large number of musicians volunteered their services, including many not named on the committee. The use of Music Hall was given, without charge, for the occasion, as well as the pianos and printing. The programme included Beethoven's " Fifth Symphony," Schubert's " Twenty-third Psalm," a concerto from Bach, Schumann's Concert-stueck, a selection from Beethoven's " Fidelio," and an overture from Mendelssohn. This concert awakened great enthusiasm among the musicians of Boston and vicinity, it was largely attended, and the occasion proved an ovation to one who had toiled for musicians so many years. It proved to him that his work was appreciated, and that there were many people ready to do him honor. The committee was able to put into Dwight's hand the sum of $6,000 as the result of the concert and the contributions of his friends.

Of this concert Dwight said in the *Journal of Music:* " Greetings and warmest signs of recognition, kindliest notes of sympathy (often from most

unexpected quarters), prompt, enthusiastic offers of
musical service in any concert that might be arranged, poured in upon the editor, who all at once
found himself the object of unusual attention.
Hand and heart were offered wherever he met an
old acquaintance. Everybody seemed full of the
bright idea that had struck somebody just in the
nick of time. We never knew we had so many
friends . . . who, through the press, as well as by
voice and pen in private, created an interest in
others, and helped to organize the plan so beautifully realized on Thursday of last week. . . . For
such a testimonial, so sincere and hearty in the inception, so admirably prepared, with such consum-
mate tact and delicacy, so beautiful, resplendent in
the full flower, and so fraught with *solid* tokens of
esteem and friendship, we can hardly trust ourself to find fit words of thanks. We accept
it both with pride and with humility, for it is a
formidable thought to us that we seem now more
than ever bound to go on trying (perhaps in
vain) to perform any service that shall in any degree vindicate the faith which hosts of friends have
in this touching way reposed in us.

"But, leaving all we wished to say to be im-
agined, as it readily will be in a social and musical
atmosphere so sympathetic as this in which we just
now have the happiness to live and move and have
our being (although it seems like passive dreaming), let us come at once to the concert itself,
which was in every way a signal, memorable suc-

cess, and which we flatter ourself we could and
did appreciate about as keenly as any other man or
woman in that great and really distinguished audience.   Both programme and performance were of
so exceptionally fine a character as to claim special
mention among the many good things we have
heard or shall hear this winter.   Never was a
finer programme, either intrinsically or in its fitness for the occasion, presented in Boston; never
a more conscientious *con amore* rendering, seldom
one with finer means, and all by artists who had
kindly, eagerly, offered their co-operation freely, including the orchestra of the Harvard Symphony
Concerts, with Mr. Carl Zerrahn, conductor, and
Mr. Bernhard Listemann, violin leader, besides
a small army of our best vocalists, pianists, violinists, more than could possibly find place in a single
concert. . . . Now was not that a concert to be remembered all one's life ? "

As Dwight seems in some measure to have anticipated, the continued effort proved to be in vain.
In the number of the *Journal* for July 16, 1881, he
announced that one more number would bring the
paper to an end, and said: " Instead of the promised increase, the income from subscribers and
from advertisers has fallen off, showing for the first
half of the year a serious loss, which falls entirely on
the editor himself, who has no heart to ask or to accept any further guarantee from friends.   Prudence
counsels him that it is better to stop now than to
risk double loss by letting the paper run on to the
end of the year."

From all sides came the warmest expressions of sympathy, and regret that the *Journal of Music* should be at last obliged to give up its brave struggle. There was the warmest recognition from the press of the country of its able efforts to further the cause of music, mingled with some criticism of the editor's conservative attitude. The last number of *Dwight's Journal of Music* bore date of Sept. 3, 1881. In his valedictory article the editor said that he was convinced there was no real demand in the country for a high-class journal devoted to the interests of music; and he spoke of the severe competition which made the publication of such a journal impossible, of the fact that musical criticism was presented in the daily and weekly papers to an extent which satisfied most people, and of the wide diffusion of musical knowledge since he began his work. Parts of this final estimate of his editorial labors make it clearer than anything else he ever wrote what were Dwight's ideals, and what the task which he set before him, at which he had labored for so many years.

"There is no putting out of sight the fact," he wrote, in discussing the causes why it was desirable to discontinue the paper, and why he had grown weary of his task, "that the great themes for discussion, criticism, literary exposition and description, which inspired us in this journal's prime, the master works and character and meaning of the immortal ones, like Bach and Händel, Mozart, Beethoven, Schubert, and the rest, although they

cannot be exhausted, yet inevitably lose the charm
of novelty. . . . The thoughts we then insisted on
from inmost conviction, with a zeal for inciting
others to seek, and helping others to appreciate the
divine power and beauty and great meaning of
those inspired art creations, are now become the
common property of all the world. Of course, we
never owned them; but we felt them, and endeavored,
somewhat successfully within a narrow, slowly wid-
ening circle, to make others feel their truth. All
true thought, truly stated, inevitably crumbles in the
course of time into the smallest current coin. Lack-
ing the genius to make the old seem new, we can-
didly confess that what now challenges the world
as new in music fails to stir us to the same depths
of soul and feeling that the old masters did, and
doubtless always will. Startling as the new composers are, and novel, curious, brilliant, beautiful
at times, they do not inspire us as we have been inspired before, and do not bring us nearer heaven.
We feel no inward call to the proclaiming of the
new gospel. We have tried to do justice to these
works as they have claimed our notice, and have
omitted no intelligence of them which came within
the limits of our columns; but we lack motive for
entering their doubtful service, we are not ordained
their prophet. If these had been enthroned the
Dii majores of the musical Olympus, and there had
been no greater gods; if the contributions of the
past thirty years to musical production were the
whole of music,— we never should have dreamed of

establishing a musical journal, nor would music have been able to seduce us from other paths, in which, by persevering, we might possibly have done more good. It may be all a prejudice, perhaps we are one-sided, perhaps too steady contemplation of the glory of the great age has seared our eyeballs for the modern splendors; but we prefer to leave these and their advocacy 'to whom it may concern.' Doubtless here is one secret of much of the indifference to this journal: the 'disciples of the newness' feel that it has not been in sympathy with what they would call the new musical spirit of the times, and innocent inquirers take the cue from them. . . .

"But whatever may have been the causes of our failure to make this journal what it should be, we are disposed to find them mostly in the editor himself. . . . We have long realized that we were not made for the competitive, sharp enterprise of modern journalism. That turn of mind which looks at the ideal rather than the practical, and the native indolence of temperament which sometimes goes with it, have made our movements slow. Hurry who will, we rather wait and take our chance. The work which could not be done at leisure, and in disregard to all immediate effect, we have been too apt to feel was hardly worth the doing. To be the first in the field with an announcement or a criticism or an idea was no part of our ambition. How can one recognize competitors or enter into competition, and at the same time keep his eye upon truth? If one have anything worth saying, will it not be as good to-morrow as to-day?" . . .

All which needs to be said in the way of comment on this final word of Dwight's as an editor is expressed in a letter to him from Richard Grant White, written on receipt of the closing number: " The sight of the last number of your *Journal,* and the reading of your valedictory article, were not pleasant," wrote this able critic; "and this was the first time that either the *Journal* or your writing gave me any other feeling than one of pleasure. I had regarded the *Journal* as a Boston institution, one of the spokes of the Hub. What will musical Boston, what musical New England, do without it? For surely there is nothing that will fill its place. I note with sadness the intimation that musical New England does not want its place filled; but, if there is to be a special musical journal that is worthy to be published, of what other sort can it be than yours?

"Your article is filled with manly good sense. You mourn without whining, and yet say severe things in a mild way. The sort of musical journal which you describe as your successful rival is detestable. A mess of gossip and ' newsy ' paragraphs,— hideous word for a disgusting thing. But I came long ago to the conclusion that what professional people want is merely that you should serve their interests. Your discussion of art, and your endeavor to teach the public, they care nothing about. The singer wants you to tell how she was applauded at Boston, so that she may have a larger audience at her Providence concert. The pianoforte maker wants you to help him sell twenty more pianofortes next year than he did this, and the publisher wants you to make his publications popular. All natural enough, and right enough; but they want you to do this directly. They have no respect, or little, for the indirect influence which elevates and diffuses taste. They are not willing to play the long game.

"I regret very much this close of your valuable editorial labors. You have done great work, and have that consciousness, to be sure,— some comfort, but it should not be all. There is not a musician of respectability in the country who is not your debtor."

In *Harper's Magazine*, George W. Curtis spoke in the most appreciative way of the work which Dwight had done for music, and said of his closing word in the last number of his paper, " A more delightful valedictory it would not be easy to find in the swan song of any journal." There will be found elsewhere the first part of a letter in which Dwight asked Curtis to give an address before the Perkins Institution for the Blind. The last part of it was an expression of his warm appreciation of the friendly tribute which Curtis had paid him, as follows : —

"George, how many times I have been on the point of writing to you since that delightful week we spent at dear old Tweedy's! To me it was a sweet renewal of good old days, and I came away feeling that it must have added some time to my life. Then, too, I wished to thank you for your most friendly, hearty, and delightful talk about me and my *Journal* in the ' Easy Chair.'   It was so like you, like the dear old George.   I tell you, it made me feel well, as if life wasn't all a failure.   And now I am finding laziness agreeing with me too, too well.   You know I was always lazy in the matter of correspondence.   I let you write me so many nice long letters from Europe, and so seldom answered. Now I am indulging in society much more than ever before, and with a zest; and truth is, society here takes the form of music to a great extent of late.   And if I were not so very, very *old*, if it were not my fate to have been sent into the world so long before my time, I verily believe I should confess myself over head and ears in love.   At any rate, I love *life*.   Yet nearly all my old friends seem to be dead or dying, Robert Apthorp chief of all. When I write you again, I hope to be able to say that I am well at work again; but how? on what? Thank God, I am not a 'critic'!"

CHAPTER IX.

THE AUTOCRAT OF MUSIC.

A BIOGRAPHY of John S. Dwight, on a comprehensive plan, would be a history of music in Boston
from 1840 to 1890. His sketch of the history of
music, in the last volume of " The Memorial History of Boston," simply recited that with which he
was personally familiar, and in a large part of which
he was in some way a participant. He not only
reported the musical events of all these years, and
discussed them critically in the *Journal of Music*,
but in many of them he was an actual participant
in their inception and direction. This was emphati-
cally true in regard to the Harvard Musical Association and its symphony concerts, the professorship of music in Harvard University, the giving of
musical instruction in the public schools, the building of the Boston Music Hall and the securing of
its great organ. These are only indications of his
influence,—an influence which was for half a century
potent for good.

His life was so intimately connected with the
Harvard Musical Association that it is impossible
to separate the two. As has already been seen, it
was largely through his enthusiasm and his earnest
efforts that this society was organized. He was its
first vice-president, and chairman of the board of
directors. In 1841 he was chairman of the nominating committee, and he proposed that some one be
invited each year to give an address on music before

the society. At this meeting he gave an address on " Music as a Means of Culture," which was soon after published in pamphlet form. In succeeding years similar addresses were given by George B. Emerson, William W. Story, and Christopher P. Cranch. In 1842 Dwight was again elected vice-president, and he also held the office the two succeeding years. In 1848 he was one of the directors, and chairman of the committee for the purchase of books for the library. In 1849 he was chairman of the nominating committee, and was elected a director, as well as chairman of the library committee. On his motion the time of holding the annual meeting was changed from Commencement Week to the month of January; and the place was changed to Boston, in order that the society might be more nearly in touch with the musical life of the members.

Dwight was active in providing an attractive musical programme for the meetings of the association, the first effort in this direction being made in 1841. There soon after followed a number of Chamber Concerts in Cambridge, given under the auspices of the association. From 1844 to 1850 three series of such concerts were held in Boston, the first two at Chickering's warerooms, and the last in Cochituate Hall. These were then quite a novelty, proved attractive, and were widely imitated.

The coming of Jenny Lind to this country in 1850 made it apparent to the lovers of music in

Boston that a large music hall was greatly needed in the city. At the annual meeting of the Harvard Musical Association, held in Boston, Jan. 31, 1851, this need was considered; and a committee, of which Dwight was a member, was appointed to make inquiries and report. In November, 1852, the great Music Hall was opened with a grand musical festival. Eleven years later, in November, 1863, the great organ provided for this hall was dedicated. In the *Journal of Music* both these events were followed step by step, and with great enthusiasm. Its pages contain a complete record of their inception and consummation. For their time they were events of much importance to the musical growth of Boston, though both of them have quite lost their significance in the changed conditions of more recent years.

In 1853 Dwight was again elected vice-president of the Harvard Musical Association. From 1855 on to 1873 he was continuously elected to fill this position. Almost as continuously he was at the head of the library committee. He took much interest in the effort to build up a musical library which should contain the works of all the great masters of music, as well as such works of history, criticism, etc., as would make a helpful reference library for those interested in the thorough study of music. He was hindered for many years by lack of money, by want of a proper place for such a library, and by the absence of interest on the part of most others. For a time the library was given an alcove in the

Boston Athenæum. In 1867 the association secured a room for the library; and from that time
on it grew steadily, increasing in value with each
year. The interest which Dwight took in the association during all these years was by no means confined to the library; but it included every phase of
the work of the society, and all which concerned
the furtherance of the interests of music. He was
active in providing for the meetings held in Cambridge during Commencement Week, in making sure
that the annual meeting in January, now held in
Boston, should be attractive, that the dinner should
be excellent and the speaking of the best, and that
the society should draw into its membership all the
college graduates in Boston who were lovers of
music, and especially those of Harvard.

In 1865 Dwight brought before the association
the question of doing something for orchestral
music in Boston. It was proposed to form a Phil-
harmonic Society among the members, for the practice of such music. It was decided to hold four
orchestral concerts, and the committee in charge
had Dwight for its chairman. Now, for the first
time, Dwight was able to carry out his own ideas as
to what should be done for the education of musical
taste. It was not the aim to make money, the
receipts being faithfully devoted to the improvement
of the concerts. A fit audience was guaranteed by
subscriptions secured before the concerts began;
and only the best works of the great masters — those
of an established reputation — were to be presented.

The first of these concerts was given the last week in December, 1865, and for the first time realized the wish Dwight had expressed in the *Dial*, that there might be given in Boston a series of popular concerts of a high artistic order. Six concerts were given in all, and with eminent success. The next season the number was extended to eight; and they went on steadily for seven or eight years, increasing in popularity and success. Then came a change. The fund already accumulated became necessary to meet expenses, and the concerts were finally abandoned in 1882. This was due to the popularity of the Theodore Thomas concerts, the Symphony Concerts sustained by Mr. H. L. Higginson, and to the rapid growth of musical interest in many other directions. The association accomplished the object with which it set out. It had thoroughly trained the Boston public to know good music, and to demand that which was better than it could itself produce with its limited resources. It is to be said, however, that the "Symphony Concerts" of the Harvard Musical Association form a most important phase of the growth of musical culture in Boston. They prepared the way for much which has followed, and for the first time almost gave complete expression in Boston to the musical genius of our century. They were largely the outcome of Dwight's taste in music, and they developed his conceptions of music as a means of true culture for the people. So long as these concerts continued, he was the chairman of the concert committee, the programmes were largely prepared by him, and he had charge of the details of the management of the concerts. Whatever success they achieved and whatever influence they exerted for musical culture was primarily due to him. He had the valuable help throughout, however, of such men as B. J. Lang, Otto Dresel, John C. D. Parker, and others of like ability.

In 1869 the Harvard Musical Association secured rooms at 12 Pemberton Square for its meetings, for the better using of its library, and for social gatherings of its members. In 1873 Dwight was elected president of the association,— a position which he continued to hold until his death. On June 15 of that year he took up his residence at the rooms of the association, and henceforth he acted as its librarian. From this time until his death he was most intimately associated with everything connected with this society, and he gave to it much of his attention and interest. It was his wife and child, claiming the warmest affections of his heart. In 1886 the association moved to 11 Park Square, and in 1892 to 1 West Cedar Street.

It would be difficult to say to what extent the Harvard Musical Association was directly instrumental in bringing about the chief object of its existence,— the introduction of music to a recognized place in the curriculum of Harvard University. It certainly never wholly lost sight of this object; and it was urged from time to time with such skill as the association could command, and through such means as seemed most likely to lead to success.   In time what Dwight and the association desired was brought to pass, partly through constant agitation of the subject and partly through criticism of the music which was presented at the university.   For a number of years Levi P. Homer was employed by the university as instructor in music and organist at Appleton Chapel.   On his death, Mr. John K. Paine was called to this position, in 1862.   In 1873 he was made an " adjunct " professor of music; and in 1876 he was made full professor, this being the first instance in an American university of the establishment of a professorship of music.   These steps forward were carefully discussed in the *Journal of Music*, which did not hesitate to point out what was needed to put music on a true footing as an academic discipline and as a means of higher culture.   In the " Memorial History of Boston," Dwight wrote with great satisfaction of this triumph of musical culture in this country, and of the noble results which have been secured through the means of Professor Paine's labors at Harvard.   This was in a large measure a consummation of what he had urged as the true purpose in organizing the Harvard Musical Association, in his preliminary report of 1837.

Dwight was not less interested in the progress of music in the public schools; and this was a topic frequently discussed in the *Journal of Music*. He had no official position which enabled him to aid in this important movement; but by means of addresses and lectures, and through his editorial influence, he was able to do much to promote the interests of this form of musical instruction. All which could be done by enthusiastic approval of the efforts of others, Dwight did for this cause.

For many years he was a trustee of the Perkins Institution for the Blind in South Boston. He devoted much time to promoting its interests, used his influence for bringing to it the help of others, gave much attention to the musical instruction, aided in making the programmes of its commencement exercises, at which he sometimes presided, and on several occasions wrote its annual reports. His interest in this institution may be seen in a letter which he wrote to George William Curtis, in March, 1882, inviting him to give an address before it, which was duly delivered.

" *My dear George*,— With this I send you formal invitation, on the part of the committee of arrangements, for the celebration of the fiftieth anniversary of the foundation, by Dr. Howe, of the Institution for the Blind. The day appointed is Tuesday, June 13; the place, Tremont Temple. The whole blind school will be present and the exercises will consist of music by the pupils (which, I assure you, will be excellent), specimens of the way they read from raised print, brief exhibitions of the various classes, some of their original compositions, declamations, etc., a contributed poem or two, short address by Governor Long and perhaps other New

England Governors, etc.   But, chief of all, we wish
to have an address,— not long, say half an hour,—
partly historical; and we all (committee, director,
teachers, pupils) have set our hearts upon having
you perform that service.   It would delight us all;
and I know that you would find the occasion, the
very sight of those sightless children made so
happy, most inspiring, Director Anagnos (admirable continuer of the good Doctor's work) has
doubtless sent you the last annual ‘ Report,’ containing his most interesting history of all the efforts
made, in Europe and this country, for the education
of the blind.   With that for a guide you will easily
make yourself *au niveau* of the theme historically.
A more responsive audience than the blind themselves cannot be found.   Dear George, do think
seriously of it, and tell me you will come.   Your
own wishes in respect to the arrangements and conditions shall in all respects be consulted.   But
come, if you wish to have a good time, a memorable
time, and make a good time for us.”

Of his connection with the institution the super-
intendent, Mr. Michael Anagnos, said : —

“ Mr. Dwight took a most profound interest in the
institution and its ministry to the needs of the
blind.   For eighteen years he served as a trustee,
with rare assiduity and devotion.   It was chiefly
due to his influence that very little so-called popular music was used in the school, and that the time
was mostly given to the classics from Bach to the

masters of the present day. He not only urged this policy upon our teachers with persuasive earnestness, but devoted his time and talent to the translation and compilation of books in raised characters for the purpose."

Another way in which Dwight served the interests of music in Boston was by the earnest and enthusiastic welcome which he always gave to musicians, especially to young men of talent and genius. He saw their merits, he praised their work, and he urged their claims upon the public. It is sometimes hinted, in conversation, that he did not welcome such men if they were favorable to the newer schools, and if they did not follow the methods which he most admired. No one will find anything of this in the *Journal of Music*, not even the faintest hint of it. When such men as John C. D. Parker, John K. Paine, Benjamin J. Lang, George W. Chadwick, Arthur Foote, and William F. Apthorp came forward, the *Journal of Music* gave them unstinted welcome, cordial, unprejudiced, and enthusiastic. In that paper, for the years 1861 and 1862, will be found as appreciative notices of the organ-playing of John K. Paine, and of his appointment to the position of instructor of music at Harvard, as any young man, at the opening of his career, could desire. When Mr. Paine was made a professor of music in that university, when his important musical compositions were published, and when his works were given fit interpretation in Cambridge and elsewhere, these events were welcomed by Dwight as true indications of the development of music in this country. In one of the last numbers of his paper he spoke of the presentation of the Œdipus Tyrannus of Sophocles at Harvard, with Professor Paine's music, as "the most complete and thoroughly artistic presentation of a work of pure high art that this part of the world has ever yet achieved out of its own resources." And he also spoke of "the beautiful, strong, fitting, manly music composed by Professor Paine." Had not the *Journal* come to its end so soon after this event, there is no doubt this music would have received fit interpretation at his hands.

One more illustration of Dwight's treatment of young men may be seen in the case of Mr. George W. Chadwick. His "Rip Van Winkle" was presented in Boston in December, 1879. Dwight gave his opinion of it in these words: "Mr. Chadwick's overture more than justified the interest with which it was anticipated. It is a fresh, genial, thoroughly well-wrought, consistent, charming work. As in most overtures with titles, and no opera to follow, it may be hard to trace the story of Rip Van Winkle through it. . . . But all this is of slight account compared with the musical themes and progress and symmetrical unfolding of the work. The slow introduction impressed us as the finest part. It opens rich and broad; and, when the horns come in, it is positively stirring. The two principal themes, worked up singly and together throughout the long *Allegro*, are happily chosen and effective. The instrumentation is rich and varied, full of pleasing contrasts, never glaring, but all artistically blended. Indeed, the young man seems entirely at home in the orchestra." This is certainly a most friendly and appreciative approval of the first work of a young man, and it does not justify the tradition that Dwight opposed Mr. Chadwick because of his Wagnerian and new-style tendencies. Most of the traditions in regard to Dwight's attitude towards other musicians and composers, whom he is said to have opposed, probably have as little foundation in fact.

Not less sympathetic was Dwight's welcome to musicians from other countries who came to reside in Boston. Among these may be mentioned Rackemann, Fries, Kreissman, Zerrahn, Jaell, Eichberg, Henschel, Perabo, Listemann; and there were many others. These were welcomed, good words said for them in the *Journal of Music*, and their way made easy, so far as a kindly interpretation and an understanding approval of their work could do so. Especially was Dwight's attitude towards Otto Dresel, one of the earliest of the Germans to settle in Boston, that of sincerest and most appreciative friendliness. In Dresel he found a man after his own heart, an intimate friend, one whose musical convictions and appreciations were of close kin to his own, and a true intellectual comrade. Otto Dresel came to Boston in 1852, was a cultivated and highly trained musician, a man of a most sensitive and refined nature; and there naturally sprang up between the two men an intimate friendship.

After his death, Dwight said of him: "With an un-
qualified conviction we are bound to say he was the
best accompanist we ever heard,— the most refined,
poetic, sympathetic,— the most loyal to the composer, subordinating and forgetting his own person-
ality entirely, the most sure to catch and express
the spirit of the music, the most helpful to the
singer. . . . When all was right, and when he felt at
home, then his playing was in the best sense admirable, inimitable, so exquisitely delicate, so full of
fire and strength and a poetic unction, so crisp in
its long-sustained staccato, so song-like in its beautiful legato, and went so directly to the heart and
soul, that one wondered that he ever could be
eclipsed by even the world-wide celebrities among
pianists." Again: "Perhaps no artist ever had
in greater purity and strength, ever obeyed more
uncompromisingly, more humbly, more unselfishly,
what may be called the artistic conscience, than
Otto Dresel. It reigned in him unconsciously by
the whole bent and force and habit of his nature.
His intensity in his devotion to a high ideal, in
his work and study and performance, in his unfolding of the truth of art to others, was phenomenal."

Enough has perhaps been already said in regard
to Dwight's attitude towards the music of Wagner
and others of his school. His opposition was not
always clearly understood, and he was sometimes
misjudged. On one occasion he expressed himself
strongly on the subject in a conversation which
caused Mr. Georg Henschel to write him a letter

of frank criticism in regard to his reported asser-
tions. In reply, Dwight explained his own position,
and showed that he did not wish to stand in the way
of the music of Wagner being heard in Boston.

"Your informant," he wrote, "must have wholly
misunderstood my half playful and (I admit) quite
extravagant remark. I had not and could not
have the slightest wish to prevent your making a
memorial concert of Wagner music, and I should
be the last man in the world to vote for any prohibi-
tory committee or board of censorship. You have
a right to make your own programme according to
your own feeling of the occasion, and I admired the
earnestness and energy with which you set about it.
What I said (either to or in the hearing of Mr.
Dannreuther) had no reference to this concert or
this orchestra, but was in continuance of some conversation which began before Mr. D. joined us, in
which I expressed the *depressing* influence which so
much of the more ambitious modern music had
upon my mind,— so many big words which, by their
enormous orchestration, crowded harmonies, sheer
intensity of sound, and restless, swarming motion
without progress, seem to seek to carry the listeners
by storm, by a roaring whirlwind of sound, instead
of going to the heart by the simpler and divine way
of 'the still, small voice.' And then it occurred to
me that it might even justify a high court,— a
world's court of censorship,— composed of the greatest musicians, to pass upon such works before they
should come out, thus clearing the musical atmos-

phere of many heavy clouds and of much murky musical malaria.   It was a sudden freak of thought, and of course an utterly impracticable extravaganza. But, when I meet a 'red-hot' Wagnerite, I am some-times tempted in a humorous way to say the worst I can upon the other side; and I fear it is some-times, as in this case, taken seriously."

A curious episode in his connection with "the Music of the Future" was that in 1880 he was appealed to in behalf of Wagner, who had a project of coming to this country to take charge of the presentation of his music-dramas.   In the summer of that year he received a letter from Dresden, written by Mr. N. S. Jenkins, who said: "Some time ago I received a letter from my friend, Mr. Richard Wagner, of which I beg to enclose you a translation.   Upon passing through Italy some weeks ago, I stayed in Naples (where Mr. Wagner is now residing), and talked over with him the sub-ject upon which he had written me.   I found that he was sincerely desirous that his friends in America should be made acquainted with his feelings regard-ing a possible emigration to America, and prom-ised, so soon as I had returned from a journey to the East, to communicate with you.   As I am not specially interested in music, and am also by rea-son of a long residence abroad incapacitated from giving an opinion upon the subject of Mr. Wagner's letter, I felt that I could only advise my friend to consult the first musical authority in America, and therefore take the first opportunity of sending you the enclosed translated copy. May I beg you to kindly send a reply to Mr. Wagner, Villa Augri, Naples. Mr. Wagner is not averse to having this subject discussed among his friends, but he does not wish it to become matter for newspaper comment."

"Your letter of June 11 was duly received," Dwight wrote in reply, "and should have been acknowledged before this. But, being puzzled what to say, I have waited to consult various musical people on the subject of Herr Wagner's letter, feeling that I had received it in confidence and could not publish it.

"I find that it affects almost every one who has read it, even those most inclined to Wagnerism, as an extraordinary and almost insane proposal. You do me too much honor in alluding to me as 'the first musical authority in America'; and you will smile, no doubt, to hear that I by no means am counted here among the enthusiasts for Wagner's music, but have been more identified with the opinions of such dissenters as Dr. Hanslick, Ferdinand Hiller, Ambros, etc. I cannot, therefore, very well write (as you request) to Wagner himself.

"The most practical thought that occurs to me is this: Mr. Theodore Thomas, the famous orchestra conductor, and thus far the most active representative of the Wagner movement in this country, is just now in Europe; and it is said that he went there with the express purpose of visiting Herr Wagner. Probably by this time they have met and talked over the whole matter together. Mr. Thomas can speak from a much wider observation of musical matters in all the States than has been possible to me, who hardly ever go away from Boston; and he can better judge how far the soil is ready for such a planting.

"Your friend, the Rev. Mr. Twining, has written me a very courteous letter, saying all manner of good things about yourself; but of this assurance I had no need, since several of my friends here, who have resided in Dresden, knew you well. Among these are Mr. Otto Dresel (now on his way back to Europe) and the family of Mrs. John A. Andrew.

" Naturally, Herr Wagner's letter, which I have shown to a few, has got pretty widely talked about; and already the 'irrepressible reporters' have begun to put paragraphs about it in the newspapers. This *may* make it necessary for me to print the exact thing. Mr. Twining in his letter to me speaks of your having sent me for publication in my *Journal of Music* some statements with regard to Herr Wagner's feeling and purposes as to coming to this country."

Nothing came of this project, of course; but it is a remarkable fact that, in the midst of his success at Bayreuth, when his fame was established, Wagner had a desire to come to America. It is quite certain, however, that he would have received a greater recognition here than any he met with in Europe, had he carried out his project.

For many years John S. Dwight was the musical

dictator of Boston, and what he approved was accepted as right and good. He was, in a true sense the autocrat of musical taste; and no one questioned his opinion, at least with any probability of getting his heresy accepted. He had a remarkable gift for interpreting a musical composition, bringing out its salient points as a work of art, and putting its leading motives into literary form. His æsthetic perceptions were keen, his artistic judgment sound, and his poetic appreciation of a high order. These qualities, along with a vivid imagination, and a charming gift for literary expression, made him an able critic, and one capable of impressing cultivated persons with the value and correctness of his opinions. Those who knew him most intimately felt that he had a wonderful power of expression as a literary interpreter of music, and that his æsthetic sense of what was best in music was very great. To them he always stood for the highest things in music. He held before them a high but sound musical ideal, and they felt that his judgment was not to be questioned.

At the time when he began to write, Dwight's word was of much value in making cultured people acquainted with the best musical traditions, in pointing out to them clearly what music might become as a means of culture, and in showing them how to translate music into its corresponding poetic meanings. Especially for amateurs, those who regarded music simply as a means of culture, was this task of real service; and the effect he produced everywhere upon amateurs was great. He showed them what to expect in classic music, how to find it, and how to bring it to bear upon the higher issues of daily living. He preached the gospel of beauty in a way to make it bear fruit of a truly æsthetic kind. But his influence upon musicians of the professional type was also great, in part because he was a most appreciative and sympathetic listener, and in part because he criticised without harshness or ill-will. His presence at any kind of musical programme was stimulating to the musicians; for they knew he came not to condemn, but to admire and approve. He was a personal friend to every musician of any ability in Boston; and he was ready to commend true work of whatever kind, and to see merit or genius wherever any were to be found. The musical people knew he would treat them well, that he was never unkind or unjust, and he always spoke sincerely what he believed to be the truth.

For a period of twenty-five or thirty years the general public looked to Dwight to help them form their musical opinions. What he approved was in large degree accepted as right. This leadership he acquired because he earned it and was worthy of it, because he did not abuse it and rarely offended it, because he knew what he wanted and what he believed in, and because he had the gift of convincing other people of the importance and rightness of his point of view. He brought other people to his way of thinking, in a quiet and convincing way, without dogmatism, and with the conviction that all had been cleared up and made luminous by his interpretation. In this he was a master of the art of persuasion, because he knew his own opinions and because he respected the opinions of others.

The younger men were not always satisfied with the criticisms which Dwight put forth; and their objections may rightly find utterance here, not because they are wholly accepted, but because they are necessary to a faithful estimate of the man whose labors are under discussion. In the growing period when Dwight was most influential, one of these men has said, it needed a man of literary attainments, of good social standing, respected by every one, to supply a pointer, to direct the way to what was best. Dwight filled this place admirably, and influenced the public to see the value of music as a means of culture. Without him Boston would not to-day have reached its high stage of development in music. He had an enormous influence for good, did the real thing for the advancement of music in his day, was strong in that he never stultified himself, always was on the side of what was best and noblest, morning and night was faithful to his own convictions, and finally made the public see with him what was good by his sheer love of it, his true appreciation of its merits, and his immense persistence in presenting what was genuinely true. He never cared for what was poor or in any way false, but he had an indomitable loyalty to what is genuine and right.

Dwight's influence was very important in rousing

the musical tastes of young people. They read his paper with enthusiasm, and a goodly number of them were guided to a musical career by the stimulus of his writings and personal influence. His pure and lofty ideals of music quickened their æsthetic appreciations and stimulated their imaginations. Yet the time came when he ceased to be a leader to the young, when the age left him behind. His work would be of little value to-day, because his methods and his ideals are outgrown. He had an excessive loyalty to those he learned early in life to appreciate, but he was not able to take up the newer and abler men. He enjoyed music because it was produced by the men he loved, and anything from them he approved; but, if the name of Wagner, Brahms, or Chadwick, were given to the same composition, he would not accept it. He was not able to make true comparisons in music, his technical knowledge was very limited, and his musical judgment was not trained and skilful. He was stubbornly set in his own way, his mind was fixed, and he would not move out of the way in which he had begun to travel. He had made up his mind that such men as Bach and Otto Dresel were right; and he had no patience with the newer men, was not ready to give them a fair and honest hearing. Not only did he think the music of Wagner ugly, but he had little faith in American composers. Twenty years before he died, Dwight had come to the end of his usefulness, and the age had left him behind. He was not in touch with the newer time, would not move forward with the development of musical taste, and could not understand the rapid growth of music as an art.

These are the judgments of approval and dissent one may hear about Dwight and his work. In part they are sound, and in part they are the result of pique and jealousy. Without doubt Dwight held his opinions very firmly and with earnest conviction. By temperament he was not a Wagnerite, and would not have been so, had he grown up in a Wagner atmosphere. He was by nature an idealist, and belonged to the age when music was the voice of the interior life. The quiet, mystical, introspective mood was his; and he preferred the music which grew out of the same spirit. The more realistic music of the later time he did not care for, because it did not appeal to him, because it was objective and spectacular, because it grew out of another mood than that in which he lived and had his being. This fact must exonerate him from the charge of a stubborn unwillingness to give heed to the newer music; for, having given honest attention to it, he deliberately rejected it. Here was Dwight's limitation as a critic,— that he could not rise above personal preference, and judge a work of art by the standard of universal canons. Yet it was because of this very limitation, this intense personal interest and enthusiastic love, that his musical criticisms carried conviction to others. Dwight's power as a critic lay in what he approved, not in what he antagonized. He was able to convince others through his love and enthusiasm; and, where he could not admire, he was powerless.

Could Dwight have received a thorough musical training, could he have had the wealth which would have enabled him to visit the music centres of Europe freely, and to devote himself without a question of income to writing what he felt and believed about music, he would have given us as important and permanent work as any that has ever appeared in the way of musical interpretation. He would have become the great interpreter of music to the English-speaking world. The work he did for a few years in Boston, however, is needed for America to-day, and always will be needed. Such men as Apthorp and Krehbiel, with a technical knowledge and training which Dwight did not possess, because of the very fact that they write for trained musicians, and use the technical vocabulary of the musician, do not reach the general public. Dwight translated music into literary form, showed the public what to find in it, and how to discover its profound spiritual charm and power. This is what no one else has done with anything like such beauty of language or such persuasive skill to convince and enlighten. A score or more of his essays on general topics connected with music, scattered through the pages of the *Journal of Music* and other periodicals, deserve a place alongside the best writings of Ruskin. They have power, insight, grace, and charm. They are not less needed to-day than when they first appeared; for they discuss the primary and eternal significance of music as an art, its power to enlarge the meanings of life and to purify the soul.

CHAPTER X.

THE SATURDAY CLUB.

DWIGHT had a taste for club life; and he was successively connected with the Transcendental, Town and Country, Saturday, and St. Botolph Clubs. The first of these clubs began in the house of George Ripley, in Boston, in September, 1836; and at the first meeting there were present Ripley, Emerson, Hedge, Francis, Clarke, and Alcott. To the next meeting there came Bartol and Brownson, and soon after Dwight and W. H. Channing were added to the membership. In time came also Theodore Parker, Margaret Fuller, Elizabeth Peabody, and others. Those who attended were drawn together by their common philosophy, and for the sake of the fellowship and sympathy they were able to give each other. Out of this club grew *The Dial* and Brook Farm; but, when they were fairly under way, it came to an end.

When Alcott was living in Boston, in 1849, he brought together at his house a number of his friends for purposes of conversation; and this meeting grew into the Town and Country Club. Its membership included all of those who had been connected with the Transcendentalist Club, and about one hundred others. The club came together at first in order to give a hearing to Mr. Alcott, and it was named by Emerson. There were no dinners. A paper was read in the morning, and a discussion was held in the afternoon. This club was described by Lowell, who was a member, as a "singular agglomeration. All the persons whom other folks think crazy, and who return the compliment, belong to it. It is as if all the eccentric particles which had refused to revolve in the regular routine of the world's orbit had come together to make a planet of their own." This statement was perhaps more witty than truthful; for among the members were Emerson, Garrison, Phillips, Hedge, Howe, King, Whipple, Higginson, Dwight, Frothingham, and Alger. Higginson early attempted to introduce women into the membership, but this movement Emerson brought to an end by crossing off their names from the list of proposed members. In a few months the necessity of having a very small sum from each member, with which to meet the expenses of the club, brought it to a sudden death.

The Saturday Club originated in Emerson's custom of visiting Boston on the last Saturday of each month to take a look at the new books in the " Old Corner Bookstore" of Phillips & Sampson, who were soon after succeeded by Ticknor & Fields. He was also in the habit of dining on these occasions with a few intimate friends at the Albion restaurant or the Parker House. This practice began with him so early as the time of the Town and Country Club, and was perhaps one of the results of the manner in which its meetings were conducted. In his diary, under date of October 14, 1854, Alcott made this record: " Dine at the Al-

Sat. Club (Parker House) May 31, 1873.

Longfellow

R. Dale Owen	o	o	Emerson
Fr. Parkman	o	o	H. W. Bellows.
Eyre Ms Perkins	o	o	Rev. Dr. Hedge.
R. H. Dana, Jr.	o	o	Henry James.
T. G. Appleton	o	o	J. T. Fields.
J. S. Dwight	o	o	Pres. Eliot.
Judge Kent	o	o	Judge Hoar.
O. W. Holmes	o	o	Count Corti.
Chas. Fr. Adams	o	o	C. C. Perkins.
Sen. Boutwell	o	o	J. Eliot Cabot.
J. M. Forbes	o	o	Rev. Chas. Brigham
Jeffries Wyman	o	o	H. G. Denny.
Prof. Gurney	o	o	E. P. Whipple.
~~[scribbled]~~		o	Dr. E. H. Clark.

Present:
21 members
5 guests

Agassiz.

Absent.

Martin Brimmer	C. E. Norton
Wm. M. Hunt	Prof. B. Pierce
Estes Howe	S. W. Rowse
Dr. S. G. Howe	Chas. Sumner
J. R. Lowell	S. G. Ward
J. L. Motley	H. Woodman.

***
J. A. Andrew.
C. C. Felton.
N. Hawthorne

Facsimile of a Diagram of a Saturday Club
Dinner, in the handwriting of John S. Dwight.

[OVER]

Sat. Club (Parker House), April 1873.

O. W. Holmes.

R. H. Dana   Pres. Eliot.
C. F. Adams   Judge Hoar.
Dr. S. G. Howe
J. S. Dwight

                    Dr. Estes Howe.

bion with Emerson, Lowell, Whipple, Dwight, Hayne (of South Carolina), and Woodman; and we arrange to meet there fortnightly hereafter for conversation." Mr. Frank B. Sanborn records in his Life of Alcott that in December, 1854, he was at the Albion with Emerson, Dwight, Alcott, and an Englishman by the name of Cholmondeley, when various literary topics were discussed. A few months later, during the last week in May, 1855, a dinner was given to Lowell, at the Revere House, by his friends. At the head of the table on this occasion sat Longfellow, and at the foot Felton. On Longfellow's right were Lowell, Agassiz, George T. Davis, F. H. Underwood, Holmes, T. W. Parsons, Estes Howe, Charles W. Storey, H. Woodman, and B. Rölker. On his left were Emerson, Edmund Quincy, Charles E. Norton, J. S. Dwight, Thomas G. Appleton, William W. White, John Holmes, Robert Carter, Henry Ware, and Professor Benjamin Peirce. It is evident that the personal and intellectual associations begun in the Transcendentalist and Town and Country Clubs continued even after those clubs had ceased their existence, and that from time to time there came together the men who composed them, with others of the same intellectual and literary interests.

In his biography of Richard Henry Dana, Charles Francis Adams says that, when Emerson visited the bookstore of Phillips & Sampson on the last Saturday of each month, he met there Horatio Woodman; and by degrees they got into the custom of going to the old Albion restaurant or to the Parker House to dine. At this time Dwight was accustomed to dine at the Parker House, and he probably joined Emerson whenever he was there. Then Woodman invited others, including Samuel G. Ward, a banker and one of Emerson's friends. The next person added to the group seems to have been Edwin P. Whipple, the essayist and lecturer, then a rising literary man in Boston. Woodman was a lawyer, a man of attractive social qualities, and one who had a gift for managing such dinners as these.   Mr. Sanborn says : " He had no particular sympathy with the Transcendentalists, except as they became famous, but a certain love for literature and literary men. He was also an epicure, knowing how to provide good dinners and at which Boston tavern his friends ought to dine."

It will thus be seen that the Saturday Club owed its existence to accidental causes or to the demands of intellectual fellowship. In 1854 it had taken a definite form, so far at least as it had become an established custom for a few literary friends to meet once a fortnight or once a month for a dinner and literary conversation. Longfellow recorded in his journal that he dined with the club Feb. 28, 1857, at the invitation of Agassiz, and was asked to join it, which he thought he would do. At the meeting of the club in April the fiftieth birthday of Agassiz was recognized. Longfellow presided, and read the poem beginning, —

> It was fifty years ago,
> In the pleasant month of May.

Clever and humorous poems were also read by Lowell and Holmes. In September, Longfellow says that Charles Mackay dined with the club, that the session was a quiet one, and that the heat of the room took away all life and animation. He mentions that in May of the next year he again dined with the club, and that he felt vexed on finding plover on the table, and proclaimed aloud his disgust at seeing the game laws thus violated. He added that, if any one wanted to break a law, let him break the Fugitive Slave Law, as that is all it is fit for.

The fullest and most explicit account of the origin of the Saturday Club was that set down in his journal by Richard Henry Dana, the younger, under date of Aug. 6, 1857. "It has become an important and much valued thing to us," he wrote. "The members are Emerson, Longfellow, Agassiz, Lowell, Peirce, Motley, Whipple, Judge Hoar, Felton, Holmes, S. G. Ward, J. S. Dwight, H. Woodman, and myself. We have no written rules, and keep no records. Our only object is to dine together once a month. Our day is the last Saturday in every month, and we dine at Parker's. A unanimous vote is required to elect a member. The expense of the dinner is assessed upon those present, and charged at the office, so we have no money affairs to attend to. Guests are permitted, but each man pays for the guest he invites. The club had an accidental origin, in a habit of Emerson, Dwight, Whipple, and one or two more dining at Woodman's room at Parker's occasionally; for Woodman is a bachelor, a literary quidnunc and gossip, or, as Gould says, 'a genius broker.' Ward is a friend of Emerson's, and came. From this the club grew, Ward, Dwight, Woodman, Whipple, and Emerson being the originals. Agassiz, Peirce, and I were early invited to meet with them. This made it more of a regular thing; and we established our verbal rule as to membership, guests, and expenses. Lowell came in soon after, and then Motley and Longfellow. The first formal vote we had for members was at this stage, for up to this time unanimous consent was obtained by conversation. The vote brought in Holmes and Felton, which made the number fourteen, as many as we think it best to have."

The Saturday Club was sometimes known as the Atlantic Club; but the two were quite distinct from each other, as Dr. Holmes pointed out. Longfellow says that on May 5, 1857, he dined at the Parker House with Phillips, the publisher, to talk about the new magazine the latter was proposing to publish. The other persons present were Emerson, Lowell, Motley, Holmes, Cabot, and Underwood.

A letter written by Moses Dresser Phillips, the head of the firm of Phillips & Sampson, and given in Dr. Hale's "James Russell Lowell and his Friends," describes this first dinner given by the publisher to his contributors. Dr. Hale says that this was "the first of a series which the Saturday Club of Boston has held from that day to this day," but in this statement he is mistaken. Mr. Phillips wrote to a relative in these words: " I must tell you about a little dinner party I gave about two weeks ago. It would be proper, perhaps, to state that the origin of it was a desire to confer with my literary friends on a somewhat extensive literary project, the particulars of which I shall reserve till you come. But to the party. My invitations included only R. W. Emerson, H. W. Longfellow, J. R. Lowell, Mr. Motley (the ' Dutch Republic ' man), O. W. Holmes, Mr. Cabot, and Mr. Underwood, our literary man. Imagine your uncle at the head of such a table, with such guests. The above-named were the only ones invited, and they were all present. We sat down at 3 P.M., and rose at 8. The time occupied was longer by about four hours and thirty minutes than I am in the habit of consuming in that kind of occupation, but it was the richest time intellectu- ally by all odds that I have ever had. Leaving my- self and 'literary man' out of the group, I think you will agree with me that it would be difficult to duplicate that number of such conceded scholarship in the whole country besides. Mr. Emerson took the first post of honor at my right, and Mr. Long- fellow the second at my left. The exact arrange- ment of the table was as follows : —

MR. UNDERWOOD.

CABOT.		LOWELL.
MOTLEY.		HOLMES.
LONGFELLOW.		EMERSON.

PHILLIPS.

" They seemed so well pleased that they adjourned, and invited me *to meet them* again to-morrow, when I shall again meet the same persons, with one other (Whipple, the essayist) added to that brilliant constellation of Philosophical, Poetical, and Historical talent. Each one is known alike on both sides of the Atlantic, and is read beyond the limits of the English language. Though all this is known to you, you will pardon me for intruding it upon you. But still I have the vanity to believe that you will think them the most natural thoughts in the world to me. Though I say it that should not, it was the proudest day of my life."

In 1860 James T. Fields, of Ticknor & Fields, then the publishers of the *Atlantic Monthly*, breakfasted Longfellow, Bryant, Holmes, and others. Such gatherings as these, called together by the publishers of the magazine to bring about acquaintance and good fellowship amongst its leading contributors, and that suggestions might be secured as to its management, formed what has properly been called the Atlantic Club. It included many of the members of the Saturday Club; but they were not only not the same, but they had no connection with each other except as the same persons belonged to both. In his biography of Emerson, Dr. Holmes says that the Atlantic Club never had an existence, and that there had erroneously been supposed to be some connection between the Saturday Club and the *Atlantic Monthly*. On the other hand, Francis H. Underwood, who took an active part in bring-

ing the magazine into existence, and who was the
assistant or office editor for some years from its
very beginning, said in a letter to Dr. Holmes:
"You remember that the contributors met for dinner regularly. It was a voluntary, informal association. The invitations and reminders were from my
hand, as I conducted the correspondence of the
magazine. I have hundreds of letters in reply, and
it is my belief that the association was always
spoken of either as the Atlantic Club or the Atlantic dinner. Your very decided statement seems
to me (in the ordinary use of phrases) erroneous."
In his biography of Dr. Holmes, Mr. John T.
Morse confounds the Atlantic dinners and break-
fasts with the meetings of the Saturday Club,
though Dr. Holmes himself did not fall into such
an error. He did somewhere speak of the Atlantic
Club as "supposititious," and it is this statement
against which Mr. Underwood protested. The fact
seems to be that the Atlantic Club consisted only
of the gatherings of the contributors to the *Atlantic
Monthly*, on invitation of the publishers, who on
such occasions gave them a breakfast or a dinner.

It was natural that the Saturday Club should
have been given the name of the Atlantic on the
part of outsiders, who recognized the fact that many
of the members contributed to the magazine. The
Saturday Club was also sometimes spoken of as the
Literary Club, and it was popularly designated as
Emerson's or Agassiz's club. It was also now and
again laughed at as "The Mutual Admiration So-

ciety," probably by those who would have been rejoiced to have secured entrance to it. Of this designation of the club Dr. Holmes wisely said, " If there was not a certain amount of mutual admiration among some of those I have mentioned [as members], it was a great pity, and implied a defect in the nature of men who were otherwise largely endowed." In 1859 Richard Henry Dana dedicated his " To Cuba and Back " to " the gentlemen of the Saturday Club," and this fact sufficiently fixes the name made use of by the members from the beginning.

In his account of the club, Dana says that it was thought best not to have more than fourteen members. His biographer tells us that this limit was imposed by Dana himself, and in a somewhat arbitrary manner. " In other words, Dana, in this as in other cases, held himself high, and believed in exclusiveness. Accordingly, though never allowing his position to be misunderstood, he had been liberal with his blackballs. The result was that, in order to elect any one, it became necessary for the other members to watch for some occasion when Dana was away, and then rush in their candidate before he got back."

The original fourteen members of the club appear on its printed lists in this order: Emerson, Whipple, Woodman, Dwight, Ward, R. H. Dana, Jr., Agassiz, Peirce, Lowell, Longfellow, Motley, Felton, Holmes, Hoar. In 1857 the club seems to have been somewhat more fully organized, and members were admitted by a formal vote. Prescott and Whittier were admitted in 1858; Hawthorne, Thomas G. Appleton, and John M. Forbes, in 1859; Charles E. Norton, in 1860; James Elliot Cabot, Samuel G. Howe, Frederic Hedge, and Estes Howe, in 1861; Charles Sumner, in 1862; Henry James, in 1863; Martin Brimmer, James T. Fields, S. W. Rowse, and John A. Andrew, in 1864; Jeffries Wyman, in 1866; Edmund W. Gurney, in 1867; William M. Hunt, in 1869; Charles Francis Adams and Charles W. Eliot, in 1870; Charles C. Perkins, in 1871; Francis Parkman, Alexander Agassiz, Richard Henry Dana, Sr., Wolcott Gibbs, Horace Gray, and Edward N. Perkins, in 1873; Asa Gray and William Dean Howells, in 1874; Edmund Quincy and Edward L. Godkin, in 1875; William B. Rogers, William Amory, James Freeman Clarke, Phillips Brooks, William W. Story, and George F. Hoar, in 1877; John Lowell and Oliver Wendell Holmes, Jr., in 1880; Theodore Lyman and William James, in 1881; Francis A. Walker and Charles F. Adams, Jr., in 1882; Frederick Law Olmsted, Raphael Pumpelly, H. H. Richardson, and William Endicott, Jr., in 1883; William C. Endicott and William W. Goodwin, in 1885.

Before this last date the club had adopted an informal organization; and Dr. Holmes was the president, with his son as secretary and treasurer. In 1886 William Amory made a gift of five hundred dollars to the club; and, in order to hold this sum of money, it was incorporated. The act of incorporation was dated Feb. 1, 1886, and says that "Oliver Wendell Holmes, J. R. Lowell, John S. Dwight, Ebenezer R. Hoar, Charles W. Eliot, E. P. Whipple, and J. M. Forbes have associated themselves with the intention of forming a corporation under the name of The Saturday Club, for the purpose of the establishment and maintenance of a place for social meetings, and for having conversation and discussion upon historical, literary, scientific, and artistic subjects, and to hold and expend any funds given or bequeathed for its support."

Two days previous to the date of incorporation the club adopted a simple form of organization, which provided for a president, three directors, a clerk and treasurer, to be elected at the annual meeting in January in each year. New members are to be elected by ballot; the regular meetings are to be held on the last Saturday of each calendar month, except July, August, and September, at the Parker House in Boston; and the corporation is not to make any assessment upon the members nor incur any debt. Following the incorporation of the club, John C. Gray and Edward C. Pickering were admitted in 1887; Thomas B. Aldrich, in 1888; Edward Waldo Emerson, in 1889; Walbridge A. Field, in 1891; Henry L. Higginson, Edward W. Hooper, and Henry P. Walcott, in 1893. During the three years following, William Sturgis Bigelow, Samuel Hoar, Charles S. Sargent, and Moorfield Storey were admitted. More recent additions have been Charles Francis Adams, 2d, Charles R. Cod-

man, James M. Crafts, William G. Farlow, John
Fiske, Richard Olney, and Roger Wolcott.

When the club was incorporated, Dr. Holmes was
elected president, which position he held until his
death.   He was succeeded by Walbridge A. Field,
chief justice of the Supreme Court of Massachusetts.   Among those who have served as directors
have been Ebenezer R. Hoar and Charles W. Eliot.
Professor William W. Goodwin, of Harvard University, has been the clerk and treasurer for a considerable number of years.

An interesting incident in the early history of the
club was that Emerson, Hawthorne, and E. Rock-
wood Hoar, living at Concord, to which the Fitch-
burg Road then had no train running after the club
broke up, were obliged to leave in the midst of the
session or remain in town over the night and Sunday.   Under these conditions, Judge Hoar provided
a remedy by having his carryall meet them at Wal-
tham, and convey them to their homes.   It may be
supposed that this last part of the journey may have
had in store the best wine of the feast; for Lowell
describes Agassiz at the club meetings as listening
intently to Hoar,

> Pricked with the cider of the Judge's wit
> (Ripe-hearted homebrew, fresh and fresh again).

The reason for this night ride will be seen from a
note made by Emerson in his journal in 1862:
"Cramped for time at the club, by late dinner and
early hour of the return train,— a cramp which

spoils a club.   For you shall not, if you wish good
fortune, even take the pains to secure your right-
and-left-hand men.   The least design instantly
makes an obligation to make their time agreeable,
— which I can never assume."

Another incident was the formation of the Adirondack Club, which in August, 1858, made an excursion into the wilderness of the Adirondack
Mountains.   The party consisted of Emerson,
Lowell, Agassiz, Hoar, John Holmes, Wyman,
W. J. Stillman, Estes Howe, and Woodman.   Lowell
was the leader and planned the excursion, though
Woodman seems to have been the practical guide
and factotum.   A rough hut was built on the shore
of Follansbee Pond, flannel shirts were worn, fir
boughs and blankets furnished the beds, and the
fare was the fish and game of the wilderness.
After breakfast each morning a mark was shot at,
which Agassiz once hit, having never before fired
a gun, and steadily refusing to do so again.
Emerson bought a rifle which he seems not to have
used.   A guide one night paddled him into the
lake, and a deer was pointed out to him ; but he did
not shoot.   This trip was described by Emerson in
his poem called " The Adirondacks," published in
his " May-day, and Other Pieces," 1867.   He fitly
described the wild life of the woods, saying that

> No placard on these rocks warned to the polls,
> No door-bell heralded a visitor,
> No courier waits, no letter came or went,
> Nothing was ploughed or reaped or bought or sold.

He describes how Agassiz and Wyman dissected the deer, trout, and other creatures slain in wood and water; and he thus speaks of the manner in which the other members of the party spent their time : —

> All day we swept the lake, searched every cove,
> Watching when the loud dogs should drive in deer,
> Or whipping its rough surface for a trout;
> Or bathers, diving from the rock at noon;
> Challenging Echo by our guns and cries;
> Or listening to the laughter of the loon;
> Or, in the evening twilight's latest red,
> Beholding the procession of the pines;
> Or, later yet, beneath a lighted jack,
> In the boat's bows, a silent night-hunter
> Stealing with paddle to the feeding-grounds
> Of the red deer, to aim at a square mist.

Longfellow refused pointedly to go on this excursion, because he had heard that Emerson had bought a gun, and he keenly felt the danger which might arise from such an instrument in the hands of a philosopher,— one more familiar with the infinite than with powder and game. When asked why he would not join the party, he said, " Somebody will be shot."

During the earlier years of the Saturday Club, Horatio Woodman was its purveyor, giving voluntary attention to the menu and the other necessities of its existence. He was a clever and a witty man, and by his genial comradeship won the friendship of men who were drawn to him because of his kindly qualities. Dr. Holmes says that the club

had no Boswell, and its golden hours passed unre-
corded.   Mr. Adams expresses the regret that Woodman did not serve it in this capacity, for he had all
the qualities that would have made him successful
in such a rôle, adding that " he had a craving for
the acquaintance and society of men of reputation,
and indeed lacked only the industry to have been
a sort of Boswell.   In connection with the Saturday
Club, also, an abundant field of interesting gossip
and reminiscence opened before him, had he known
enough to labor in it.   An amusing story-teller,
with a natural eye for character and a well-developed
sense of humor, Woodman had at his command an
almost inexhaustible fund of anecdotes relating to
the men who in those days made the Parker House
and its somewhat famous restaurant a sort of headquarters.   Though during the Rebellion he was sufficiently active and prominent to have been offered
the position of Assistant Secretary of War, yet, in
his own mind, the great achievement of his life
was the founding of the Saturday Club, and his
connection with that club, which could only have
come about through his being its founder, was the
thing of which he most prided himself."

Horatio Woodman was born in Buxton, Me.,
March 18, 1821.   He studied law in Boston, and
after his admission to the bar devoted himself to
land-warrant business, and became a large owner of
Western lands.   After the Civil War, through the
influence of Governor John A. Andrew, who was
his warmest friend, he carried on an extensive busi-

ness before the claims and pension departments at
Washington.   He was lost from the Sound steamer
on his way from New York to Boston, January 2,
1879.

After the marriage of Woodman, in 1877, it
seems to have in part fallen upon Dwight to man-
age the affairs of the club.   Writing to a friend in
October, 1877, he said: "We had a delightful club
dinner yesterday.   William Story sat at my side.
J. F. Clarke, too, was there as a new member, and
seemed radiantly happy; also Bayard Taylor, who
is giving a course of Lowell lectures on German
literature,— how that would have interested you!
I had a long talk with him and Dr. Hedge on the
Nibelungen Lied; and in the evening I heard him
lecture on that subject, which was very interesting.
His lectures are crowded."   Some of Dwight's plans
for seating the members and guests, preserved by
him, indicate who were present or expected on certain dates.   Thus, in April, 1873, his sketch pro-
vides for Holmes, Dana, Adams, Howe, Dwight,
Eliot, Hoar, and Estes Howe.   In May of the
same year twenty-one members were present and
eight guests.   On this occasion Longfellow sat at
the head of the table and Agassiz at the foot.   On
the right of the chairman were Robert Dale Owen,
Parkman, Perkins, Dana, Appleton, Dwight, Judge
Kent, Holmes, Adams, Senator Boutwell, Forbes,
Wyman, and Professor Gurney.   On his left were
Emerson, H. W. Bellows, Hedge, Henry James,
Fields, Eliot, Hoar, Count Corti, C. C. Perkins,

Cabot, Rev. Charles H. Brigham, H. G. Denny, Whipple, and Dr. E. H. Clark. The journal of Richard Henry Dana gives the reason for so large an attendance. " Our club dined to-day," he wrote, — " the largest number we ever sat down, partly as the last of the season, to which many come, but chiefly to welcome Emerson on his return from Europe and Egypt. It was really rather a brilliant gathering. Yet, as we sit at a long table, and the room is on the street and, being warm, the windows open, we have no general conversation. All the talking is in sets of two to four each. Towards the end of the dinner we change places a little. Emerson looks years younger for his European tour, and is in good spirits."

Dana was wrong in saying that this was the last meeting of the season, for at the June dinner Emerson sat at the head of the table and Agassiz at the foot. There were present Holmes, Brimmer, Peirce, Forbes, Cabot, Dwight, Howe, and Hoar, with Weiss and Barnard as guests. At the January meeting of 1877, Judge Hoar was at the head of the table, and opposite him was Edmund Quincy. On the right of the chairman were Holmes, Harding, C. C. Perkins, Brimmer, Estes Howe, and Dwight; and on his left were Emerson, Parkman, Gibbs, Gray, Godkin, Norton, and Edward N. Perkins.

A pleasant episode in the history of the club was the admittance of Richard Henry Dana, Sr., the author of " The Buccaneer," " The Idle Man," and other works in prose and poetry, as an honorary member of the club, the only person accorded such distinction. Under the date of Oct. 28, 1873, the younger Dana wrote in his journal: "Yesterday my father had a great success and pleasure. I took him to the club to dine. We had Emerson, Longfellow, Agassiz, Charles Francis Adams, Sumner, Holmes, Judge Hoar, President Eliot, and others, our usual set; and, after a while, Emerson rose and asked a moment's attention, and said: 'We are gratified to-day by the presence of Mr. Dana. He has a higher as well as an older claim on the respect and honor of men of letters and lovers of literature than any of us here, and we must not let the occasion go by without an expression of our feeling towards him. I propose that, instead of nominating him for election as a regular member of the club, which we would gladly have done years ago, we unanimously declare him an honorary member and permanent guest of the club,' etc. Agassiz put the question, and they all rose to their feet in response, and gave him a hearty cheer. It was very gratifying, touching, and in the best possible taste."

During the first decade of its existence, at least, before other clubs in great numbers had been organized, the Saturday Club was of real service to its members. It gave them social recreation, and it brought them mental stimulus. It brought together many distinguished people, as Dr. Holmes mentions; and it was a place where the intellectual leaders of the city could meet men from other cities and other countries in a friendly and happy way.

"At one end of the table," says Dr. Holmes, "sat Longfellow, florid, quiet, benignant, soft-voiced, a most agreeable rather than a brilliant talker, but a man upon whom it was always pleasant to look, — whose silence was better than any other man's conversation.   At the other end of the table sat Agassiz, robust, sanguine, animated, full of talk, boy-like in his laughter."   Mrs. Agassiz says that her husband was especially attached to the club; and Dr. Holmes remarks that "the most jovial man at table was Agassiz, his laugh was that of a big giant." Around him were usually grouped the men of wit, and those who most enjoyed laughter and fun.   In this connection Jules Marcou, the biographer of Agassiz, has said that the members "lingered long round the table, while hour after hour passed in animated conversation, in which *bon mots* and rep-artees were exchanged as rapidly as a discharge of fireworks,—an encounter of anecdote, wit, and eru-dition.   At such times Agassiz was at his best, with his inexhaustible *bonhomie*.   With a lighted cigar in each hand, he would force the attention of every one around him.   Excited by the pyrotechnic wit of James Russell Lowell, Judge Rockwell Hoar, and Dr. Holmes, Agassiz, whose vivid imagination was always on the *qui vive*, was not a man to let others eclipse him.   Then would come one of his made-up stories,— a mixture of dream and science.   If he thought any one in the company was doubting its truth, he would look at him with a dumb request not to betray him.   On the next occasion he would repeat the same story without any hesitation; and the third time he told it he was sure that it really happened, and was true."

Lowell said nothing about the club in his letters, so far as they have been published; but he wrote to Motley, when ambassador of the United States to Great Britain, "I have never seen society, on the whole, so good as I used to meet at our Saturday Club." In his memorial poem to Agassiz, however, he described the club with a poet's appreciation and sympathy. Of Agassiz and his place at the table these are his words: —

Once more I see him at the table's head
When Saturday her monthly banquet spread
   To scholars, poets, wits,
All choice, some famous, loving things, not names,
And so without a twinge at others' fames;
   Such company as wisest moods befits,
Yet with no pedant blindness to the worth
Of undeliberate mirth,
Natures benignly mixed of air and earth,
Now with the stars and now with equal zest
Tracing the eccentric orbit of a jest.

Again he says of Agassiz: —

Ample and ruddy, the board's end he fills
   As he our fireside were, our light and heat,
Centre where minds diverse and various skills
   Find their warm nook and stretch unhampered feet.
I see the firm benignity of face,
   Wide-smiling champaign, without tameness sweet,
The mass Teutonic toned to Gallic grace,

> The eyes whose sunshine runs before the lips
> While Holmes's rockets curve their long ellipse,
> And burst in seeds the fire that burst again
> To drop in scintillating rain.

Later on in the poem he describes the breaking up of the club meeting, and says : —

> Now forth into the darkness all are gone,
> But memory, still unsated, follows on,
> Retracing step by step our homeward walk,
> With many a laugh among our serious talk.

Then follows an account of his conversations with Agassiz as they find their way homeward, and of the reluctant " Good-night " with which they parted from each other when the end of their walk had been reached.

Dr. Holmes said that he was not able to forget the very modest, delicate, musical way in which Longfellow read his charming verse addressed to Agassiz on the occasion of his fiftieth birthday; and Mrs. Agassiz says the poet had an exquisite touch for occasions of this kind, whether serious or mirthful. If the wit and laughter of the club flowed around Agassiz, the quieter conversation secured its opportunity near Longfellow, on whose left Emerson most often found his place. Longfellow often spoke of the club in his diary, and with evident enjoyment and appreciation of its meetings. He seldom does more than mention his attendance, with perhaps some brief word as to who was present and what was done of special importance; but his frequent reference to it indicates how much it was in his life for some years.

Emerson was described by Dr. Holmes as usually sitting near the Longfellow end of the table, "talking in low tones and carefully measured utterances to his neighbor, or listening and recording any stray word worth remembering on his mental photograph." "I went to the club last Saturday," wrote Holmes to Motley in April, 1870, "and met some of the friends you always like to hear of. I sat by the side of Emerson, who always charms me with his delicious voice, his fine sense and wit, and the delicate way he steps about among the words of his vocabulary, and at last seizing his noun or adjective,— the best, the only one which would serve the need of his thought." "I well remember amongst other things," says Dr. Holmes again, "how the club would settle itself to listen when Dana had a story to tell. Not a word was missed, and those who were absent were told at the next club what they had lost. Emerson smoked his cigar and was supremely happy, and laughed under protest when the point of the story was reached." Probably no one attended the club more regularly than Emerson, for he greatly enjoyed the meetings; and he was wont to praise the brilliant conversation he heard there. His own attitude was that of an eager listener, and he took less satisfaction in speaking himself than in hearing the clever men about him. In 1864, when the club held a Shaksperean anniversary meeting, he rose to speak, stood for a

minute or two, and then quietly sat down.   Speech
did not come, and he serenely permitted silence to
speak for him.   Emerson continued his connection
with the club until about 1875, always taking a
warm interest in the meetings until his failing
speech and memory made them no longer attractive to him.

No one can doubt that Dr. Holmes furnished his
full share of the wit and wisdom of the club.   He
has written of it in his biographies of Motley and
Emerson, as well as on other occasions.   In his
letters it was a frequent subject of mention, especially to those correspondents, like Motley and
Lowell, who were themselves members of the club.
He first mentioned it in his biography of Motley,
and then said that "it offered a wide gamut of in-
telligences, and the meetings were noteworthy occasions.   The vitality of this club has depended in
a great measure on its utter poverty in statutes and
by-laws, its entire absence of formalism, and its
blessed freedom from speech-making."   His biographer says that outside of his own front door there
was nothing that gave him so much pleasure as did
the Saturday Club.   " He loved it.   He hugged the
thought of it."   He could not keep its affairs out
of his letters, and he gossiped about its doings with
a flowing pen.   Evidently, it had a large place in his
heart, because of the fellowship it gave him, and
because of the noble men with whom it brought
him into frequent contact.

In writing to Motley in February, 1861, Holmes

shows how important the club had already become in his life; for he says: " The club has flourished greatly, and proved to all of us a source of the greatest delight. I do not believe there ever were such agreeable periodical meetings in Boston as these we have had at Parker's." Writing to the same friend in 1865, he again expresses his interest in the club meetings. " What a fine thing it would be," he says, " to see you back at the Saturday Club again! Longfellow has begun to come again. He was at his old place — the end of the table — at our last meeting. We have had a good many of the notabilities here within the last three or four months, and I have been fortunate enough to have some pleasant talks with most of them." " We come together on Saturdays and have good talks, and pleasant," he says in 1871, "rather than jolly times. Many of your old friends are commonly there,— among the rest, Sumner, not rarely. There is a great deal of good feeling, I think, in our little circle of literary and scientific people. I find Longfellow peculiarly sweet in disposition, gentle, soothing to be with, not commonly brilliant in conversation, but at times very agreeable, and saying excellent things with a singular modesty." Ten years later many changes had taken place in the club. Some of the members had died, and others had gone away to Europe or were too far away from Boston to attend the meetings. " I go to the Saturday Club quite regularly," wrote Dr. Holmes to Lowell in 1883; "but the company is more of

ghosts than of flesh and blood for me." He lamented the fact that Longfellow, Agassiz, Emerson,
Lowell, Hawthorne, Motley, and Sumner no longer
attended, and added, " I feel as if I belonged to the
past." He proposed, however, with the aid of the
younger members, to keep the club alive until
Lowell could return to give some fresh life to it.
He had already lamented that the club was not
what it was when Lowell had attended its meetings.
Finally, in 1890, he complained that he hardly saw
a face of the old times except those of Dwight and
Hoar, " where we used to have those brilliant gatherings." His biographer says that probably no other
member of the club felt about it as Dr. Homes did,
and adds that, of all who sat at its table, he was by
far the most brilliant talker. We may accept this
opinion without admitting the truthfulness of Mr.
Morse's statement that, if Holmes had travelled
largely, he would have held the club in less esteem.
Such a statement falsely assumes that more of cos-
mopolitanism would have made Dr. Holmes another
man, and would have saved him from enjoying the
men he met at the Saturday Club.

Mr. Samuel G. Ward, a resident of Washington, is the only original member of the club now
living. The other oldest members are Senator
Hoar, Professor Norton, President C. W. Eliot,
Judge Gray, E. L. Godkin, and Wolcott Gibbs.
There is not in the club at present so large a number of literary men as formerly. A member said
of the club, in 1884, that Dr. Holmes was then

president; and he was always present at the dinners, and so were Judge Hoar and Mr. J. M. Forbes. These three, with a few intimate friends, like Lowell and James Freeman Clarke, who came less frequently, kept up a steady fire of bright sayings and jokes, to which the younger generation were often glad to listen in silence. Since the death of Dr. Holmes and Judge Hoar everything is changed in this respect; but the dinners of the club still remain as social and perfectly informal as ever, though the old leaders are gone.

For twenty years, beginning about 1856, the Saturday was the leading club of Boston; and it contained most of the men of wit, brilliant parts, and literary reputation, who lived in or near the city. It was a gathering of genial friends, who sought good-fellowship and intellectual relaxation. The meetings were social, and not literary. No essays were read, and no lectures were given. At one meeting of the club, when a reporter forced his way into the room before dinner, and asked Dr. Holmes what subjects were to be discussed, he received the reply: "We do nothing but tell our old stories. We never discuss anything."

Except on rare occasions the literary part of the meeting consisted of conversation only. The dinner was the central object, and that was expected to bring out quite enough of social chat and conversational stir of thought to give the meetings a real interest. There being no rules to observe and no red tape to follow, the meetings were purely informal, and therefore cheerful and cordial. All the members knew each other intimately, and consequently felt quite at home with each other, and ready for the free expression of thought and sentiment. Already the club has assumed a considerable importance in the literary history of Boston, and that importance is likely to increase as the history of the club is more fully known, and as its members are looked at from a time more remote.

CHAPTER XI.

PERSONAL TRAITS.

Dwight was a small man, short, slender, with a most genial face, kindly and benevolent. He had great sweetness of nature, was most companionable and sympathetic; but he was sometimes irritable, and one of his friends said that he was on occasion "pretty peppery." He was self-conscious, bashful, sensitive, and extremely diffident. It was not unusual for him, especially as a young man, to blush painfully; and this trait he never wholly overcame. In general society he was shy and retreating, and he never outgrew this extreme sensitiveness. On the occasion of his first performing the marriage service he was so much impressed that he broke into tears, and had to pause to recover himself. Undoubtedly, this extreme bashfulness, want of self-confidence and self-assertion, had much to do with his retirement from the pulpit. One of his intimate friends in the same profession says he had faith enough, and his beliefs were positive enough, but he was too diffident.

One who knew Dwight for many years, and came into close business relations with him, says that he was very quiet and mild-mannered, had no bitterness in his nature, but that he was very positive in his opinions. He wasted no time on trivial matters, told no stories, but was very enthusiastic about everything which interested him. This reserve or exclusiveness was not in any degree the result of hauteur or contempt for others. At heart he was one of the most thoroughly democratic of men.

Like all men of vivid æsthetic appreciations, he was essentially an aristocrat in his intellectual preferences and in the exquisite love of beauty which guided his tastes. He had the artistic temperament, and he had that keen sensitiveness to what is happy and beautiful which that temperament usually gives to those who possess it.

Mrs. Ednah D. Cheney, who knew Dwight at the period of his married life, says that he went into society much, and that he greatly enjoyed it. He was a favorite in the cultured society of the Boston of that time, because of his easy way of accepting things, and because of his literary and musical gifts. He was a quiet, sunny, beaming person. If she met him in the street, he always stopped to talk in a cheery way, but always about subjects of intellectual interest, not about the gossip of the day. His usual topic was books or music.

Dwight had very little practical talent, was almost helpless about the simple details of daily living. During the time of his married life his wife watched over him almost as a mother would over her wayward boy, for she had the practical gifts in which he was so deficient. He had no faculty for making money, had little appreciation of its value, was all his life poor, and was not capable of getting on in a thrifty and saving way of life.

The genial and sympathetic nature of our subject has been well described in a contribution for these pages from the pen of the venerable and incisive preacher, Cyrus A. Bartol, who knew Dwight through many years of intimate association. "John S. Dwight was as gentle as the apostle whose name he bore," says Dr. Bartol. "Sixty years ago he startled the audience he addressed by declaring that God is not to be feared, as the Bible exhorts, but only loved. When blamed for his opinions, he could not make a harsh, but only a smiling reply. He was musical in his writing and in every mood of his mind, which was copied in all the strokes of his pen. A more harmonious feeling than he expressed could not exist. If he had any fault, it was that he did not resent blame, and was thus not quite fit for this warring world. As he sat and listened, he seemed part of the symphony or song. Such a nature seems to come and go as unnoted as sunshine or the summer's breath. But, like the genial elements, it moulds and softens the universal frame, outlasting every storm. Without a word comes nature's bloom or fruit. Our subject had as little sound or show."

The sunny and hopeful nature of Dwight's character has been spoken of, and that cheerfulness appeared in every phase of his life. He could not be conquered by disappointments or failures, but persistently looked on the bright side of life, and continued to believe steadfastly in its underlying good. He was one of the most hopeful of optimists who ever lived, and persistently refused to surrender to the evil and the gloom of life.

Dwight's keen enjoyment of everything healthy, beautiful, and loving, was a noticeable feature in his character. Mrs. John A. Andrew, who knew him intimately for many years, has said that he had a great capacity for enjoyment, finding pleasure in the little things about him, being keenly alive to their beauty or fitness or the mere charm of their existence. He found pleasure in watching the fireflies, when on a visit to the country in summer, or the apples on the trees. His little country walks would give him exquisite enjoyment, as he gazed at the water, watched a beautiful sunset, or took an interest in the katydids. Another woman saw the same thing in him, and has thus borne testimony to it: " I think one of Mr. Dwight's finest traits was his keen instinct for and appreciation of the highest and noblest things in life, whether in art, literature, or the character of men and women whom he knew and met. He seemed to gravitate naturally towards the beautiful, and to have a responsiveness towards all the most ideal and finest sides of life."

One of Dwight's lifelong friends has said that his "love of flowers was a passion. He made us first acquainted with the Northampton flowers," she writes, " which were of any rarity. None of us young people had ever seen an Arethusa until he brought us handfuls of them; and I might say the same of countless flowers of literature." Although city born and bred, and a man of the city nearly all his life, yet he was a genuine lover of nature. His delight in the simpler forms of the outward world was of an almost exuberant character. Certainly, it was intense and never-failing. His fondness for flowers was that of a poet, and he could never enjoy them too often or too keenly. All living, growing, happy things appealed to him; and he seemed to appreciate them as if they were persons who could respond with love for love.

What one has called "that benign, intellectual, sunlit face of his" attracted many persons. John Holmes, the most intimate of his friends from the time of their college days, has said: "Dwight used, at rather long intervals, to visit me in the classic Appian Way; and the beaming benevolence of his aspect made quite an impression on my household, which still remains." "He was more than a friend to me, and I revered him as I would a father," says the principal of the Perkins Institution for the Blind. Another of his lifelong friends has said of his letters: "They were always interesting, and I was always glad to get them. How could they be otherwise from a writer whose spirit was so profoundly impressed with not only the deepest musical harmonies, but those also of the great world itself in all its relations? He was very often my guest, and his visits were always most welcome."

One who was a member of Dwight's family for a time has written of him: "I do not know any one who can do justice to his character. He was unique, as pure and lovely a soul as I ever met in man. He needs many biographers, he was so many-sided." One of these many sides of Dwight's nature has been interpreted by another friend, who has written: " I could weave my thoughts of him into a romance. He was surrounded with a glamour from my youthful discipleship, when he was the apostle of music; and, when I came to know him, I never could feel in his company that Pan was dead. His touch with life — with sunshine, music, poetry, flowers, even food and wine — made me feel inclined to look for the 'furry ears.' I am the victim of imagination, and perhaps John Dwight was something very different from this; but he had this suggestion, too, I know,— and this was why I loved him."

Dwight was not a student in the sense of being a persistent questioner of any special form of truth. He was not even a student of music in the technical sense. His habitual life was not that of the intellect, but rather that of imagination and feeling. He lived to enjoy rather than to know. He cared less for truth than for æsthetic fulness of being, to feel and to love what is beautiful.

Dwight's voice was pleasant and winning. He spoke slowly, with poise and equilibrium. He shrank from speaking in public, except in the circle of his own intimate associates. Yet, when he did speak, it was with apparent readiness, slowly, with evident desire to find the right word, and with care to state his argument with precision. His conversation was joyous, almost exuberant with intimate friends, hopeful and cheerful in the highest degree.

He had a charming, playful humor, quick and sympathetic enjoyment of all around him, the keenest relish of free social intercourse, and a warm interest in all that was sparkling, bright, and amusing.

It may be truly said that Dwight had a gift for friendship. The circle of his friends was a wide one, and it included many of the noblest men and women in New England and New York during his time. In early life he sat at the feet of Dr. Channing, and imbibed the spirit of that great preacher. Among his friends, during the period of his life as a minister, were Samuel Osgood, Frederic H. Hedge, Henry W. Bellows, and Charles T. Brooks. He was a great admirer of Hedge, was much influenced by his thought, and continued his regard for him to the end of his life. With Brooks the intimacy was a very close one, and was never broken. He came close to Parker in his intellectual convictions, though so wide apart from him in his sympathies. For a few years they saw much of each other, and sought each other's society with warm regard. All the men and women who were at Brook Farm came into the circle of Dwight's friends, and the cordial relation between them was continued throughout life. One of the closest of these friendships was that with George W. Curtis. Until Curtis settled in New York, their correspondence was frequent; and never many months, so long as Curtis lived, passed without an interchange of letters. They confided in each other, and poured out the secrets of the heart. From this time, too,

dated most friendly relations with Emerson, Lowell, Holmes, Fields, Underwood, and how many
more!

From the days of the Associationists and
Dwight's connection with the Boston *Chronotype*
dates his friendship with Dr. S. G. and Mrs. Julia
Ward Howe. Dr. Howe had a general sympathy
with the associationist movement, enough so to at-
tach Dwight to him; and the acquaintance ripened
into the warmest friendship. In the Howe family
Dwight was almost domesticated, and was trusted
and loved. This regard passed into warmest attachment and veneration on the part of the children and grandchildren of the family. Almost as
cordial was his relation with the family of Governor
John A. Andrew and several other of his more intimate friends. He won their confidence, he secured their love, and they became most warmly
attached to him. This was due in no small degree
to his own sympathetic and affectionate nature,
which drew others to him, because he gave himself
to them with such fidelity and appreciation.

One source of Dwight's attachment to the families of his friends was his love for children. This
love was almost unbounded in its devotion and
quickness of sympathy. Children trusted and
loved him, clung to him with passionate attachment, and confided to him their hopes and griefs.
This fondness for him remained when the girls had
grown into maidenhood; and he had always two or
three maidens to whom he was devoted, with whom

his friendship was intimate, who trusted him as a comrade, and who had an unbounded admiration for him. It was usual for him to take one or two of these girls with him to concerts. He advised them as to their intellectual pursuits, and he exercised an important influence on their lives. It is quite unusual for old persons to have so many warm friends among those of the younger generations as he did. It was a great delight to him to take the children of his friends to concerts, and give them their earliest hearings of the music of the great masters. He was never so happy as when with congenial companions, young or old; and it is no wonder if at times this pleasure colored a little too highly his enjoyment of events, but it never warped his judgment when in a serious mood. He was greatly dependent on such associations for his relish of life, and friendship was to him an essential of his being. He lived in those he loved, and found life momentarily good or bad according to his personal associations.

It shows one of the nobler sides of human nature when we consider the cordial way in which Dwight was sustained by his friends. Without money himself and without the gift for making it, his friends stood by him in his enterprises for the promotion of the interests of music, again and again helped him to the financial means to carry on his labors. They rallied around him whenever a pinch came, making sure that his labors should not come to an end, and giving freely to him in such a way as to make the interests of culture, and not his own personal needs, the object of their help. Their devotion to him through many years shows his own winning personal qualities in the brightest light, partly because he could win and hold such loyalty, and partly because he could so completely lose sight of himself in that for which he lived,— the promotion of the highest interests of art. Even the young people who loved him so well felt that it was an honor to help such a man in his devotion to music; and some of them once held a concert, from the proceeds of which they handed him six hundred dollars.

It may be said of Dwight that he knew how to give with enthusiasm, as well as how to receive with self-respect. No one could have been more ready to help others than he, or oftener moved to give a helping hand. When the library of one of his friends was offered for sale because ill-health had brought poverty, Dwight set to work and secured the aid which made that sacrifice unnecessary. Among the visitors at Brook Farm was Signora Elisa Biscaccianti, a beautiful Italian singer. Misfortunes came to her in later years. She wrote to Dwight of her troubles, and he did all which was possible to aid her in her poverty and sorrow. Joseph Trenkle was a young musician in Boston of great promise. Disease came upon him, and he was obliged to seek a milder climate. Dwight organized a concert, sent his friend a generous contribution, which enabled the young man to settle in California and to do much for music before consumption claimed him.

From his position as the widely known leader of the musical interests of Boston, Dwight was constantly appealed to for advice and help. He was most generous in giving his own time to the friends who thus called upon him, and not less freely to the strangers, who were many. There came requests for advice as to teachers, musical instruments, and the study of music. Facts historical, biographical, and literary were desired. Aid for this, that, and the other, was requested. Among these requests was one from George Ticknor, asking for a list of two or three hundred of the best books on music, such as ought to be purchased for the Boston Public Library. Another was from Andrew D. White, asking his aid in securing a suitable person to fill the professorship of music in Cornell University. Still another was from Henry Ward Beecher, asking advice as to a musical conductor for his church. To all these requests Dwight gave sympathetic reply, and such help as was in his power. They came frequently, because it was known that he was ready to respond, and because he gave as freely as he received. His was not a stinted sympathy, but responsive and intelligent. He was very generous, and very fond of making presents of rare books or of fine editions of Beethoven's sonatas. When Mrs. Anagnos died, he presided at a memorial service in a most sympathetic and inspiring manner, reading a poem of cordial appreciation of her gifts as a woman.

This gift for friendship put Dwight into kindly relations with the musicians of Boston, and won for him their most cordial support.   They criticised him on occasion, and sometimes sharply; but they knew his generous nature, and that he desired to help them in every way possible.   They trusted him therefore, and gave him their admiration and support.

At the Symphony concerts it was Dwight's habit to sit in the front seat of the left balcony, very near the stage.   At the Händel and Haydn concerts he always had the same seat, about the middle of the floor.   He took no notes, was always promptly in his seat, and was very impatient if obliged to wait for those he invited to accompany him.   He studied the composition beforehand, trusted to his impressions, and wrote fluently of what he had heard and felt.   His writing, when at its best, had the appearance of being produced easily and in eloquent strain, the outgushing of a full mind and deep feeling.   In fact, he often wrote slowly, with careful refinement and deliberation, correcting and rewriting with much painstaking.

When all went as he desired, Dwight was a generous and amiable presiding officer; but, when anything he decidedly disapproved came forward, he always managed to prevent its acceptance.   This feature of his character is shown clearly in some reminiscences furnished by Mr. William F. Apthorp, who says : —

" The time when I saw most of Dwight was from

twenty to twenty-five years ago,— before I was married; and I used to pass a good many evenings in his company, into the small hours, across a table in the Parker House restaurant. But with my marriage came a truce to *das Wirthshauslaufen*; and, as I got busier and busier, I found less and less opportunity to share in that *dolce far niente* which made up a good part of his life. I have no definite recollection of any of our old Parker House chats. They were too long ago, and I really don't think we talked about much of anything in particular. He never talked as he wrote.

"After his election as president of the Harvard Musical Association, I continued to meet him a good deal on committees, of several of which I was a member in those days. He always presided, and I think I could swear before a jury that in no single instance did any pressure succeed in inducing him to put a motion which he did not like. His obstinacy in this matter was so marked that it has crowded all else out of my memory.

"I do, however, remember one comical incident which well exemplified a certain mental trait of his. We were sitting in committee one afternoon, in the old Harvard Musical rooms in Pemberton Square, and discussing things rather lazily and desultorily, as was our wont. James T. Fields — who was a member of the Association, though not on the committee — happened to drop in, to get a book out of the library. Finding a committee in session, he was about to beat a hasty retreat, when Dwight called out to him : —

"'Oh, don't go, Fields,— don't go. You won't trouble us in the least.   We will make you member of the committee *pro tem.*   Sit down and tell us something.'

" Fields accepted the invitation, and, after a little chit-chat, said : —

" ' By the way, gentlemen, I have just seen something on a publisher's price-list that struck me as something out of the common.   It was the title of a song,— " Give my chewing-gum to Gerty."   I have been bothering my head ever since to try to imagine what on earth the next line can be.'

" We all laughed ; and, just as the conversation was about to turn to other topics, Dwight called out : —

" ' Fields, that was a strange freak of fancy,— that title you just mentioned.   What could have suggested such a curious connection of ideas ?   Let me see, what was the title ? ' "

" ' " Give my chewing-gum to Gerty," ' repeated Fields.

" ' Strange, very strange, indeed,' Dwight went on. ' Chewing-gum,— yes, I can understand chewing-gum being made the subject of a popular song nowadays.   People make songs on pretty much everything.   But what bothers me is the other part,— why especially to Goethe ? '

" As an instance of Dwight's immovableness, the late Otto Dresel once told me : ' The other day I made up my mind that I would, for once, force Dwight to make the first move, even at the risk of my life. It was an awful afternoon, with east wind and rain and sleet and everything horrible. I met him on Tremont Street, just opposite the West Street gate. I stopped him in the middle of the street, and began talking with him. There we stood, in the middle of the crossing, in all the wind and cold rain, with the horse-cars running on one side of us, and the carriages rushing on the other. Well,— will you believe it? — after half an hour by the Park Street clock, I had to give in, or I should be dead now with pneumonia. Dwight would not budge, nor give the faintest sign of intending ever to budge! I had to make the first move, after all.'

"Another incident occurs to me, illustrating Dwight's good nature, and his willingness to laugh at a joke against himself. It was at a meeting of the Harvard Musical Association concert committee for the purpose of assigning seats to the subscribers to the symphony concerts. The seats were to be drawn by lot. For once, Dwight made the unusual concession to parliamentary law of moving that S. Lothrop Thorndike should take the chair, as he himself would like to take part in the discussion of certain matters. When Thorndike had been voted into the chair, Dwight made a motion that, as he (Dwight) really managed the concerts, he might be allowed to select his seats before the drawing by lot, it being important to him to have seats from which he could easily leave the hall at any time during the concert, as he often had to consult with the musicians. Thorndike immediately said, 'Gentlemen, you have heard the motion, which is to the effect that, in consequence of the necessity Mr. Dwight labors under of having to go out every now and then to see a man,'— A shout of laughter interrupted him, and Dwight was the heartiest laugher there."

In religion Dwight was a follower of Emerson and Parker, with the one repudiating all formalism and creed, and with the other holding to the conviction that Christianity is the absolute religion. He was of the same mind with Emerson in his repudiation of the organized religion about him, not attending church for many years, and holding toward the churches an attitude of dislike of their methods and spirit. He hated all formality in religion; but his attitude in this respect, as one of his most intimate friends has said, was quite unlike his sweet and generous self.

If Dwight was mistaken in his religious attitude, it was in believing too much and not in believing too little. He repudiated the historic and conventional, but with the conviction that he was thereby holding all the more firmly to what is spiritual and eternal. He agreed with Emerson in holding that the communion of the soul with God is too sacred for public prayer, and he could not believe that spiritual trust gives any sanction to petitions for material blessings. He did not hold with the scientist that prayer is of no avail, but that it is the private communion of the soul with God,— too holy for any outward expression, too interior in its spiritual import for any formal utterance.

Theodore Parker's belief that in its great spiritual teachings Christianity is the absolute religion was also accepted by Dwight. This opinion he very clearly stated in his essay on Common Sense, where he asks: "What is the religion of common sense? Is not that — I ask with reverence — the proud distinction of Christianity? The simplest of all religions, the faith which Jesus of Nazareth lived and taught, finds its response and welcome in the nobler common sense of man. I mean the Christianity of Christ himself, as illustrated in the whole spirit of his own short life on earth, and not that of the churches, creeds, and artificial, subtle schemes of dogma."

It will be seen that, in these opinions, Dwight put himself into sympathy with the mystics of all ages. He was not a rationalist, for he found the centre of his faith in feeling; and the emotional life afforded him whatever is best in religion. He overlooked in some measure the great need men have for union with each other in worship, and that such union necessitates what is conventional or what all can agree upon as fit symbol for the inward conviction. He was right enough, however, in insisting that the soul is its own witness of God, and that all forms are nothing more than forms, as often hiding as revealing the interior fact. His appeal to feeling was of great interest, because he made music his chosen form for the interpretation of the soul's needs.

CHAPTER XII.

THE CLOSING YEARS.

It was not left for Dwight to undertake any great task after the closing of the *Journal of Music*. Yet the dozen years more of his life were busy ones, and quite in harmony with those which had preceded. He wrote several papers on the history of music in Boston, and he produced several essays of much value on topics which had always interested him. He continued his work as president of the Harvard Musical Association, and he gave much attention to the improvement of its library.

In July, 1880, occurred the death of his lifelong friend, George Ripley, who had perhaps been nearer to him than any other of his many friends. They were of one mind on nearly all questions which interested them both, for many years they had counselled and cheered each other, and they had been closely associated under circumstances which cemented their affection. Dwight was asked by Mrs. Ripley to act as one of the pall-bearers at the funeral, and he sent this letter in reply: —

"I feel very grateful to you for thinking of me for one of the pall-bearers at the funeral of my ever-dear and honored friend and old-time associate, the cherished noble partner of your life so many years, George Ripley. The name is sacred to me; and it seemed to me a sacred duty to go at once and join with other old friends in those last, solemn,

tender services about his grave. But a moment's
reflection showed me that, in the critical condition
of my affairs,— demanding all my time,— and in
the far from sound condition of my health, it would
be very imprudent, and might at the last moment
prove impossible for me to make the journey in the
extreme heat to New York. So, rather than answer doubtfully, I telegraphed to Mr. Reid as I did.
It was done most reluctantly. My heart yearned
to be there. It would have been good for my own
soul to share in the last words of farewell and of
peace to that hard-working, brave, true, noble friend.
As it was, I could but be present in the spirit; and
I passed that hour at my piano, playing from
Bach's ' Passion Music ' several chorals, and the
profoundly sad yet tender, hopeful Schluss-chor,
' Around thy tomb here sit we weeping.'

" Indeed, my haunting thought through all these
days has been of him. He was, on the whole, the
best friend I ever had; and, though I have not
seen him for some years, I have never ceased to
think of him with love and gratitude for all the
encouragement, the quickening influence, the wise
counsel, and the happiness which I derived from intercourse with him during so many of the best years
of my life, before and during the Brook Farm days,
with delightful (only too infrequent) meetings since.
I now repent me sadly that I never made the effort
to get on to New York during the last year or two,
and look upon his benignant face and listen to his
cheerful voice again. I had hoped even yet, after

Mr. Allen's rather favorable report of his condition some ten days ago, to see him once more alive. Alas, too late!

"It must be very grateful to you, as it is to me, to read on all sides such heartfelt tributes as his rich, beneficent, well-rounded life and labors have called forth. I trust the record will be embodied in a biography complete enough to be his worthy monument. Accept my heartfelt sympathies in your great loss,— for comfort, what could you have greater than the thought of what he was and did? — and believe me sincerely your friend."

To the end of his life Dwight continued to make his summer outings in Newport, Gardiner, and elsewhere. A letter written to one of his sisters in August, 1882, may find a place here: —

"My week at Newport was very enjoyable; and I felt very much refreshed by it, in spite of the great heat and drought there also. The Tweedys were as good and kind as ever, and I saw many pleasant people. One day Brooks and the new young pastor of the Channing Church, Mr. Wendte, dined with us; also Mrs. Howe and Mr. John Field, a most genial, entertaining man,— an intimate friend of the J. R. Lowells,— who has been living nine years abroad, knows everybody, and has much to tell. He gave us one good anecdote of Carlyle, which he had direct from Robert Browning. It seems the queen one day suggested to Dean Stanley that it would be quite nice if he would bring together at the deanery some of the literary celebrities, and ask

her to meet them in a quiet social way.   He did so.
There were present Tennyson, Carlyle, Browning,
and others.   In the course of the evening the conversation turned on poverty, its alarming increase,
and the question of the remedy. ' You must except Scotland,' said Carlyle. . ' We have no poverty in Scotland.'   Said the queen, ' I beg your
pardon, but I have frequently had occasion to relieve it there myself.'   ' Then,' gruffly returned
Carlyle, ' if there is any, it must be of your own
making.'   The queen, on retiring, passed near
Browning, and said to him in a low tone, ' What
a terrible old man ! '

Appropriate to this place is a letter which
Dwight received on the occasion of his seventieth
birthday : —

Cambridge, May 12, *or make it the* 13*th,* 1883.

My dear John,— I greet you on your arrival with
me at the Scriptural age of threescore and ten, —
you my junior by two months. Can you believe it?
We have known each other fifty years!   The
whirligig of time, with its ceaseless revolutions,
changes, absences from each other, and so on, has
not, I think, worn away in the least our old friendship. We were drawn together from the first by
intellectual sympathies, by our studies in the Divinity School, by our tendencies towards freer, fresher,
more ideal views of literature and life, in our aspirations after the true, the good, the beautiful, and,
not least, by our common love of music. We were
youths then. Are we much older now? Wiser,

let us hope, but both young at the core of our hearts.

Let us bless the good Powers that have preserved us for this meeting to celebrate your birthday. I shall be delighted to come, and am ever, with remembrance of the old days and the new, yours faithfully,

CHRISTOPHER P. CRANCH.

In 1884 Dwight's portrait was painted by Miss Caroline Cranch, and she found him a quiet and helpful sitter. It was secured by his friends, and hung in one of the rooms of the Harvard Musical Association. In a letter to her, on this occasion, he said: " I am greatly pleased on your account, as well as my own, that the picture was so appreciated by the Association of which I am president; for I could not be reconciled to the idea of having all your skill and labor bestowed upon my unworthy self with no remuneration. I know not what you have received, but I fear not half as much as you had a fair right to demand. When I am hung up on the wall (with the other old masters, Händel, Gluck, etc.), I trust you will come up and see us. In writing a day or two since to G. W. C., I told him about the portrait and the presentation."

In his reply, Curtis said: " It was very good to see your familiar hand again, and unchanged, and, best of all, to read your strong, clear, masterly, and delightful plea for the true saving grace of humanity, common sense. It is a most admirable piece of work, and a host of readers will wonder that they never thought it before. That is the effect of all wise writing, I suppose, which, like yours, lays us all under obligation. Why don't you oftener bring us reports of your interviews with Egerie? Cranch had already told us of the paper with great praise in a letter which told me also of your birthnight orgie with Boott and John Holmes. I have the photograph of Carrie Cranch's remarkable portrait of you, which is a precious possession; and, when I see Cranch, I hear of you, and, when I don't see him, I think of you, and always with the old affection."

In another letter we get a glimpse of one of Dwight's most intimate and lifelong friends, a younger brother of Dr. O. W. Holmes: "The evening before your letter came I spent in Cambridge with my dear friend John Holmes, who has been laid up lame, but is getting better. I must tell you of a little thing he related to me, as showing the delicacy of his character. I chanced to say that, driven to the last extremity, unable to write or read or think, I had taken up ' Pickwick Papers ' again. Said he: ' I never met Dickens but once: that was at James Lowell's. Mention was made of some little known book of Walter Scott, and Dickens said to me: " You ought to have that. When I get home, I will send it to you." ' John said, ' I replied: " Oh, no, my dear sir. I cannot allow that. If you make such a promise, it will bother you more than it is worth," ' — or something like that."

In 1883 occurred the death of Charles T. Brooks,
preacher and poet, who was one of Dwight's most
intimate friends, and who had been associated with
him in at least one or two literary ventures. To the
Boston *Transcript* he sent a poem expressive of
what his friend had been to him, which elicited the
following letter : —

Boston, Oct. 30, 1883.

My dear Dwight,— I can hardly express to you
how much I was delighted by your poem on
Brooks, published in the *Transcript*. Every trait
of his charming mind, every feature of his gentle
and beneficent face, rise before me as I read your
tribute to his moral and intellectual worth. What
good that man has done, considered simply as a
translator of Goethe and Richter! Yet his patriotism, in making us familiar with great works of the
German mind, is hardly yet appreciated — except
by men like you. How good the man was! Nobody could believe in original sin in his presence.
He radiated his own stainless heart and soul and
character through every company where he appeared. But, my dear Dwight, why don't you
write more poems? It seems to me that any
journal in the country would gladly accept such
a poem as this of yours.

Ever sincerely yours,

E. P. Whipple.

For " The Memorial History of Boston," the
fourth volume of which was published in 1881,

Dwight wrote a history of music in that city. In the introduction to it he gave a rapid sketch of the musical growth of the city during the seventeenth and eighteenth centuries, but this was not used because the article was of too great length. This excised part appeared in the *Atlantic Monthly* in December, 1882, under the title of "Our Dark Age in Music." The conclusion of the article, which was devoted to the teaching of music in the public schools, was also omitted.

In 1885 Dwight was asked by the publishers of Webster's Dictionary to act as one of the editors of that work, in the preparation of a new and enlarged edition. He was to revise the musical definitions, and to add such as the advance in music had made desirable. This edition appeared in 1890, as the "International." In 1885 came the two hundredth anniversary of the births of Händel and Bach, and for the *Atlantic Monthly* Dwight wrote an article on each of these great composers. That on Händel appeared in April, and that on Bach in May.

Although Dwight found in the Harvard Musical Association the chief interest of his life, in the way of an organized effort to advance the cause of music in Boston, yet he did not confine his affection or his labors to that institution. He was also warmly interested in the Händel and Haydn Society, and welcomed all its efforts to advance the cause of music. When the history of that society by Charles C. Perkins, one of Dwight's devoted

friends, came to an end because of his death,
Dwight was asked by the society to take up the
work and continue it.   He accordingly prepared
two parts, of about one hundred pages each, which
were published in 1887.   For the *New England
Magazine* he prepared a sketch of the work of the
Händel and Haydn Society, which appeared in
December, 1889.   This was the last of his several
articles on the history of music in Boston, which,
taken together, make a continuous and admirable
historical survey of the musical development of
that city.

In the summer of 1890 Dwight was asked to
take charge of the musical department of the Boston *Transcript* during the absence of the editor,
Mr. William F. Apthorp, in Europe.   He was to
write of certain concerts, and his duties were to
continue for only six months.   After much hesitation he undertook the task, which he carried
through with entire success.   To a work edited by
Professor John K. Paine, Theodore Thomas, and
Karl Klauser, and called " Famous Composers and
their Works," which was published in 1891,
Dwight contributed a paper on Felix Mendelssohn-
Bartholdy.   This was the last of his contributions
to the criticism of that art he had loved all his
life, and to which his life had been so faithfully
devoted.

In 1884 Dwight made an effort to publish his
translations of the poems of Goethe.   He consulted
Francis H. Underwood as to the best way of bring-

ing this about, who advised him to apply to a
London publisher; but nothing came of this project. In 1885 he wrote an essay on "Common
Sense," in which he discussed philosophy, religion,
and politics. He read it several times at the houses
of his friends and to club gatherings. It was much
admired by those who heard it, and it was received
with enthusiasm by many. In some degree it was
his parting word to his friends on some of the
themes he had been pondering all his life. It was
a defence of the idealistic philosophy of his youth,
and an application of its great principles to the
chief activities of humanity. This essay was given
to the public in the *Unitarian Review* for May,
1890.

In 1886 the Harvard Musical Association moved
to 11 Park Square, and here Dwight found a new
home. The janitor and his family lived in the
house, and with them he was able to take his meals,
if he did not wish to go out; and more of the com-
forts of a home came to him in this place than he
had enjoyed for many years. The removal was
made necessary by the building of the new Court
House, but it was advantageous in many ways.

In November, 1892, the Association bought the
house No. 1 West Cedar Street, and moved into
it. To Dwight the removal looked like a terrible
task, especially as the janitor and his family, to
whom he was warmly attached, could not go with
him. The move was made very easy to him, however; and he found himself better situated than ever

before.　Nov. 21, 1892, he wrote to a young friend:
"For several weeks I could only say, I eat and
breathe dust, I think dust, I feel dust, I am dust!
That means I have been getting ready to move;
and, finally, I have moved.　I write you from our
new house, which is ours (the Harvard Musical Association's).　I moved last Friday.　Thanks to the
zealous and efficient help of my friends, the Hamiltons, who took such excellent and tender care
of me in Park Square, I had everything — books,
clothes, pictures, furniture, and rubbish — brought
over here in one day.　Hamilton put up all my
books and hung all my pictures, and Mrs. H. made
my bed; and the dear little Arthur helped with
more zeal than achievement, but with a vast deal
of sympathy.　The day was very warm and sunny,
but after I got here came on a rain and fierce wind.
Yet I slept sweetly in the quiet, clean neighborhood; and I woke the next morning refreshed, in
the sunshiniest room I was ever in.　And so it has
been for three nights and days.　The house is full
of carpenters, painters, electric-light men, who are
straining every nerve to get all ready for a grand
opening social musicale, with many guests, next Friday evening.　Our committee have worked like
dragons, getting the library over and setting it up,
not just in my old order; for they sacrifice much to
their acoustic hobby.　But we shall have a beautiful long room, three parlors end to end, with solid
pine floor, uncarpeted; and I think that eye and ear
will find it very agreeable.　We shall have a very

choice selection of music : Beethoven's great B-flat
Trio (Lang, Kneisel and Schröder of the Symphony Orchestra); 'Adelaïde,' sung by W. J.
Winch; and a Bach bass aria, sung by Lamson. I
could not have chosen better myself.

"The saddest thing about moving was leaving
our good Hamiltons behind; but I find a good
Scotch couple in charge of the house, and she furnishes me breakfast, and makes (what is a great
matter with me) excellent coffee, and also toasts
muffins well. Chater's headquarters for muffins is
right round the corner. The Symphony concerts
are getting on apace. Orchestra admirable, programmes might be better. But we had a good one,
with Beethoven's Second Symphony (the slow movement was played at my wedding, in 1851, on the
piano by a friend)."

"Your beautiful note, with its most cheering
contents, came at the right time, when I was sick
and much depressed by loss of working days," he
wrote Jan. 18, 1892, to Mrs. Otto Dresel. "I have
been for a week, and I am still, confined to the
house by a cough, with all manner of painful accompaniments,— even the old enemy, gout, has
seized the opportunity to come back on me when I
am helpless! — else I should have made grateful
acknowledgment before now of the most friendly
favor. All day yesterday I had proof to correct,— a
long article on Mendelssohn, which, I flatter myself,
dear Otto would have approved. How thoughtful
and how kind you are! And how such sweet sur-

prises quicken one's feeling that an unfailing friendship is very nearly the best thing in life ! "

On the occasion of Dwight's eightieth birthday, May 13, 1893, the Harvard Musical Association gave him a birthday party, and his friends gathered in large numbers. This was a red-letter day in Dwight's life, and he enjoyed the occasion greatly. All through the morning came to him congratulatory letters and telegrams from friends who could not be present, and many gifts. He took the deepest pleasure in the flowers that showered in upon him throughout the day, and often afterward he referred to them as the most beautiful he ever saw. Though the afternoon was very rainy, a host of friends gathered to do him honor, among others five who were over eighty years of age; and Dwight was fond of alluding to the six old gentlemen, whose ages rose in uninterrupted succession from eighty to eighty-five. These were John S. Dwight, 80; John Holmes, 81; Henry W. Pickering, 82; Oliver Wendell Holmes, 83; Robert C. Winthrop, 84; Epes Dixwell, 85. The party was entirely social, with just enough music, chiefly furnished by Mr. Arthur W. Foote and Mr. Wulf Fries, to make it a most fitting occasion. Four of Dwight's favorite young lady friends poured the tea. The whole afforded a happy expression of the esteem in which Dwight was held by his many friends and admirers. Among the messages of friendship and congratulation was this from Mrs. Ednah D. Cheney, who thus recalled the many years of her acquaintance with Dwight : —

1853.

Forty years since : the way has been long, but not dreary :
The limbs may grow feeble and faint, but the heart is not
    weary ;
And the music has now the self-same melodious ringing,
And high thoughts as then on their own lofty pinions are wing-
    ing,
As when we were young, and I listened, and found with de-
    light
That music itself sounded fuller and clearer through Dwight.

1893.

Early in August a very sudden, acute illness
prostrated him, from which he only partially rallied.
Although suffering much, he always wore a peaceful face, and was made very happy and grateful by
the tireless devotion of his friends, who kept him
well supplied with flowers, fruit, etc. They called
upon him frequently, and his days of suffering were
brightened so much by their presence that it was
almost impossible to realize that he was dan-
gerously ill. He had the constant and tender care
of relatives, and his brother Frank was with him in
the last hours. During the last days, friendly messages came to him from all directions. He died on
Sept. 5, 1893.

The library of the Harvard Musical Association
on September 8 was for a second time a gathering
place of his friends,— this time for the service
which, some one beautifully said, was less "like a
funeral than a meeting of friends to bid him God-
speed." Dr. O. W. Holmes said to Mrs. Julia Ward

Howe, as they sat by each other on this occasion,
" Mrs. Howe, if we could see everything that is,
don't you think we would see about that casket a
group of angels very much like those who sang a
certain morning in Judea?" " Doctor, why do you
not put that into a poem?" was the reply. The
usual religious service was held; and the music,
under the direction of Mr. B. J. Lang, was touching
and beautiful. The King's Chapel Quartet sang
Bach's chorale, " Ein' feste Burg"; and the con-
tralto song, " Oh rest in the Lord," was most feel-
ingly sung by Miss Lena Little. Mrs. Howe read
the following poem as a tribute to her friend of
many years: —

TO JOHN S. DWIGHT.

O Presence reverend and rare,
  Art thou from earth withdrawn?
Thou passest as the sunshine flits
  To light another dawn.

Surely, among the symphonies
  That praise the ever-blest,
Some strophe of surpassing peace
  Inviteth thee to rest.

Thine was the treasure of a life
  Heart-ripened from within,
Whose many lustres perfected
  What youth did well begin.

The noble champions of thy day
  Were thy companions meet,
In the great harvest of our race,
  Bound with its priceless wheat.

Thy voice its silver cadence leaves
  In Truth's resistless court,
Where of thy faithful services
  Her heralds make report.

Here thou, a watchful sentinel,
  Didst guard the gates of Song,
That no unworthy note should pass
  To do her temple wrong.

Dear are the traces of thy days
  Mixed in these walks of ours:
Thy footsteps in our household ways
  Are garlanded with flowers.

If we surrender earth to earth,
  The frame that's born to die,
Spirit with spirit doth ascend
  To live immortally.